Social Psychology of Self-Referent Behavior

Social Psychology of Self-Referent Behavior

Howard B. Kaplan

Baylor College of Medicine
Houston, Texas

Plenum Press • New York and London

Library of Congress Cataloging in Publication Data

Kaplan, Howard B.
  Social psychology of self-referent behavior.

  Includes bibliographical references and index.
  1. Self—Social aspects. 2. Social psychology. 3. Interpersonal relations. I. Title.
HM291.K19   1986   302.5   86-25371
ISBN 0-306-42356-1

© 1986 Plenum Press, New York
A Division of Plenum Publishing Corporation
233 Spring Street, New York, N.Y. 10013

Printed in the United States of America

To my family:
Diane Susan, Samuel Charles, Rachel Esther

Preface

This book is about human behavior and, more particularly, about a class of human behaviors—those behaviors by people that have themselves as the object of their behaviors. These self-referent behaviors are social in nature in the sense that in large measure, they are the outcomes of pervasive social processes and are themselves major influences on social outcomes. As such, self-referent behaviors have the potential to be significant organizing constructs in the study of the broader field of social psychology. In any case, they are regarded here as of intrinsic interest and are the focus of this volume. Four broad categories of self-referent behaviors are considered with regard to their social bases and consequences as these are revealed in the social psychological and sociological literature. With appropriate discriminations made within each grouping, the four categories are: self-conceiving, self-evaluating, self-feeling, and self-protective–self-enhancing responses. Following a consideration of the social antecedents and consequences of each category of self-referent behaviors, I present a final summary statement that outlines a theoretical model of the additive and interactive social influences on and consequences of the mutually influential self-referent behaviors. The outline of the theoretical model reflects my synthesis of the apparently relevant theoretical and empirical literature and is intended to function as a framework for the orderly incorporation of new theoretical assertions and more or less apparently relevant empirical associations.

Acknowledgments

My intellectual debt is to many of the investigators I cite and to many more whose influence on me was never consciously recognized or has long since been forgotten. I do recall vividly, however, that the preparation of this volume was accomplished in the course of research supported by a grant (R01 DA02497) from the National Institute on Drug Abuse, a grant from the Hogg Foundation for Mental Health, and a Research Scientist Award (K05 DA00105) from the National Institute on Drug Abuse.

I thank Pamela K. Derrick for her efforts in the typing of the manuscript and my colleague, Robert J. Johnson, for his suggestions and other aid in the production of the final draft.

Contents

CHAPTER 1

Introduction

In the course of a day, we look at ourselves, describe ourselves to others, form concepts of ourselves, attempt to present ourselves to others in ways that will create certain impressions, try to protect ourselves against threats to our psychological or physical well-being, judge ourselves to be more or less successful, feel more or less kindly toward ourselves, and (more or less overtly) communicate with ourselves. These responses are examples of self-referent behaviors. They are behaviors in the sense that they refer to changes in the energy system of an organism. They are reflexive or *self-referent behaviors* in the sense that they are behaviors that refer back to the very people who are performing the behaviors. The people who perform the behaviors are, at the same time, the objects of the behavior. The person is the knower and the known, the one who feels and the object of the feeling, the person who judges and the one who is evaluated.

Whether or not we might profitably study self-referent behaviors from other perspectives as well, such responses are most appropriately considered within a social psychological framework because of the social nature of these self-oriented cognitive, affective, and conative responses.

THE SOCIAL NATURE OF SELF-REFERENT BEHAVIORS

Self-referent behaviors fall into the more inclusive category of human social behavior. Human social behavior may be defined as any behavior by a person or collectivity that more or less directly serves as a stimulus for, or response to, the (real or imagined, past, present, or future) behavior of another person or collectivity. The parenthetical material reminds us that behavior need not be "real" in order to be social by our definition. A contrary-to-fact belief about one individual's behavior may stimulate, or be a response to, behavior of another individual or collectivity. (A false belief regarding another person's hostile intentions will lead us to react accordingly.) Nor need the behavior be contemporary in order to be considered "social." Either the memory or the anticipation of one person's behavior may serve as the stimulus for, or response to, the behavior of another person. (Our recall of how others have responded to us in the past influences how we behave, as does the anticipation of another person's probable response to our own behavior influence our decision to so behave.)

Self-referent behaviors fall under the rubric of human social behavior, as we have just defined it, whether one focuses on the structure of self-referent behaviors or on the undifferentiated self-referent behavior as a stimulus for, or response, to the behavior of others.

Structure of Self-Referent Behavior

The structure of self-referent behavior is such that a person can be conceptualized as two separate individuals—one who acts and one who reacts to the behavior of the actor. Human beings have the ability to perceive, evaluate, and otherwise respond to their own characteristics and behavior; and these behaviors serve as stimuli for further responses by the very same people. A person anticipates how he will behave in a given situation and responds to this self-perception with a particular self-feeling which in turn stimulates further self-awareness. Insofar as these reflexive processes represent responses by a person to himself or stimuli for further responses by the person or both, self-referent responses may be considered social behavior. Indeed, we might plausibly redefine human social behavior as any behavior by one human being that serves as a stimulus for, or response to, either *his own* (real or imagined, past, present, or future) behavior or the behavior of another human being.

Self-Referent Behavior as Undifferentiated Stimulus-Response

Even more plausibly, however, self-referent activities are appropriately termed social behavior insofar as self referent activities (1) stimulate responses (including the structures that emerge from individual social response patterns) by *another* human being and (2) are themselves responses to (or the product of) the socially patterned responses of others.

Self-Referent Behaviors as Stimuli. The effects of self-referent behaviors on the responses of others may be more or less direct, depending on a number of circumstances which include the mode of such
behaviors. The distinction may be made, for example, between self-
referent behaviors that are covert or private and, therefore, have no
direct stimulus value for the responses of others, on the one hand, and
more overt or public self-referent responses that are observed by and do
have direct stimulus value for the responses of another, on the other
hand. Self conceiving and self-feeling, for example, have no direct social
consequences. Others do not directly perceive the subject's self-conceiving and self-feeling activities and, therefore, do not respond to these
activities directly. However, the ways a person conceives of himself,
evaluates himself, and feels toward himself elicits other self-referent
behaviors that do call forth responses from others and otherwise have
consequences for the outcomes experienced by others. Thus, an individual's self-conception becomes a meaningful social stimulus *indirectly*
when it motivates him to present himself to others in particular ways.
Self-evaluation influences others' behaviors indirectly when it elicits visible expressions of self-feeling and self-hate stimulates responses from
others or otherwise has consequences for the social system, by stimulating such overt responses as attacks on others or by avoiding role performance in a social institutional context.

However, such reflexive behaviors as self-representational responses more directly influence others' behavior, as when the individual communicates to others his conception of himself in order to elicit
responses desired by the individual (e.g., identifying oneself as a superi-
or in order to elicit deferential behavior from a subordinate).

In short, self-referent behaviors may have direct effects on social
outcome or be mediated by effects on other self-referent behaviors. In
either case, the social outcomes (the responses by others) may have
additional more or less direct ramifications. Thus, in order to reduce
negative self-feelings, a person may engage in the self-protective device
of deviating from the norms of the group subjectively perceived as occasioning feelings of self-rejection. A *direct* effect of this self-protective
pattern might be reciprocal rejection of the subject by the group members, either individually or collectively. This response in turn might lead
to further outcomes of (1) attenuation of the emotional ties between the
subject and the group, thereby weakening the subject's amenability to
social controls and (2) negative reinforcement of deviant behavior on the
part of some group members who observed rejection of the deviant actor
by the group. Thus, *indirectly* the self-protective response might lead
both to stabilization of a deviant outgroup and increased conforming
behavior on the part of the members of the ingroup.

To summarize, self-referent behaviors elicit social responses either directly or indirectly through their initial impact on other self-referent behaviors which in turn influence social outcomes. The initial social outcomes are likely to have further effects on the outcomes of others in either case. Thus, even where self-referent behaviors directly impinge on the outcomes of others, these behaviors are likely to have other indirect social consequences as well.

Self-Referent Behaviors as Responses. Just as self-referent behaviors more or less directly stimulate responses by others, so do such behaviors emerge *in response to* the behaviors of others. The self-referent behaviors may be a relatively direct response to the behaviors of others, as when negative self-evaluations are elicited by the perceived punitive behavior of parents. Alternatively, the self-referent behaviors may be more indirect responses to the behaviors of others. The behavior of others may (1) first influence other self-referent behaviors which in turn influence the self-referent behavior under consideration, or may (2) initially influence other social outcomes which then influence the self-referent behavior. To pursue an earlier example, the first situation is illustrated by the introduction of a person as someone in authority, which leads the actor to conceive of himself as a subordinate and to a self-conception that ultimately influences the actor to present himself deferentially. The deferential self-presentation is an indirect response to the introduction, mediated by self-conception and other self-referent responses. To illustrate the second situation, patterns of differential association may influence the decision to train for a particular career, entry into a particular professional socialization sequence, and, ultimately, a self-conception as a representative of that profession. The influence of the patterns of differential association on one's self-concept as a professional is indirect, mediated by a number of other social responses (e.g., patterns of differential association, professional socialization experiences).

Although I tend to illustrate the response patterns in which self-referent behaviors serve as social stimuli and responses in terms of individual responses, it must be emphasized that self-referent behaviors may also elicit or respond to the *collective* responses of others. Since the remaining chapters abundantly illustrate this, only a few illustrations are given here. Later discussions, for example, will highlight the role of cultural systems in (1) providing the system of cognitive categories that elicit particular self-conceiving responses and (2) defining the normative order (including the hierarchical system of values and the system of variously applicable sanctions) that influences self-definitions, self-judgments, and affective responses to self. Consensual definitions of social identities directly influence self-conception and mediate responses by others to the subject. These responses, in turn, further influence self-conception and self-evaluation (and, thereby, self-feelings). The role expectations associated with social positions provide the definition of the identities influencing a person's self-conception and provide a set of performance standards against which the person evaluates himself. Shared definitions of social relationships will be observed to be useful in understanding the ways in which the person is moved to present himself to others and to otherwise behave; to ascribe particular identities to himself; and to evaluate himself as more or less closely approximating the standards appropriate to the relational context and, consequently, to feel more or less accepting of himself. In short, self-referent behaviors are appropriately conceived as a subset of patterns of human social behavior, since self-referent behaviors serve, more or less directly, as stimuli for, or responses to, the (real or imagined, past, present, or future) patterns of behavior of other people, either individually or collectively.

SELF-REFERENT BEHAVIORS AND THE SELF

In the preceding discussion, I have been careful to specify that my interest is in self-referent behaviors. I have avoided any use of the term *self* that might imply a stable psychological structure that could be studied objectively. In focusing on self-referent behaviors, I associate myself with those scholars (e.g., Wells & Marwell, 1976) who urge

> that self not be used as a noun, to describe a psychological entity or structure. Instead, it should be used as a modifier, signifying a reflexive activity or process, when talking about specific behavioral phenomena like self-conception, self-evaluation, self-perception, and self-esteem. (p. 231)

The decision to focus on self-referent behaviors rather than on the "self" was made, generally, because it appeared that this was a more useful way to study human behavior, in general, and human beings as reflexive organisms (organisms that behave toward themselves), in particular. More specifically, I felt that focusing on self-referent responses (1) more easily permitted self-relevant phenomena to be studied both as active forces, exerting an influence on others, and as the consequences of other influences (and, thereby, permitted conceptualization of these phenomena as *social* forces); (2) offered the promise of reducing the confusion attendant on the multiple and (often) ill-defined meanings assigned to self or self-relevant phenomena; (3) facilitated the formulation and testing of theoretical statements; and (4) was more compatible with what behavioral scientists, in fact, investigated, regardless of the terminology they employed.

Self-Referent Behaviors as Active Forces

The previous discussion illustrates the ease with which particular self-referent behaviors may be thought of as actively exerting influence on particular social outcomes, whether directly or indirectly (via their influence on other self-referent responses or social outcomes or both). The self, treated as an objectified psychological entity, appears to inhibit the examination of self-related phenomena as active forces (social or otherwise). Although this concept easily suggests something that could be the product of social forces, how can such a private psychological structure be thought of as influencing others if it cannot be known by others? Presumably, such influences could only be exerted through the self-generation of mutually influential self-referent *behaviors* which ultimately impinge on the outcomes of others. Our experience tells us that the person's behaviors with reference to his own person and experience (i.e., with reference to the self) do have a significant influence on others. How someone thinks about, feels toward, evaluates, and presents himself does indeed affect (directly or indirectly) the outcomes of others. If this is our experience, then we must have a convenient way of expressing it; and the language of self-referent behaviors more easily permits this expression than the language of the self. It is to connote the *active* influences of self-referent behavior that frequently, throughout this work, I will express self-referent behavior in the active mode (self-conceiving, self-feeling, self-enhancing responses, and so forth). It is to emphasize the active influence of cognitive and affective responses (as well as the motor responses that are more traditionally thought of as "behavior") that I designate these reponses with the term *behavior*.

Conceptual Confusion

The decision of many scholars to focus on self-referent activities as the appropriate object of inquiry was in part the result of growing dissatisfaction with the confusion caused by the term *self*. Although the term has a long history in the behavioral sciences, there is increasing recognition that this undifferentiated concept has impeded understanding of the phenomena subsumed under its label by virtue of its diverse meanings for scientists and laymen alike. Others have commented on the range of meanings associated with this term, extending from the total person to particular feelings (such as esteem) held by the person toward himself, and have noted that "no theorist has been able to work consistently with this term and/or concept" (Wells & Marwell, 1976, p. 231).

Much of the confusion surrounding this concept has involved the failure to distinguish between the person and its attributes, as they are objectively given, and the same person's experience of and response to those personal attributes. The decision to focus on self-referent behaviors helps resolve that confusion by forcing this basic distinction between self-referent responses, on the one hand, and the object of those responses (the person's own behaviors and attributes, including his possessions, and any aspects of the physical and social environment with which he is identified), on the other hand. These self-referent behaviors, the distinction having been made, became increasingly associated with this notion. Out of the many meanings still associated with *self*, Wells and Marwell (1976) have noted that

> the common elements are that the phenomenon of self involves some process of *reflexive* activity (thoughts, feelings, or actions in which the agent and the objects of the behavior are the same person), that the self is typically regarded as an experiential (rather than objective) phenomenon, and the self is generally an acquired structure. (p. 229)

Just as the distinction between self-referent behaviors, on the one hand, and the person or personal attributes that were the objects of the self-referent behaviors, on the other hand, aided in the clarification of the concept of self, so did the notion of self-referent behaviors acquire refinements of meaning. When self-referent behaviors are viewed as a subcategory of behaviors, it is possible to distinguish among various modes of self-referent response that are similar to those that have been made among behaviors in general. Thus, semantic confusion may be diminished by drawing increasingly fine distinctions among the range of responses a person makes to himself.

Frequently, three broad categories of self-referent responses are recognized. For example, Stryker (1968) conceives of the self as a set of responses of an organism to itself that are differentiated along cognitive–conative–affective lines and notes that it will make a difference with respect to behavior whether the organism responds to itself with cognitive (I am), conative (I want), or affective (I feel) responses (p. 560). Similar distinctions have been made by others, as by Secord and Backman (1964), when they distinguished among the cognitive, affective, and "behavioral" aspects of a person's attitudes toward himself.

However, even finer distinctions may be made. Although numerous commentators appear to confuse evaluative–judgmental responses to self with affective responses to self, using a term such as self-esteem to refer to both sets of responses, the literature as a whole reflects a difference between self-evaluation and self-feeling. According to Wells and Marwell (1976),

> descriptions of self-*evaluation* tend to stress how people regard themselves in terms of their facility in achieving valued ends and in eliciting social rewards. . . . In contrast, descriptions of self-*affection* emphasize the emotional concomitants of self-evaluation. How persons feel about themselves and their personal worthiness is not entirely determined by how good they think they are in a utilitarian sense. (p. 232)

Similar distinctions might be made within the cognitive category, with self-cognitions referring to beliefs held by the person about himself, self-conceptualization referring to the organization or structuring of self-perceptions, self-awareness referring to relative consciousness of self and nonself, and self-perception referring to sensory awareness of personal attributes.

Within the conative or behavioral categories, a distinction might be made between self-presentation (with self-description as a subclass of self-presentational activities) and a variety of other self-protective or adaptive responses that have, as their more or less conscious purpose, to forestall or reduce the intensity of subjective distress associated with self-devaluing circumstances. Such self-referent activities include self-direction and self-control. These activities imply, respectively, the person's orientation of self toward the achievement of some positively desired goal and the avoidance of the expression of a behavior that would be intrinsically or instrumentally undesirable.

Formulation and Testing of Theoretical Statements

Both the distinction between personal attributes and self-referent behaviors and the increasingly fine distinctions made among self-referent behaviors facilitate the formulation and refinement of testable theoretical statements accounting for any of these elements. Once the distinction has been made, the genesis of particular personal attributes in part can be accounted for by self-referent responses (e.g., self-hatred leading to seclusiveness or hostile attitudes), just as self-referent responses are accounted for, in part, by personal attributes (e.g., physical characteristics of a person influence self-conception which in turn evokes particular self-evaluations and self-feelings).

Similarly, theoretical statements regarding particular self-referent activities may incorporate other self-referent responses as explanatory factors. For example, insofar as self-evaluation and self-feeling are correlated, but less than perfectly so, it is possible to employ self-evaluation in an explanation of self-feeling and to inquire about the conditions under which the correlation will be strengthened or attenuated. Thus, the degree to which affective responses are elicited by our evaluation may depend on the salience of the object of our evaluation and the priority of the dimensions along which we are making judgments in our hierarchy of values. If we evaluate ourselves or an aspect of ourselves negatively, if we are motivated to think well of ourselves, and if that aspect of ourselves we evaluate negatively is considered to be a significant basis for self-evaluation, then the self-evaluative process will have a profound influence on the nature of our self-feelings. Under mutually exclusive conditions, the self-evaluative acts may have appreciably less influence.

In short, focusing on self-referent behaviors stimulates the making of distinctions between self-referent behaviors and objectively given personal attributes and behaviors, as it stimulates increasingly fine distinctions among modes of self-referent responses. These distinctions in turn permit more sophisticated theoretical statements by virtue of the proliferation of explanatory factors.

Operational Definitions of "Self"

Finally, the decision to focus on self-referent behaviors is more continuous with past research operations than the conceptualization of self as some objective structure. This is true for those researchers who conceive of the self as an objective structure as well as for those who explicitly study self-referent responses rather than the self. In fact, behavioral scientists generally do not study the nature of the self but rather how an individual behaves toward himself. An examination of the literature dealing with the self will reveal that generalizations made about the self refer to operationalized self-referent behaviors rather than the self as an objectified phenomenon. Behavioral scientists study not the determinants and consequences of the self but rather the determinants and consequences of self-referent behaviors. They are not primarily interested in how the self comes to be, but rather how the person comes to perceive himself (his own person) in a certain way, to hold certain beliefs about himself, to feel positively or negatively about himself, to evaluate himself as of great or little worth, and to present himself to others the way he does. Nor, as students of the self, are they interested in how a person comes to be short rather than tall, amiable rather than belligerent, well liked rather than disliked, a professor rather than the occupant of some other occupational status (i.e., they are not *directly* interested in these associations). Rather, they are interested in how a person comes to perceive or to evaluate himself as tall or short, how he comes to feel pride in being a professor or to present himself to others in a way that will communicate his occupational status, how he feels loss of esteem by virtue of being disliked. The determinants of a person's rejection by others or of his professional status are regarded as indirect determinants, then, of the person's own responses to his self (i.e., his self-perceptions, self-evaluations, self-feelings, self-presentations). Behavioral scientists are further interested in the influences among, and the consequences of, the mutually influencing self-referent behaviors.

The study of self-referent behaviors rather than of the self may have been purposive, for such reasons as those noted above, or it may have been the result of research decisions that the only way to operationalize the objective self is in terms of how an individual behaves with reference to himself. In the former case, the investigator is truly interested in studying what an individual says about himself because it is of interest in its own right, or because what he says about himself or what he otherwise expresses toward himself is taken as an operational indicator of an otherwise nonobservable self-referent response such as self-feeling or self-conceiving. When the self is conceptualized in terms other than self-referent behaviors, the end result is the same. The decision is generally made that the self is not knowable but may only be inferred through the observable behaviors (including self-descriptions) of a person toward (aspects of) his own person.

The decision to focus on self-referent behaviors may be the result of both processes: the conclusion that it is "more important" to study self-referent behaviors and the conclusion that self-relevant phenomena may only be studied as self-referent responses. The following statement by Gergen (1971), for example, appears to reflect both processes:

> In the final analysis, one's personal conduct is based upon one's conception of "reality" rather than upon reality itself. And it is the *process* of self-understanding that is more important than the "self" which the individual attempts to understand. The "self" may always elude our comprehension, but the process of comprehension is open to understanding. (p. viii)

The preceding observations do not necessarily imply a positivistic denial of the self but rather reflect a recognition that, whatever the meaning of the self (as some internal structure of the person or otherwise), what we in fact study as sociologists or social psychologists are individuals' behaviors with reference to the self: how these behaviors influence each other, how these behaviors are influenced by the behaviors of others, and how these self-referent behaviors influence the responses of others.

PURPOSE AND ORGANIZATION

The purpose of this volume is to consider the state of our under-standing of the social psychology of self-referent behaviors—that is, the social antecedents and consequences of mutually influential self-referent behaviors. Given the tenuous state of knowledge in this area, our in-ventory of "knowledge" will incorporate what is currently accepted as working hypotheses regarding the antecedents, consequences, and mu-tual influences of self-referent activities more frequently than what is known beyond all doubt about these relationships; and the ordering of this knowledge will reflect an attempt to impose the outline of a the-oretical structure on unrelated findings more often than it will reflect preexisting theoretical statements. These circumstances are occasioned by the ambiguous concepts, use of unvalidated instruments, flawed research designs, and lack of theoretical guidance that is said to charac-terize much of the literature on self-referent constructs (Wylie, 1974, 1979).

For simplicity of presentation, the state of our understanding will be organized around a limited number of modes of self-referent responses, those modes of response that have been most studied as stimuli for or responses to the social responses of others. Among the more prominent self-referent behaviors in the literature are self-conceiving (the cognitive structuring of perceived self-referent experiences); self-evaluating (judg-ments regarding the approximation of self-conceptions to more or less highly valued criteria); self-feeling (more or less intense positive–nega-tive affective responses to self-conception and self-evaluation); and what we can conceptualize as self-protective–self-enhancing responses since the self-referent behaviors appear to relate more or less directly to the achievement of personally (instrumentally or intrinsically) valued goals and to the avoidance of personally disvalued states. This last category of responses encompasses self-referent adaptive, defensive, and coping patterns, including those that have been labeled self-presentation, self-description, self-control, self-determination, and self-protection in vari-ous contexts.

The social nature of these self-referent behaviors will be considered in the next four chapters. One chapter will be devoted to each of the four categories of self-referent behaviors. It is argued above that self-referent behaviors comprise a subset of social behaviors (1) by virtue of the structure of reflexive activity (the person behaves and responds to his own behavior) and (2) insofar as the self-referent behavior is a stimulus for (an influence on) and a response to (a consequence of) the individual or collective (patterned) responses of others. This being the case, it follows that both self-referent response patterns and the individual or collective responses of others must be considered as contributing to the social basis and as reflecting the social consequences of a particular mode of self-referent behavior. Thus, self-cognition is influenced in part by self-protective mechanisms that distort the subject's self-perceptions or sensitize him to self-enhancing aspects of himself or both, and, less directly, is influenced by self-feelings that motivate the putative self-protective responses. In addition, however, self-cognition is influenced by the social context in which personal attributes and behaviors are perceived; by the collective (shared) conceptual systems that are transmitted to the subject in the course of the socialization process; and by the social processes that influence the attributes, behaviors, and experiences that are the objects of self-referent cognition.

Generally, in each of the four chapters, I focus on the social influences (whether other self-referent responses or the individual–collective responses of others) on the self-referent mode of interest in that chapter. I note only in passing the consequences of that self-referent mode for other self-referent responses, since these are considered in the chapter(s) devoted to those categories of self-referent behaviors. For example, whereas the chapter on self-cognition notes that self-cognition has consequences for self-evaluative responses, this relationship is considered in greater detail in the chapter on self-evaluative responses, in which these responses are treated as the direct outcome of the conjoint influence of self-cognition and the personal need-value system and (less directly) of the determinants of these phenomena. However, the chapter on self-protective–self-enhancing responses has a somewhat different form. First, the consequences of these responses are necessarily considered in greater detail since the formal properties of the responses *are* the consequences. Self-protective responses *do not influence* changes in self-referent cognition, personal value systems, and person–environment relations. Rather, they *are reflected* in these transformations. The self-enhancing–self-protective responses (i.e., the responses motivated by the need for positive self-evaluation and consequent positive self-feelings) *are* changes in self-referent cognition, personal value systems, and person–environment relations. To describe self-protective–self-enhancing responses is to describe their "consequences" for self-referent responses, the person, and the person's relationships to the environment. Second, in Chapter 5, unlike the earlier chapters, the consequences of the self-referent behaviors are concerned with transformations of phenomena in addition to those reflecting self-referent responses. These phenomena include person–environment relations. Although in Chap-

ter 5 I focus on individual level changes, the implications of self-protective–self-enhancing responses for the functioning of interpersonal systems in which the person participates and for the stable social institutional structures that are exemplified by the interpersonal systems will
be apparent. These effects are made more explicit in the final chapter.

Finally, in Chapter 6, I consider, simultaneously, the direct and
indirect additive and interactive social antecedents and consequences of
the four categories of mutually influential self-referent behaviors. The
result reflects the broad outline of a tentative theoretical model of the
social significance of self-referent behaviors viewed both as products of
social influences and as influences on social patterns.

SUMMARY

The purpose of this volume is to consider, from the social psychological perspective, the state of our understanding of a special category
of human behaviors. This category of behaviors includes all behaviors
by individuals that have themselves as objects of their behavior. These
behaviors include feelings toward oneself, evaluating oneself, conceiving the self, and personal responses consciously or unconsciously directed toward protecting the person from threatening circumstances or
enhancing the person's positive self-feelings.

The social psychological perspective views psychological patterns
as human social behavior. Patterns of human social behavior are defined
as behaviors (including feeling, thinking, and acting) that serve as stimuli for, or responses to, the (real or imagined, past, present, or future)
behavior of other people. To connote the idea that cognition and affect,
as well as overt responses that are more traditionally thought of as
behavior, actively influence (whether directly or indirectly) the responses of others and are themselves responses to stimuli, these otherwise qualitatively distinct responses are grouped together under the
rubric *behavior*. *Self-referent* behavior *is* human social behavior (and,
hence, is an appropriate object of study from the social psychological
perspective) in two senses. First, the reflexive nature of much human
behavior is such that the person may be treated as if he were both the
actor and the object of the action. The person's behavior directed toward
himself stimulates further response from himself. Thus, conceiving the
person as both one who acts and as one who responds to the action, the
self-referent behavior is essentially social in nature—that is, the behavior by the person is a stimulus for or response to the behavior of another
organism or both. Second, the social nature of self-referent behavior is

inherent in the observation that self-referent responses by specified kinds of people in specified circumstances do serve as stimuli for, or responses to, patterns of behavior by other people. The reciprocal relationships between specified self-referent behaviors and specified behaviors by others may be relatively direct or mediated by other self-referent behaviors or behaviors of others or both.

Although the *self* has been defined variously in the history of the behavioral sciences, the decision was made here (as by others) to focus on self-referent behaviors after considering at least four issues.

First, our experience tells us that how an individual behaves toward himself more or less directly influences the responses of others. Yet it is difficult to think of the self, conceived of as a private intrapsychic structure, as influencing others except by first influencing self-referent responses that ultimately are communicated to or otherwise influence the outcomes of others. Only by conceptualizing the self in terms of self-referent behaviors can the self be thought of as exerting social influence as well as being influenced by social forces.

Second, the self has been associated with numerous, often ill-defined meanings. The focus on self-referent behaviors helps to reduce the confusion and ambiguity associated with this concept by (1) distinguishing between the responses of the person to himself and those aspects of the person to which the person is responding and (2) by distinguishing among various modes of self-referent behaviors.

Third, these conceptual distinctions facilitated by focusing on self-referent behaviors permit more sophisticated theoretical statements. A particular pattern of self-referent response, whether as an antecedent or a consequence, could then be hypothesized to enter into reciprocal relationships with personal attributes and other mutually influential self-referent responses.

Fourth, whether the self is conceptualized as self-referent behaviors or otherwise, the study of the self has traditionally involved the investigation of such behaviors. Either observable (including self-reported) self-referent behaviors were taken as the appropriate object of study or they were understood to be operational definitions of an otherwise unknowable self. Thus, whether the conceptualization of the self in terms of self-referent behavior departs from traditional model of determining this concept, it remains congruent with traditional research operations.

The following chapters treat each of the specific modes of self-referent behaviors as the antecedent and outcome of other mutually influential self-referent patterns and other social forces. The modes of self-referent responses are self-cognition (Chapter 2), self-evaluation (Chapter 3), self-feeling (Chapter 4), and self-protective–self-enhancing responses (Chapter 5). The summary chapter (Chapter 6) may be taken as the broad outline of a tentative theoretical model derived from a consideration of the common and unique, direct and indirect, additive and interactive social antecedents and consequences of the mutually influential self-referent behaviors.

CHAPTER 2

Social Antecedents and Consequences of Self-Referent Cognition

Here we consider what we know (with varying degrees of certainty) about the social influences on self-referent cognitive (self-conceiving) processes and, to a lesser degree, about their social consequences. *Self-conceiving processes*, for our present purposes, is meant to encompass the range of self-referent cognitive activities—imagining oneself, holding beliefs about oneself, self-perception, self-conception, sensing oneself, and being aware of oneself. Self-referent cognitive responses collectively define what others have called the *phenomenal self*, that is, "a person's awareness, rising out of interactions with his environment, of his own beliefs, values, attitudes, the links between them, and their implications for his behavior" (p. 716) (Jones & Gerard, 1967).

In accordance with the approach described earlier, the following inventory examines the factors that influence and are influenced by self-conceiving *processes* rather than those that relate to the *products* of reflexive activity. As noted by Wells and Marwell (p. 46) (1976), this approach is akin to that of Mead (1934), who is said to regard the self not so much as the object of reflexive behavior as the act of experiencing that object through the person's reflection in the behavior of others. This is in contrast to the view that defines the self as the content or products of reflexive behavior. The focus is more on continuing interpretative responses to self than on the resulting structure of self-conceptions (Gordon, 1968). We consider, in turn, the social antecedents and consequences of modes of self-conceiving responses.

SOCIAL ANTECEDENTS OF SELF-CONCEIVING RESPONSES

The focus on the *social* basis of self-conceiving responses, how an individual becomes aware of and conceives of himself, whether in present circumstances, in memory, in anticipation, or in imagination, is a function of the effects of four sets of variables: (1) the (in large measure, socially influenced) personal attributes, behaviors, and experiences (including the responses of others to the person); (2) the (in large measure, socially defined) perceived situational context in which the personal attributes, behaviors, and experiences are manifested; (3) the person's conceptual system, learned in the course of the socialization process that is used to structure self-relevant as well as all other experiences; and (4) the self-enhancing disposition of the subject that influences the person to attend to value-relevant aspects of his person and to be aware of personal traits, behaviors, and experiences in more or less undistorted form toward the goals of forestalling the threat of self-devaluing experiences, reducing the distress associated with the occurrence of self-devaluing experiences, and maintaining self-accepting attitudes.

Personal Traits, Behaviors, and Experiences

To understand the factors that determine how people conceive of themselves, it is necessary to begin with what the person is, for it is the nature of the person's traits, behaviors, and experiences to which symbolic significance is assigned, and which, thereby, stimulates the self-conceiving processes.

The Nature of Personal Traits, Behaviors, and Experiences. A person is characterized by a complex of interrelated traits, behaviors, and experiences, including physical aspects (six feet tall, small nose, weight 150 pounds), behavioral predispositions (argumentative, ambitious, depressed, logical), ascribed or achieved social positions (mother, Protestant, friend, secretary, motorist, member of the middle class), characteristic role behaviors (affectionate father, an active member of civic organizations, a person who is willing to do anything for a friend), abilities (leadership, musical, organizational), specific behaviors in specific situations (someone who just had an argument with her mother), and personal attributes (loyal, honest, sensual, successful). An important subclass of personal behavioral tendencies consists of patterned responses to self, which, in turn, may be the stimulus for other self-referent responses or for responses to the person by others. Thus, a person may characteristically devalue his athletic ability, momentarily perceive himself as self-depreciating, or positively evaluate himself because of his ability to depreciate himself (insofar as this self-evaluative behavior approximates such personally held values as the ability to be "realistic" about one's limitations).

Included among personal traits and behaviors are personal *extensions*, that is, aspect of the environment, including membership groups and physical possessions the person identifies as belonging to him or that are identified by others as belonging to him. Both James (1890) and Cooley (1902) early recognized the extensions of the person as influential in self-conception. James referred to the material *Me* as one part of the self, the material Me including the person's body, as well as his material possessions and those groups of which he is most intimately a part, such as the family; and Cooley's (1902) discussion of self-conception referred to "that toward which we have the 'my' attitude" (p. 40).

In addition to what a person is and does, it is important to consider, among his traits and behaviors (including his self-referent behaviors), what *happens* to him as well as what he *causes* to happen. An individual may, for example, be one who normally experiences adverse life circumstances, who is deferred to, or who is rejected by others. The fact of having had these experiences becomes part of what the person is.

Among the personal attributes, behaviors, and experiences of an individual are those that (when the individual becomes aware of them as personal attributes) will be defined and evaluated as characteristics that deviate from the personal evaluative standards. In another context, these attributes, behaviors, and experiences have been defined as unmotivated deviance, since the individual fails to conform to social and personal expectations of appropriate behavior while still desiring to conform to the expectations (Kaplan, 1972b, 1980, 1982). He will possess disvalued attributes, although he would wish it otherwise; he will fail to conform to personal and social expectations; and he will experience unfortunate circumstances that he would have prevented if he could. (Deviant behaviors, attributes, and experiences that are purposely attained, performed, or invited are considered in Chapter 5 in connection with self-protective–self-enhancing patterns.)

The Social Origins of Personal Traits, Behaviors, and Experiences. The person's traits, behaviors, and experiences as influences on self-conceiving processes are social in nature in two senses. From a synchronic point of view, the symbolic significance (the stimulus value) of the person's traits, behaviors, and experiences is determined by the social setting. From a diachronic point of view, the person's traits, behaviors, and experiences are, in large measure, a result of his experiences during the socialization process.

To treat a subject as vast as the social origins of personal traits and behaviors in any detail is beyond the scope of this work. The study of social influences directly impinging on personal traits and behaviors would encompass a large part of what is traditionally covered by social psychology; and the study of the mutual influences among the social factors that influence personal attributes and behaviors encompasses much of traditional sociology. Nevertheless, it is necessary to emphasize and illustrate that those personal traits and behaviors (whether normative or deviant) that profoundly affect cognitive self-referent responses are themselves affected by mutually influential social factors. This point with reference to normative traits and behaviors was made well by Wylie (1979), while commenting on the general theoretical dependence on the concepts of identification and social learning in considerations of the developmental aspects of the self-concept:

> Both direct parental reinforcement and the reward value of imitating the parental model presumably play important parts in shaping the children's "actual" characteristics and behaviors. Partly as a function of these actual characteristics (especially as they are reflected to the child by others' reactions) children develop self-conceptions. (p. 332)

Among the actual traits of the subject are such biological characteristics as sex, which form the basis for social differentiation (that is, assignment to different social positions). Given the sexual nature of the subject, the person's social experiences will determine what associated role dispositions he will display. He or she will be rewarded for displaying certain behaviors and characteristics, but not others—those displayed by certain role models with which the child will be asked to identify, depending on a number of social conditions. For example, the establishment of an appropriate sex-role identity may be motivated by the need to identify with a model in order to command the attractive goals possessed by the model. The child appears to assume that if he possessed some of the external characteristics of the model, he would also possess the desirable psychological properties, such as power or love from others (Kagan, 1964).

Both the stimulus value of the social reinforcement and the nature of the characteristics the child is asked to adopt presume the operation of social forces that more or less directly influence the child's actual sex-related social role characteristics. The effectiveness of parental reinforcement, for example, depends on the ability of the parent to command rewards and punishments that are meaningful to the child. Such a condition is assured by the early placement and prolonged tenure of the dependent child within the socially defined family unit and by the socially prescribed authority that is a parental prerogative. The actual characteristics that define the sex-related roles are reflected in cultural stereotypes, and these correspond to appropriate sex-related self-descriptions. Thus, Wylie (1979) writes that

> the self-descriptions of men correspond with the male stereotype on such qualities as self-confidence, leadership, independence, ambition, aggression, and ruggedness. For women an analogous correspondence between self-descriptions and the female stereotype is suggested with respect to such attributes as kindness, interest in others, sympathy, sensitivity, and cultural interests. (p. 303)

The culturally defined role behaviors associated with a given sex, however, change over time, and subcultural differentiation has been noted as well (Kagan, 1964).

The social origin of *unmotivated deviance,* as well as normatively defined attributes, behaviors, and experiences is also noteworthy (Kaplan 1982). Instances of unmotivated deviance arise as a result of three general categories of circumstances.

In the first category, individuals will fail to conform to the expectations of others when they are unaware of or mistaken about the social identities of others with whom they interact or when they are aware of the others' social positions but are unaware or mistaken about the role expectations defining their own social identity or that of those with whom they are interacting. In the former case, not knowing the social positions of those with whom one is interacting, the person is unable to identify his own complementary position and therefore cannot play the appropriate role. Such circumstances are most likely to arise when a person is moved to a new set of interpersonal relationships and when situational cues are vague or ambiguous or both. Members of the more mobile segments of our society would be more vulnerable to these circumstances. In the latter case, the subject may know both his identity and the identity of the other person but have no expectations, or have erroneous expectations, regarding the roles that the interacting parties should play. Such circumstances are most likely to arise during times of rapidly changing role definitions, as a consequence of improper role models or other inadequate socialization experiences, and following life events that require the occupancy of unfamiliar roles.

The second category of circumstances influencing the subject's unwilling failure to perform in accordance with the expectations of others relates to the subject having status sets or role sets that impose conflicting expectations. Although the person wishes to conform to the expectations of all the other parties with whom he is interacting, the nature of the conflicting expectations are such that he can conform to one set of expectations only at the cost of not conforming to another set. In the case of the status set, conflicting expectations are occasioned by the subject simultaneously occupying two or more social positions and, in those capacities, engaging in two or more social relationships. In the case of the role set, the conflicting expectations are also occasioned by the subject simultaneously participating in more than one relationship. Here, the subject is expected to play different roles while acting in the same capacity, that is, occupying the same social position or status in each relationship. Such situations are likely to occur during periods of rapid and uneven rates of sociocultural change in diverse sectors of the more inclusive social system.

The third category of circumstances influencing unmotivated deviant behavior concerns the absence of instrumental resources to achieve legitimate goals. The absence of instrumental resources derives from (1) congenital inadequacies, as in strength, dexterity, or intelligence; (2) a failure to acquire the skills and experience necessary for adapting to or coping with the environment as a result of faulty socialization experiences or the disruption of already acquired adaptive or coping patterns by various life events; (3) the lack of adequate social support systems; (4) the occurrence of life events that impose legitimate requirements on an individual that cannot be met by his heretofore adequate resources; and (5) deviant attributions by other social systems. This last set of influences on legitimate instrumental resources relates to an alternative conception of deviance other than that of motivated and unmotivated deviance. This conception takes into account the existence of more or less inclusive and interlocking social systems.

As a result of the interdigitation among systems, it is possible for a subject to conform successfully to the expectations of his membership group in his own view and that of other group members and yet to be judged deviant by other groups because the same behavior that conforms to the socionormative system of the membership group is judged to be deviant from the perspective of the other group's system of normative expectations. To the extent that the other group judges the subject's behavior to be deviant (and has the power to do so), the group will implement negative sanctions. These negative sanctions will adversely affect the availability of legitimate instrumental resources that are required if the subject is to be able to conform to the expectations of his own membership group. In failing to conform to these expectations against his will, the subject, by definition, manifests unmotivated deviance. Thus, unmotivated deviance is the indirect result of the attribution of deviance and the consequent implementation of effective negative sanctions by a nonmembership or reference group for behavior by a person that is normative in the context of that person's own membership or reference group.

The empirical basis of the social origins of various personal traits and behaviors is not uniformly well established. For example, Wylie (1979) has noted that "it has been frequently hypothesized that parents from different socioeconomic classes use different techniques of child rearing which could conceivably lead to personality in the children as a function of socioeconomic class, which in turn could lead to differences in self-description and self-evaluation as a function of class" (p. 73). However, she goes on to note that studies relating to this hypothesized sequences are not notably in evidence. Generally, it appears that definitive empirical statements regarding associations between child-rearing practices by parents of varying socioeconomic level, on the one hand, and children's behaviors or attributes, on the other hand, are not possible on the basis of existing literature (Hess, 1970).

Nevertheless, although the presumed social origins of personal attributes, behaviors, and experiences are all too frequently more a matter of faith than of observation, the sociological literature on the subject is sufficiently rich to justify that faith and, at least, to provide illustrative material.

Having illustrated the social influences that affect such personal traits and behaviors as sex-based role dispositions and unmotivated deviance, we now look at the effects of mutually influential personal attributes, behaviors, and experiences on self-referent cognitive behaviors.

Personal Attributes, Behaviors, and Experiences and Self-Cognition: Empirical Associations. Up to this point, it has been assumed that personal attributes or behaviors indeed influence self-referent cognitive responses. However, no empirical justification for this assumption has yet been established. Before we present further theoretical statements regarding the relationship, the research literature will be evaluated with regard to the justification for presuming an etiological relationship between antecedent personal traits, behaviors, and experiences and subsequent self-cognition.

The empirical literature does include numerous reports of associations between personal traits and behaviors and self-conceiving responses, although these reports frequently permit very different interpretations regarding the casual relationships among these variables, and the associations reported are far from perfect. A person's sex and race are associated with apparently self-referent cognitive responses early in life. Sweet and Thornburg (1971), for example, reported that black and white three-, four-, and five-year-olds were able to choose as the picture that looked most like them a picture of the child of their own sex and race from among a set of pictures of six males and six females equally divided among black, white, and oriental categories. Specifically, with regard to sex identity, one of the most stable of all social identities (Kohlberg, 1966), the labeling of one's own sex (one of the early steps in the acquisition of sex identity) appears to occur late in the second year of life (Kohlberg, 1966).

With regard to self-conception of race, Wylie (1979) summarizes the research data as follows:

> In general, some notion of racial differentiation (between black and white) seems to begin to appear before the third birthday, with classification of clear-cut examplars and self-classification by doll identification or verbal self-labeling being virtually errorless by age seven. Recent evidence suggests no racial difference in this sort of conceptual development, especially if socioeconomic level and general cognitive developmental level are taken into account. (p. 160)

In addition to reports detailing relationships between self-conceiving responses and such congenital characteristics as sex and race, the empirical literature also offers conclusions regarding the relationship between self-referent cognitive responses and a range of other personal traits and accomplishments. For example, grades obtained in school have been observed to be correlated with self-concept of school ability or intelligence (Bachman, O'Malley, & Johnston, 1978; Purkey, 1970). Additional evidence of the influence of actual personal attributes, behaviors, and experiences on self-conceptions comes from studies of the effects of experiences in the occupational sphere. Experiences relating to the attainment of greater or lesser income, promotion, demotion, employment, and like experiences affect the individual's self-perceptions of internal control, sense of competence, and of being more or less highly regarded (Cohn, 1978; Elder, 1969). For example, individuals who apparently have experiences of work-autonomy tend to perceive themselves in terms of self-efficacy. According to Mortimer and Lorence (1979a),

> the results, therefore, suggest that autonomous and challenging work experiences, requiring a high level of self-directed thought and independent judgment, have important impacts on the individual's conception of self. (pp. 317–318)

Consistent with this, Staples, Schwalbe, and Gecas (1984) report that the degree of supervision and routinization that an individual experiences on the job influences self-perceptions of occupation-related self-efficacy.

Another illustration of the influence of personal experiences on self-cognition is a study by Pitts (1978), which reports that in Sherbroook, Quebec, French males who had attended schools in which instruction was in English (in which presumably they were more likely, in fact, to be the objects of prejudice) were more likely than those who had attended schools in which instruction was in French to record that they were the object of ethnic prejudice, a self-cognition that may have implications for self-evaluation, since the French who had attended the former schools tended to have lower self-esteem.

These findings, although they suggest a relationship between personal traits or behaviors or both, on the one hand, and cognitive self-referent responses, on the other hand, must be interpreted with great caution. Not all these observations may be said to demonstrate unequivocally the influence of personal traits or behaviors or both on self-conceiving responses. Although the correlation between self-concept (for example, of school ability) and a behavior or attribute (for example, good grades) may indicate that the behavior or attribute influences the self-concept by providing a cognitive basis for self-attribution, it may also indicate that people behave or acquire attributes on the basis of their self-concept, as when thinking of one's self as being academically able influences behavior that is consistent with the (presumably valued) self-concept. Alternatively, the relationship might be accounted for in terms of common antecedents. However, the temporal relationship between sex or race and self-conceiving responses is less problematic.

In any case, other reported research suggests an uncertain relationship between certain personal experiences and the person's self-perceptions with regard to those experiences. For example, other persons' perceptions of the subject are not always highly correlated with the subject's self-perceptions as the object of others' perceptions. These circumstances tend to be accounted for in terms of impediments to the communication of others' perceptions of the subject to the subject. Shrauger and Schoenemann (1979) observe

> that there is minimal agreement between individuals' judgements of others' perceptions of them and their actual perceptions suggests that the communication of feedback to others may often be infrequent or ambiguous. Although norms regarding the evaluation of other people's behavior probably vary widely across different subcultures and situations, strong sanctions are often maintained against making direct appraisals, particularly when they are negative. In some of the only research on the communication of evaluations, Blumberg (1972) found that people report inhibiting the direct communication of all types of evaluations to others, particularly if it is negative or if the recipient is not known well. Barriers to direct expression can be found in intimate relationships as well as in more impersonal social interactions. This "not-even-your-best-friend-will-tell-you" phenomenon has been noted by Goffman (1955), who pointed out that unfavorable evaluations of close associates are typically given only when directly solicited and that in such a situation, chances are that the asker has already made some negative self-appraisal. (p. 565)

In this connection, Felson (1985) asks,

> Why are the relationships between actual and reflected appraisals not high-
> er? Why do persons tend to be fairly inaccurate in their own perceptions of
> what other people think of them? Evidence . . . suggests that the answer has
> to do with barriers to communication. People do not usually communicate
> their appraisals of others to those others. Even young children, who are
> supposedly rather blunt, showed evidence of these communication barriers.
> First, most of the effect of actual or perceived appraisal was not due to
> explicit communication, and therefore must have been communicated by
> more subtle means. Second, children reported receiving more communica-
> tion about their appearance through third parties than directly, face to face.
> That is, children had to rely upon messengers and "spies" to find out how
> good-looking their peers thought they were. Finally, more positive messages
> were received than negative messages. (p. 73)

Nevertheless, it appears reasonable, on the basis of many empirical
observations, to hypothesize that personal traits or behaviors or both do
(more or less directly) influence self-referent cognitions under some conditions. However, the personal traits, behaviors, or experiences may be
more or less isomorphous with, and may exercise more or less direct
influence on, the self-referent cognitive responses. Further, the influence on self-referent cognitive responses may occur at a more or less
conscious level.

We expand on three features of these propositions: first, the stimulus value of particular traits, behaviors, or experiences in evoking self-
conceiving responses, either by entering the person's consciousness as a
face-valid indicator of the personal trait, behavior, or experience in question or by signifying to the person the presence of another, perhaps not
directly observable trait, behavior, or experience; second, the mutual
influence of various personal traits, behaviors, and experiences over
longer and shorter periods of time and, thus, the more or less indirect
influence of the trait, behavior, or experience in stimulating self-conceiving responses; and, third, the level of conscious self-awareness at which
the self-referent cognitive responses occur.

*The Formal Relationship between Personal Traits, Behaviors, and
Experiences and Self-Referent Cognition.* The trait, behavior, or experience that stimulates self-cognition may be taken at face value (one might
conceive of oneself exactly in terms of what is observed) or one may
interpret the observed traits and behaviors so as to infer other, perhaps
nonobservable self-relevant characteristics. The personal experiences of
physiological responses are cases in point. The subject may become
aware of himself as one who experiences certain physiological responses
(my skin is tingling) or infer from these responses that he is experiencing
particular emotions: "My skin is tingling—I must be afraid." There is a

good deal of disagreement regarding whether the person tends to attribute specific emotional experiences to specific physiological patterns or whether general physiological responses interact with particular behavioral contexts (the sight of a person with a gun aimed at the subject) to elicit self-attributions of a particular emotional experience, such as fear (Kemper, 1978). In either case, regardless of the significance of the behavioral context, it appears reasonable to assume that subjectively experienced physiological responses do play a part in the self-perception of inferred emotional responses.

The delineation of the process whereby the subject interprets his *attributes* or *responses* as implying nonobservable traits or behaviors is the special contribution of self-perception theory. Central to self-perception theory (Bem, 1972) is the statement that individuals come to know their own attitudes, emotions, and other internal states, in part, by inferring them from observations of their own behavior or the circumstances in which the behavior occurs; and, thus, to the extent that internal cues are weak, ambiguous, or uninterpretable, an individual, like an outside observer, must rely on external cues to infer his own inner state. To this might be added "or any other nonobservable state," such as having a particular social identity. Thus, although a male's skill with tools might influence the self-cognition only of being skilled at using tools, it might also be interpreted as an appropriately masculine trait, that is, as a confirmation of a male identity. Traits that have no *necessary* connection with social identities permit inferences regarding that class of self-cognitions known as "identifications," that is, beliefs "that some of the attributes of a model (parents, siblings. relatives, peers, and so on) belong to the self" (p. 146) (Kagan, 1964). The personal attributes presumably facilitate the subjective perception of some objective basis of similarity in external attributes or psychological properties between the child and the model, a perception that is said to be a condition for establishing an optimally strong identification (the two other conditions being the perception of the model as being in command of such desired goals as power or love from others or task competence in areas regarded by the child as important).

Just as a person may interpret his traits and behaviors in face-valid terms or as indicators of unobserved self-relevant phenomena, so are the *experiences* of the person interpretable in either of these ways by the person. A large class of the experiences of the person are the outcomes of others' individual or collective actions. These actions may have been stimulated by the person's traits or behaviors or by the responses of yet other people to the person. The responses of others to the person's traits and behaviors that, in turn, influence self-conception include the acts of recognizing or ascribing to the person various social identities and, on the basis of those identities, holding complex sets of expectations about how the person will and should behave. Also included are the evaluative responses elicited from others by the person's attributes and behaviors. However, the actions may have occurred independently of the antecedent traits, behaviors, and experiences of the person but still have influenced the person's outcomes, as when the person may not have stimulated an economic depression but was still affected by it. In any case, once the person becomes aware of the actions of others or of the effects of these actions on him, the actions will influence his self-referent cognition in precisely the same ways that personal attributes and behaviors had a more or less direct influence on self-referent cognitive responses.

First, others' responses to the person may influence his subjective awareness of himself as an object of other persons' particular responses; and he will, thereby, conceive of himself as one who evokes those particular responses. Having been shown deference by others, the person comes to conceive of himself as one who is deferred to by others; and having been identified by others as male, having been expected by others to display masculine traits, and having been evaluated by others as "a real man," he comes to think of himself as a person who other people identify as masculine, expect to display masculine traits, and evaluate as a real man. In a sense, others' responses to subject traits and behaviors become face-valid manifestations of the person's attributes and behaviors. Responses by others *are* the person's traits as he perceives them. It is particularly noteworthy that evaluative responses by others constitute a basis for self-conception as well as self-evaluation and self-feeling. Thus, a person, as a result of negative responses from others, may conceive of himself as having a negative or deviant identity independent of any negative self-evaluation or negative self feelings that may be evoked by the deviant self concept.

Second, others' responses similarly will influence subjective awareness of the person as an object of, or as experiencing the effects of others'particular responses; but, in this instance, he interprets the responses of other people as implying the presence of other subject traits or behavior patterns and comes to conceive of himself in terms of the *implied* attributes and response patterns. If others respond to the person by expressing affection for him, he may well come to think of himself as a person others like. However, in addition to or instead of this outcome, the person may infer from the others' response that he is worthy of these affectional responses, that is, that he is likeable, and he thereby comes to think of himself in this way—as a likeable person. As another illustration of this, unlike the situation in which the self-cognitions may take the exact form of the others' responses, as when others' deferential responses to the person lead to the self-cognition "I am a person who is deferred to," the others' responses, in contrast, may be interpreted as implying other traits or behaviors, as when self-awareness of being the object of deferential responses by others leads to the self-cognition "Therefore, I must be a powerful person."

Direct and Indirect Influences of Personal Traits, Behaviors, and Experiences on Self-Referent Cognition. Having considered the stimulus value of personal traits, behaviors, and experiences in eliciting self-referent cognitive responses that interpret the personal traits, behaviors, or experiences, either in face-valid terms or as indicators of other unobserved traits, behaviors, or experiences, we turn to the second feature of the general propositions that inform this discussion. The second feature of the general propositions stated above relates to the more or less indirect influence of personal traits, behaviors, or experiences on self-cognition.

A direct influence of personal traits, behaviors, or experiences on self-referent cognition is said to occur when the person immediately becomes aware of or conceptualizes them. However, personal traits, behaviors, or experiences may also influence self-referent cognitive responses indirectly by virtue of their effects on intervening personal traits, behaviors, and experiences that may, ultimately, stimulate self-referent cognitive responses.

That the person's past, present, anticipated, or imagined attributes, behaviors, and experiences (including responses by others that are directed toward him or that otherwise affect him) are mutually influential is easily illustrated. Individuals who have certain attributes, such as those defined in terms of sex or race, will be socialized to behave in different ways that will, in turn, evoke differential responses from others. The responses of others to the person will motivate him to behave in certain ways and will lead to the development of certain personal characteristics.

The mutual influences among personal traits, behaviors, and experiences may be described precisely by the following three propositions.

1. The possession of certain traits will increase the likelihood that the person will develop other traits, will behave in certain ways, and will evoke particular kinds of responses from other people or experience other outcomes.
2. The performance of particular behaviors will influence the development of particular traits and the performance of other behaviors, and will stimulate responses by others toward the subject or other outcomes.

3. The responses by others or other outcomes (whether or not the
   responses are intended to influence the subject's experiences)
   will affect the person's traits, behaviors, and other individual or
   collective responses to the subject (or other outcomes).

The mutual influences among the person's traits, behaviors, and
experiences may occur over longer or shorter periods of time. Over the
long term, socializing experiences of childhood may ultimately influence
the person's current traits, behaviors, and experiences. Over the short
term, the manifestation of a particular trait and behavior may evoke
more immediate responses by others or influence other outcomes (e.g.,
risk of accidental injury).

Any particular current personal trait, behavior, or experience may
stimulate self-referent cognitive responses directly. However, over the
short term, because of the mutual influences exercised by the person's
current traits, behaviors, or experiences the same trait, behavior, or
experience may *indirectly* influence self-conceiving processes as well, by
initiating a more or less lengthy chain of influences among traits, behaviors, or experiences that, ultimately, may directly stimulate self-referent
cognitive responses. Of course, any earlier personal traits (including
behavioral dispositions) that do not maintain their currency and any
past behaviors or experiences (by definition) may only exercise indirect
effects (through their influence on current personal traits, behaviors, or
outcomes) on current, self-referent cognitive responses. It is such an
indirect chain of influence on current traits, behaviors, and personal
outcomes that justifies the study of earlier personal traits, behaviors,
and experiences in an attempt to account for the self-referent responses.
And it is the largely social nature of these responses that justifies the
formulation of explanations in social psychological terms.

Whether the effect of a current personal trait, behavior, or experience (interpreted in face-valid terms or as indicators of unobservable or
unobserved phenomena) on self-referent cognitions is more or less direct will be a function of the nature of the trait, behavior, or experience
in question. For example, the awareness of some traits or behaviors
depend on the responses of others (one is aware of his popularity because people express the desire to be in his company). Popularity influences self-awareness of popularity indirectly, through the responses of
others. In contrast, certain physical talents may stimulate self-recognition in terms of these talents more directly, without the intervening
responses of others. The likelihood that the person will possess traits
and perform behaviors that directly stimulate self-referent cognitive responses will depend on strategic personal characteristics. Sex-based so-

cial identities are cases in point. A girl requires feedback from the social environment to influence her awareness of many of the traits associated with her sex-related role (such as attractiveness, social poise). However, the situation is different for a boy. Many of his important sex-related behaviors are developed while alone. Many such skills involve solitary practice and, at the same time, permit direct awareness of the skills in question. He does not require the reactions of others in order to become aware of, for example, when he has reached a level of achievement in certain gross motor or mechanical skills. The boy receives, from these private activities, direct information that stimulates self-recognition of performing these activities or of acquiring appropriate masculine traits or both (Kagan, 1964, p. 152).

When the influence of a personal trait, behavior, or experience on self-referent cognition is indirect, the relationship will be mediated by the range of, consistency of responses by, and the value systems of the others with whom the person interacted in the course of his socialization experiences or with whom he is interacting in current social situations (and less directly, by the social–structural arrangements and social processes that influence these variables). We briefly consider each of these in turn.

Early in life, the *range* of others who respond to the person is relatively narrow. The identification of self as a distinct object occurs at about the same time as other-awareness—the recognition that there are perspectives other than those of the child that must be taken into account. The most significant others in the child's life at this time are his parents. The child begins to respond to his own actions in ways that parallel and imitate parental actions, and a sense of self-identity crystallizes. Parental selves and behavioral repertoires become a part of the child's identity. The self becomes more differentiated than it was at an earlier stage (Denzin, 1972).

Between the ages of three and five, the range of significant others appears to be constant. In a study of three-, four-, and five-year-old children, Kirchner and Vondracek (1975) found no age effect in terms of the number of people mentioned in response to the request "Tell me who really likes you." Thereafter, however, the child, by force of circumstances, is exposed to a whole new set of significant others and to a concomitant variability in responses by these others to himself—responses he must become aware of if he is to adopt successfully to his environment. Thus, does change in the range of significant others responding to the subject influence his self-referent cognitive responses, that is, his awareness of himself as an object of various others' responses. The situation occasioning expansion (or contraction) of the range of responsive others varies with time of life. Entry into elementary school and, later, the transition to junior high school, for example, occasions new responses to the person by networks of peers and teachers (Simmons, Brown, Bush, & Blyth, 1973).

Just as the range of others' responses to subjective attributes and behaviors influences self-referent cognitions, so does the *consistency* of others' responses to the person affect how he will conceive of himself. Over time, other people may be more or less alike in the ways they respond to the subject. The same group of people may be consistent in the way they respond to the subject at different points in time. A person's relatives, for example, may remain relatively constant in the way they respond to him between youth and young adulthood. Or different sets of significant others at different points in time may respond in similar fashion to the subject's traits and behaviors. Those people constituting the subject's significant others when he is five years of age (perhaps parents and siblings) may respond in a fashion similar to that of the people comprising the subject's social circle when he is nine years old (perhaps teachers, schoolmates, neighborhood friends, in addition to parents and siblings).

In like manner, at any given point in time, the range of others in the subject's social circle may be more or less uniform with regard to the nature of their responses to his attributes and behaviors. The degree of consistency of (the same or different) others in their responses to him over time and at the same point in time will affect the processes of self-awareness and self-conceiving.

The subject is more likely to become aware of and to conceive of himself in terms of others' responses to him to the extent that the responses of others are relatively persistent over time and are uniform at any given point in time. If the differential responses are observed on a day-to-day basis and uniformly from diverse significant others, the subject is more likely to become aware of the responses than if they are given only occasionally and by only some of the significant people in his environment. In like manner, when there is a perceived consensus on the part of the others, self-conception is more profoundly influenced than where consensus is perceived to be low. Congruent with this conclusion is the observation that it is easier to change the subject's concept of himself when he believes that the perceptions of others are in disagreement with his own opinions than where he believes that the perceptions of valued others are in agreement (Backman, Secord, & Pierce, 1963; Kinch, 1963).

Given these principles, it is to be expected that, for example, sex-based social identities would be a salient aspect of self-concept, since such identities appear to be the earliest to develop (Kohlberg, 1966;

Mussen, Conger, & Kagan, 1969). A wide range of others over a long period of time consistently and continually respond to the subject in terms of that identity and give evidence of expecting that the person will respond in accordance with the expectations imputed to others on the basis of that presumed identity. From the developmental point of view, if the responses to the subject in terms of that identity began early in life and continued to the present (as opposed to beginning later in life), then, all other things being equal, that identity should be relatively prominent in the self-conceptualizing processes. In contemporary terms, to the extent that the identity is more frequently evoked by the responses of the range of others, that identity should be more salient. In short, the stimulus value of particular social identities for self-conceiving responses is a function of the time of onset, continuity, and contemporary prevalence of responses by others toward the subject who is displaying attributes and behaviors associated with the particular social identities. Consistent with these expectations, Thomas, Gecas, Weigert, and Rooney (1974), summarizing findings regarding the identity structures of American and Latin adolescents, noted that for American and Latin adolescents, and for both sexes, sex was observed to be the most prominent identity.

The preceding discussion does not imply, however, that consistent self-referent cognitions can only be obtained when a broad range of others respond to the subject in a consistent fashion in all situations. It is true that, to the extent others respond to the subject consistently all the time and in a wide variety of situations, he will develop a consistent picture of himself. However, it is also true that to the extent that a person elicits different but predictable responses from others in different situations, he will develop numerous, situationally based self-images, including those that are contingent on the occupancy of a specific social position and the performance of a specific social role in relationship to individuals occupying complementary positions and performing complementary social roles.

In short, when the person's traits, behaviors, or experiences are stable, whether in the sense that they are apparent in diverse situations or in the sense that they recur predictably in specific situations, the self-referent cognitive responses they stimulate are stable. However, during developmental periods or other circumstances when the person's traits and behaviors undergo major and rapid change, self-referent cognitive responses are commensurately unstable. Such a period and circumstances are associated with adolescence. As Rosenberg (1979) recalls,

> It is in early adolescence (ages 12–14), when the actual self is undergoing great physical change, when social experiences are altered as a consequence of moving from the elementary to the junior high school, and when a new

and mature stage of social intimacy is achieved, that the self-concept appears to become more unstable. (p. 283)

The nature of the indirect relationship between others' responses to subject attributes, behaviors, or experiences, on the one hand, and subject self-referent cognition, on the other hand, then, will be influenced profoundly by the range of others who respond to the subject and by the consistency of these others. In addition, and at least of equal importance, are the *meanings attributed* by the other people to subject traits and behaviors. Given a particular social context, the system of arbitrary symbols employed by group members to cognitively structure their perceptions, and the system of values shared by the group members, the phenomenal attributes and behaviors of the subject serve as cognitive and evaluative cues for other group members' responses. Other people perceive the traits and behaviors of the subject against the background of their own expectations of the attributes and behaviors the subject will and should display in particular social contexts. The expectations are reflected in the stereotypic descriptions of particular social attributes or behaviors. For example, referring again to sex-appropriate expectations, numerous studies suggest that certain traits are variously ascribed to the typical female and male. Further, apparently males and females appear to agree about stereotypic features of the typical male and female (Wylie, 1979). Regarding the content of these stereotypes, Wylie states that

the evidence across different instruments is largely consistent, revealing a common core of stereotypic characteristics. Females are described as warm and sensitive, socially skilled, inclined toward interpersonal and artistic interests; males as competent and logical, possessing self-confidence, direct in manner, dominant. (p. 289)

Compatible observations (Kagan, 1964) were made decades ago:

In sum, females are supposed to inhibit aggression and open display of sexual urges, to be passive with men, to be nurturing to others, to cultivate attractiveness, and to maintain an affective, socially poised, and friendly posture with others. Males are urged to be aggressive in face of attack, independent in problem situations, sexually aggressive, in control of regressive urges, and suppressive of strong emotion, especially anxiety. (p. 143)

Depending on the evaluative significance of these sex-appropriate expectations in the shared hierarchy of values in a particular society and depending on the extent to which the subject was perceived by others as conforming to or deviating from expectations regarding sex-appropriate traits and behaviors, others would respond variably to him. Qualitatively different responses to the subject by others are to be expected, depending on whether in particular social contexts the subject was perceived as conforming to or deviating from socially *valued* expectations relating to sex roles and as conforming to or deviating from sex-appropriate expectations that are generally not accorded particularly high value in the social order. The nature of these responses reflect indirect influences of sex-related behavior on the subject's self-referent cognitive responses.

In brief, these elements of the subject's person that are socially meaningful are most likely to elicit responses from others. Those particular responses from others, in turn, influence self-referent cognitive responses, whether interpreted in face-valid terms or as indicators of nonobservable or unobserved personal traits, behaviors, or experiences.

Conscious Awareness. The self-referent cognitive responses of the person may occur at a more or less conscious level. In the course of socialization processes, certain self-conscious cognitive responses are selectively reinforced by environmental responses. The recurrence of situational cues evokes now-habituated responses, including self-referent cognitions at or below the conscious level of awareness. Only when the automatic responses are interrupted does self-referent cognition occur at a level of conscious awareness. Jones and Pittman (1982) observe that

> a consequence of being socialized in a particular culture is that sequences of action become automatic, triggered off by contextual cues in line with past reinforcement. . . . In many of the routine social interchanges of everyday life, therefore, the phenomenal self is not aroused, does not become salient. Conflict and novelty do, however, give rise to mindfulness and self-salience. When we do not have preprogrammed response sequences, the phenomenal self becomes a reference point for decision making as we review the implications of our beliefs and values for action. (pp. 232–233)

Those circumstances that disrupt automatic self-referent responses and, therefore, that make the person self-aware, in general, are those that upset the person's system of personal expectancies. These include novel circumstances in which new demands are made on the person that cannot be met with the person's existing repertoire of responses; the failure of others to respond, in accustomed fashion, to personal expectations; and the recognition of personal failure to meet the legitimate and customary demands made upon the person by self and others. Under these circumstances, the person becomes aware of self out of a need to evolve appropriate and gratifying adjustments to these disruptions in personal expectancies. Indeed, mechanisms of social control frequently appear to be calculated to increase self-awareness, as found by Wicklund (1982):

> When society needs to bring someone under control, meaning to gain a better knowledge of the person or ensure that the person is oriented correctly in behaviors, it gives a good deal of attention to that person. The parent insists on eye contact when lecturing on a moral principle, the deviate is singled out and shamed or otherwise evaluated in the group's effort to create homogeneity, and perhaps more subtly, those who don't abide by the norms are labelled as "weird," "different," or "non-conformists." *The effect of such labelling should be one of heightening the person's self-awareness, simply by his sense of uniqueness and nonfit.* (p. 225, italics added)

Empirically, unaccustomed social demands and the self-awareness they engender is illustrated by the experience of being a first-time visitor to a foreign land (Wicklund & Frey, 1980). When the sense of being different was mitigated by traveling in groups, conscious self-awareness was less in evidence.

From the foregoing discussion, it may be assumed that personal traits, behaviors, or experiences tend, more or less directly, to influence the person to more or less consciously *attend to* (be aware of) the personal traits or behaviors or actions by others or both (whether the actions were stimulated by the person's traits, behaviors, or experiences) that influence the person's outcomes; and having attended to the personal traits, behaviors, or the responses of others or all three, the person comes to *conceive of himself* in these terms or in terms apparently implied by them. However, these relationships only hold on a probabilistic basis. To be sure, a person is more likely to become aware of personal traits or behaviors if these, in fact, characterize the person than if they do not; and a person is more likely to become aware of others' responses (whether in response to personal traits or behaviors) that impinge on the subject, if these responses, in fact, occur than if they do not. Nevertheless, not all personal traits or behaviors, and not all actions by others (whether in response to these personal traits or behaviors), enter subjective awareness. Conversely, not all subjective awareness has a basis in reality—a person may misperceive reality. In short, there is no necessary one-to-one relationship between personal traits or behaviors or others' responses to them, on the one hand, and subjective awareness, on the other hand. If that is the case, what other factors influence self-referent cognitive response? What factors determine whether subjects will attend to or be aware of personal traits and behaviors or the responses of others to them, and what factors will determine whether a person will "become aware of" personal attributes or response patterns or others' "responses" that do not exist in fact?

In like manner, having become aware of his personal traits or behaviors or others' responses to them, the person is more likely to conceive of himself in these terms—that is, with reference to personal attributes or behaviors or others responses to them—than if he did not become aware of these personal traits or behaviors and of others' responses that affect the subject's outcomes. Nevertheless, under certain conditions, self-awareness of traits or behaviors and of being the object of particular responses by others may have no influence on self-conception. Further, when self-conception is influenced by self-awareness, the self-conceiving may or may not be exclusively in the exact terms of the personal traits or behaviors or of the responses by others that prompted the self-awareness. Instead of, or in addition to, such self-conceiving responses, the personal traits or behaviors or the responses of others that prompted self-awareness might be reinterpreted so as to imply to the subject other nonobserved (or nonobservable) personal attributes or dispositions. Under what conditions, then, will self-awareness influence self-conceiving, whether exclusively in terms of which the subject became aware or, instead of or in addition to these, in terms subjectively inferred from the personal traits or behaviors or others' responses to the subject of which he became aware?

The answer to this question and those asked earlier, in large measure, may be found in three sets of factors. These factors relate to the perceived social setting within which the individual responds, predispositions to use particular conceptual systems, and motivational dispositions. Each of these sets of factors, starting with the situational context, will be considered, in turn, as influencing the nature of the relationship between personal traits and behaviors, on the one hand, and self-referent cognitions on the other hand.

Perceived Situational Context

Whether and how the person's own traits, behaviors, or experiences influence self-awareness and self-conception will depend on the situational context in which they are presented. The person potentially may conceive of himself in terms of any of countless traits that he, in fact, possesses; in terms of any of the behaviors that he, in fact, performs; and in terms of any of a range of experiences. Why does he focus on some of his traits rather than on others in a given situation? For example, why does he conceive of himself in terms of certain of his social identities rather than in terms of others? And for any given identity, why does the person define his appropriate role in one way rather than another? The answer is, in part, that the perceived situational context in which the traits, behaviors, and experiences are presented *structures the meaning* of the person's traits, behaviors, and experiences.

The situational context consists of the social identities of the people who behave toward the subject or whose actions impinge on the subject, the patterned responses of these people, and the physical environment in which the responses occur. The cognitive meanings of the person's traits, behaviors, and experiences are influenced by the situational context in the sense that the context provides the symbolic background for the person's current self-cognitions. The largely social context provides symbolic cues that help to structure the person's self-referent cognitive responses. These cues are in addition to the effects of the responses of others that influence subjective awareness of (1) being the object of the individual or collective actions of others or (2) having traits, behaviors, or experiences implied by the actions of others.

The symbolic cues that are provided by the situational context function in two ways. First, they define the relevance of particular traits, behaviors, and experiences for the person's current life space from among the myriad traits, behaviors, and experiences in his repertoire. Second, the symbolic cues provide a range and distribution of values along specific dimensions that permit and stimulate the individual to determine the particular values that characterize him along those dimensions.

Situational Relevance. Consider, first, the function of the situational context as defining the relevance of personal traits, behaviors, or experiences. The current situation consists, in large measure, of the social relationships in which the person participates and the physical setting for these relationships. These aspects of the situation stimulate the self-awareness of personal identities and other self-relevant perceptions that are appropriate to the situation. In the context of a school building, when interacting with teachers, a person is more likely to conceive of himself in terms of social identity of student (if that identity is indeed part of his repertoire). In the normal course of social interaction, a person is motivated to enter into and conform to the system of reciprocal obligations and rights that defines the relationship. In order to do so, it is necessary for an individual to understand the nature of his social identity in the situation and the nature of the social identities of those people with whom he is interacting. As a result of the socialization experience in a particular sociocultural context, each person learns what normative expectations are appropriate for particular social identities as they interact with other specified social identities. Such understandings are prerequisite to being able to conform to the consensually defined obligations that bind one in a particular relationship.

But how does one know which identity obtains in any situation? At any given time, any of a range of identities are available to a person, and in each capacity, different expectations of the person are applicable. In short, as this is articulated in symbolic interaction theory (Stryker, 1977), the self is seen

> as a complex and differentiated construction of many parts. These parts are identities. Thus one's self may consist in part of an identity as mother, sister, employee, friend, student, etc., i.e., a set of identities representing one's participation in structured social relationships. (p. 151)

Which identity the person is called on to accept and conform to in any given situation is defined by the social context, which is to say, by the identities of the other people in the situation. If the identity of the other person in a particular social context is that of the subject's employer, then the subject is likely to conceive of himself as an employee and to play the role that is appropriate to this identity.

Similarly, the "concept learning" approach (Gergen, 1971) holds that an individual acquires varying conceptions of self in different situations:

> He can learn a certain way of conceptualizing himself from his father and possibly an opposite way from his younger brothers. In the former case, he may come to see himself as "submissive" and in the latter, "dominant." When these situations recur and, more specifically, when the people within them reappear, they act as stimuli to elicit the particular conceptions learned in the past. A father may cause the son to remember himself as "submissive" and brothers may elicit the conception that he is "dominant." (p. 21).

Dimensions of Self–Other Comparison. The second function of the symbolic cues provided by the social context relates to the range and distribution along specific dimensions of traits, behaviors, and experiences of others in the situation that permits and stimulates the subject to conceptualize his own traits, behaviors, and experiences along those same dimensions. They permit self-conceptualization in the sense that certain features of self-conception have no meaning apart from the characteristics exhibited by others in the situation. Self-conceptions of being rich, tall, or beautiful or average in ability, to offer a few examples, cannot be derived except with reference to perceptions of the possessions, height, appearance, and abilities of other group members. Whether these conceptions are merely descriptive or have an evaluative component as well, they involve the judgment by the subject of being placed in the context of the range of values exhibited by the group along specified dimensions. Self-perceptions of relative achievement (I am a successful person) depend on our perceptions of the achievements of those with whom we habitually compare ourselves. For me to judge that I am a successful person depends, in part, on perceiving others to be less successful. If men are, in fact, more successful in the business world, and women compare their own success with that of men (whether or not they also compare them with that of other women), they may well perceive themselves as relatively less successful. As will be noted later, the self-perception of being relatively less successful will evoke negative self-evaluations to the extent that such a success is a relatively high-order personal value. If the person values such success and judges himself in terms of the degree to which this value is approximated, the self-perception of being relatively less successful, compared to others, will elicit negative self-evaluations.

This process is illustrated by the relationship between achievement values and self-conception, a relationship that is frequently framed within particular social contexts. A person tends to evaluate himself not according to an absolute level of achievement but rather according to the achievements of a specified reference group. That is, academic achievement influences self-concept as mediated through social comparison processes. The child compares his level of achievement of that of others in the classroom, and, depending on the favorable or unfavorable results, experiences a more or less enhanced self-concept. Rogers, Smith, and Coleman (1978) determined that

> when information regarding relative academic standing within the classroom was considered, a strong relationship between both reading and math achievement with self-concept was found; but when information regarding relative academic standing within the classroom was not considered, reading achievement showed no relationship to self-concept, and the observed relationship between math achievement and self-concept was substantially less robust. (p. 56)

The range of values along particular dimensions may be broad, whereas the *distribution* among the values may be skewed. The values may cluster near one end of a continuum or in one of a few, mutually exclusive qualitative categories. The relationship of the subject's characteristics to this distribution thus not only permits self-conceptualization, in terms of one or another value, but also stimulates self-conception, in terms of the relative distinctiveness of the value. In any given social situation, relative to others, the subject will have more or less distinctive characteristics; and the more distinctive the trait, the more likely is the person to incorporate it into his spontaneous self-concept. Thus, McGuire and Padawer-Singer (1976), applying the distinctiveness theory of selective perception to the spontaneous self-concept, argue that "we notice any aspect (or dimension) of ourselves to the extent that our characteristic on that dimension is peculiar in our social milieu" (p. 41). For example, a black woman is more likely to become aware of her womanhood when associating with black men and of her blackness when associating with white women. In support of the personal distinctiveness hypothesis, data are offered indicating that people who are atypically younger or older are more likely to spontaneously mention their ages than are people who approximate the classroom mode as part of their self-description. Foreign-born children were appreciably more likely than native-born children to mention their birthplaces. With regard to hair color, eye color, and weight, people having unusual characteristics spontaneously mentioned them more than did people with more typical characteristics. Consistent with the above, members of the minority sex in any given class were more likely to mention their sex spontaneously in self-descriptions.

Elsewhere, McGuire, McGuire, Child, and Fujioka (1978) found support for four predictions based on the general proposition that ethnic identity is salient in children's spontaneous self-concepts to the extent that their ethnic group is in the minority in their social milieu at school. The four predictions supported were (1) that in an ethnically mixed group, members of the minority groups are more conscious of their ethnicity than members of the majority group; (2) that within any ethnic group, members become progressively less conscious of their ethnicity as their ethnic group becomes increasingly more predominant in the social setting; (3) that ethnicity becomes more salient as the group becomes increasingly heterogeneous ethnically (i.e., as the number of ethnic groups in the setting increases or as the distribution of the group members over those ethnic categories become more equipotential or both); and (4) that for the minority group, ethnicity is more salient in the affirmation self-concept (in response to Tell us about yourself) than in the negation self-concept (Tell us what you are *not*), and, for the majority group, the reverse would be the case.

These findings suggest that any social pattern that effectively increases heterogeneity increases the likelihood that the social characteristics under consideration would become salient features of self-conceptualization. Social policies that aim to increase the representation of various racial, religious, ethnic, and sex groupings in economic, educational, and other social settings on the basis of the foregoing research may be expected to result in heightened self-consciousness of race, religion, ethnic affiliation, and sex (McGuire et al., 1978).

The question arises as to why distinctiveness of traits or behaviors should increase their salience in self-conception. As was suggested earlier, one possible answer, quite apart from explanations in terms of information processing (McGuire *et al.*, 1978), is that there is a relationship between distinctiveness and deviation (in a positive or negative direction) from normative expectations. That is, the more the trait or behavior deviates, in a probabilistic sense, the more it tends to deviate from what is regarded as appropriate. If this were the case, it might explain why more distinctive traits are more likely to stimulate self-consciousness. Insofar as a trait or a behavior has a normative reference point, positive or negative sanctions are more likely. Perhaps it is the reward–punishment potential of the trait or behavior that influences its salience in spontaneous self-conception.

The fact of being more or less distinctive may influence not only self-conceiving responses, in terms of the more or less unique traits, behaviors, or experiences, but also may further stimulate in the person other self-referent cognitions, such as those relating to attribution of causality to self. In effect, distinctiveness of the person, in the social context, calls attention to that person. According to objective self-awareness theory (Duval & Wicklund, 1973), the tendency to attribute causality to self as opposed to environment will be a function of the subject's focus of attention. Any element in the environment that reminds the person of his position as an object in the world will focus attention on the self to the exclusion of other parts of the environment. Thus, a mirror image, the sound of a person's voice will influence inward-turning of attention and, consequently, an increased likelihood of self-attribution of causality. In the absence of such reminders, particularly when environmental change diverts attention from self, the focus of attention and consequent attribution will more likely be outward than inward. Experimental evidence seems to support the expectation that attribution of causality to self would be a positive function of objective self-awareness.

In sum, the relationship between personal traits, behaviors, and experiences, on the one hand, and self-referent cognitive responses, on the other hand, is conditioned by the social context. The context defines the social relevance of the trait, behavior, or experience in question and thereby stimulates self-recognition of situationally appropriate traits, behaviors, or experiences. The social context, further, (1) defines the *range* of values comprising a particular dimension and, thereby, facilitates self-specification of the person's own value along that dimension and (2) reflects the *distribution* of values, thus defining the personal characteristic as more or less distinctive, a characteristic that provokes self-referent cognition in those or other related terms.

Personal Conceptual Systems

The nature of the person's cognitive self-referent responses to his own attributes, behaviors, and experiences will depend, in part, on the system of concepts that the person characteristically uses to structure his environment. The sensory data impinging on the person's sensory organs are selectively perceived and organized in accordance with these concepts or symbolic constructs and (1) sensitize the individual to common elements of otherwise heterogeneous examples, (2) categorize the diverse instances sharing the common elements, and (3) label the categories in ways that express the common elements of the diverse examples, In theory, the ways in which personal traits, behaviors, or experiences can be categorized are limitless. The ways in which these phenomena are categorized, however, are limited by the concepts available to the person. A person attends to certain traits, behaviors, or experiences (or to particular aspects of them) rather than to others because of the concepts he habitually uses. Through the use of these concepts, the person, in effect, imposes a reality on a mass of otherwise unorganized sensations. Particular activities are classified as, for example, work rather than play, and as exemplars of efficient rather than inefficient behavior. Were the concepts habitually used by the person different, he would not make such distinctions in response to his various behaviors. In this connection, Rosenberg (1979) notes that

> when society, in the course of socialization, teaches the individual the meaning of trait concepts, it profoundly affects his self-concepts by providing him with a point of view for viewing the self. Learning such ideas as smart or interesting or friendly alerts him to aspects of the self which he might not otherwise have attended and causes him to see himself within these frameworks. The adolescent's superior ability to probe beneath the surface of things, to achieve a new intellectual synthesis of the materials of experience which impinge upon his senses effect a profound change in his self-concept. The very structure of the self-concept is altered; older and younger children now see themselves within different intellectual frameworks, apply to themselves different categories of thought. (p. 221)

The system of concepts generally employed by the person to structure the environment comprises his language and, thus, is reflected in the person's verbal behavior. More particularly, the system of concepts the person uses to structure self-relevant sensory impressions is reflected in the person's *self-referent* language. Although a person will, on occasion, describe himself in ways that are contrary to his conceptualization of and beliefs about himself for the purpose of eliciting desired responses from others, generally the system of concepts he uses to structure his perceptions of personal traits, behaviors, and experiences will be reflected in his verbal self-descriptions.

From one group to another, different sets of concepts might be used to guide self-referent cognitions regarding personal traits, behaviors, and experiences. Similarly, inter-individual differences in this regard might be noted within a particular group. Further, the same individuals at different maturational stages might be observed to employ different conceptual schemes to selectively perceive from the range of sensory inputs relating to personal attributes, behaviors, and experiences. Regarding family identity, for example, Sweet and Thornburg (1971) provided three-, four-, and five-year-olds with figures of various sizes, asking them to "make" their very own family and to identify the various members of the family. Only 50 percent of the subjects included themselves in the family group. However, there was a steady increase, with age, in the tendency to include the self as part of the family. In general, in the course of maturation, children are less likely to describe themselves in terms of such concrete, objective categories as physical appearance or possessions, and as they reach adolescence, they are more likely to use more abstract, subjective descriptions such as personal beliefs and motivational and interpersonal characteristics (Montemayor & Eisen, 1977).

Much of our understanding of the development of self-conceptualization process derives from the early work of such commentators as Mead (1934). For Mead, the social genesis of self-conception involves the child's observation of the behavior of others around him and imitation of their behaviors as part of his play. A portion of these behaviors were directed toward the child himself. Thus, in imitating them at play, he was adopting the responses of others toward himself. He was, in effect, taking the role of the other toward himself and coming to think of himself in terms of others' behaviors toward him. The development of language abilities permitted the individual to take the role not only as specific others in his environment but also of a generalized other roughly corresponding to society. Through these earlier experiences, then, the person has internalized the perspectives of others and systems of shared symbols, which enable him to conceptualize his own traits and behaviors without, at that time, necessarily being aware of others' responses to him. Interaction with others, in short, is profoundly implicated in developing the subject's capacity *to later respond to himself directly.* Given these earlier experiences, the person is indeed capable of directly responding with self-referent concepts to personal attributes or behaviors.

In all historical epochs and in all cultures, it seems that once the person has matured sufficiently to internalize a system of self-referent constructs, and although intergroup, inter-individual, and intra-individual (developmental) variability in systems of concepts used to structure data on self (as well as on the world in general) may be noted at any given time, a person uses a *relatively* stable, more or less consensual conceptual system to guide his selective cognitive structuring of personal attributes, behaviors, or experiences. This cross-cultural pattern is consistent with the postulate that, universally, an individual *needs* to conceptualize himself. He has already learned that satisfaction of his needs is contingent on his environment, in particular, the responses of others. He has learned that the responses of others are contingent on his own attributes and behaviors. Therefore, in order to anticipate how others might respond to his own traits and behaviors, he must be able to rehearse the responses of others to his own hypothetical traits or behaviors, an ability that, in turn, depends on his ability to conceptualize himself in terms of a socially meaningful set of arbitrary symbols. In short, the learned need to conceptualize oneself is based on the child's recognition of a relationship between personal traits or behaviors and the responses of others.

If, as the preceding remarks suggest, a person uses some system of self-referent concepts because he needs to, the question remains as to why the person uses a *particular* conceptual scheme to organize the potentially limitless subjective sensations stimulated by personal attributes, behaviors, or experiences.

There are perhaps two broad explanations of why particular self-referent categories are used. The first explanation relates to the reward value of employing particular conceptual systems, the second relates to regularities in human behavior.

With regard to the *reward value* of using particular concepts, the employment of particular conceptual systems is associated with receiving gratifying responses from others in two ways. First, as part of the socialization process, people are taught to view the physical and social environment, and themselves, in certain terms rather than other terms, as they are taught numerous other social conventions. As in the case of any normative expectation, then, conformity (here in the form of using certain conceptual distinctions) is rewarded, whereas deviation (here in the form of using inappropriate conceptual distinctions) is punished. The nature of the appropriate sanctions administered by others will be a function of the socially defined value attached to the distinction (and this, in turn, may be associated with the functional value of the conceptual distinction for survival of the social system in its present form). In short, making particular conceptual distinctions is a socially approved pattern, and the individual's conformity to this pattern will elicit rewarding (or avoid punitive) responses from others. Second, and this was alluded to above, personal satisfactions are contingent on the responses of others to the subject. The nature of others' responses to the subject will depend on the others' perception of the subject's attributes and behaviors. If the subject is to obtain gratifying responses from others, he must be able to anticipate their responses and adjust his own presentation of self in ways calculated to elicit predominantly gratifying responses from others. The subject, then, is motivated to learn and use the particular conceptual systems of others in order to elicit, ultimately, gratifying responses from others.

In the second explanation for the adoption of particular conceptual schemes, individuals do display *regularities in their behavior*, whether out of a need to conform to expectations associated with particular social identities or for other reasons. Such regularities tend to facilitate symbolic recognition of the pattern in the form of self-referent concepts or, in the words of Markus (1977), self-schemata (the cognitive structures used in encoding one's own behavior and for processing information about one's own behavior). Self-schemata represent *"cognitive generalizations about the self, derived from past experience"* that, having been derived, *"organize and guide the processing of self-related behavior contained in the individual's social experiences"* (Markus, 1977, p. 64).

Markus's comments suggest that particular self-schemata influence a range of self-referent cognitive responses to personal attributes and behaviors. The cognitive framework generated permits inferences from little information and the efficient interpretation of complex sequences of events. Self-schemata "are useful in understanding intentions and feelings and in identifying likely or appropriate patterns of behavior" p. 64 (Markus, 1977). Once the schemata are established, they function as selective mechanisms determining which information is attended to, how it will be structured, the importance attached to the information, and what happens to the information subsequently. Once a pattern has been formed, it is used as a basis for "future judgments, decisions, inferences, or predictions about the self."

Consistent with these assertions, Markus (1977) recorded studies relating self-schemata to a number of self-referent cognitive operations. Thus, with regard to the dimension of independence–dependence, groups of individuals who thought of themselves as independent tended to endorse more adjectives associated with concept of independence than did individuals who did not so characterize themselves, required shorter processing time for "me" judgments to words concerned with independence than to other types of words, were able to supply more specific examples of independent behavior, believed they were likely to engage in future independent behavior, and resisted accepting information implying that they were not indepedent. Parallel results were observed for individuals who thought of themselves as dependent people. Those who thought of themselves as neither independents nor dependents (the aschematics) did not differ in processing times for independent and dependent words, had greater difficulty in providing behavioral evidence of independence and dependence, and believed that they were as likely to engage in dependent as in independent behavior. Further, they were relatively accepting of information about themselves on this dimension. In short, they did not seem to view themselves along an independence–dependence dimension.

To summarize, then, the influence of personal traits and behaviors on self-referent cognition is contingent on the nature of the system of concepts the person habitually uses to structure the sensations and perceptions evoked by the world, in general, and by the self, in particular. The use of particular concepts, influenced by social expectations and the ultimate utility of the conventional conceptual schemes in gaining gratifying responses from others, are, in part, derived from the subject generalizing from observed regularities in his personal attributes, behaviors, and experiences. Once derived, however, the self-referent concepts greatly influence the nature of subsequent self-referent cognition in response to the stimulation of sensory processes by personal traits, behaviors, and experiences.

Self-Enhancing Motivation

Just as the relationship between personal traits and behaviors, on the one hand, and self-referent cognitive responses and experiences, on the other hand, are conditioned by the social context and the person's conceptual system, so is this relationship moderated by the person's self-enhancing motivational disposition. Although we will consider the following in greater detail in Chapter 5, in connection with a discussion of self-protective–self-enhancing mechanisms, a full understanding of self-referent cognitive response requires that these ideas be introduced here. Motivational dispositions, in general, involve, first, experiences of needs stemming from subjective perceptions of being more or less distant from (or approximate to) affectively significant evaluative criteria. Given such experiences of needs, motivational dispositions involve, second, the (conscious or unconscious) readiness of the person to behave in ways that promise to approximate personally valued goals (or to gain greater distance from disvalued end-states), thus assuaging the dysphoric experience of need. In the case of self-enhancing motivational dispositions, the person needs to experience positive self-feelings and is disposed to behave in ways that will approximate that goal.

Direct and Indirect Effects on Self-Cognitions. Self-referent cognition is affected by this disposition, since the person is motivated (1) to be sensitive to those aspects of reality that threaten self-accepting attitudes or offer promise of self-enhancing outcomes and (2) to selectively perceive (if necessary, to perceptually distort) reality in ways that make reality congruent with self-accepting attitudes. By being sensitive to personal traits, behaviors, and experiences that are relevant to self-attitudes, the person may better act to forestall or reduce the distress associated with self-threatening phenomena; and, by correctly perceiving personally valued aspects of self and by distorting perceptions of disvalued aspects of self, the person may define himself and his situation in ways that elicit self-accepting attitudes. To illustrate the distinction between the motivation to be aware of or sensitive to particular aspects of self, on the one hand, and the motivation to distort perception of one's own traits, behaviors, and experiences, on the other hand, we refer to the social context of interaction between the sexes on a college campus where students value physical attractiveness and recognition from others that one is physically attractive. Because of the social context and the high consensual valuation of physical attractiveness in this context, the individual is particularly sensitive to his own appearance. If the person perceives himself as having a less than desirable appearance, the person may be motivated to *distort* his own perception of his appearance in a favorable direction or, contrary to reality, to perceive others as having a benign attitude toward his appearance. By so doing, the individual satisfies his need to perceive himself and to be perceived by others as attractive.

The need for positive self-feeling more directly influences self-cognition by sensitizing and distorting processes. Less directly, the person is motivated to behave in ways or to stimulate consequences that, when recognized by the person, will stimulate positive self-evaluation and positive self-feelings.

The Self-Consistency Motive. We express the motivational determinants of self-cognition in terms of the need for positive self-evaluation on the assumption (as is argued in greater detail in Chapter 4) that this need is the most inclusive one in the person's need-value system and that all more-specific motives are subordinate to the goal of approximating the criteria for positive self-evaluation or to goal states that are instrumental in the achievement of positive self-evaluation and that, thereby, come to be valued in their own right. Thus, when the need for positive self-evaluation is threatened, the person's self-referent cognitive responses are influenced accordingly. The individual is most likely to be sensitive to past, present, anticipated, or imagined personally relevant occurrences that reflect criteria for self-evaluation or that in the past were associated with or instrumental to the achievement of such criteria; and the person in such circumstances will be moved to recognize reality in ways that will facilitate positive self-evaluation.

However, a number of scholars have recognized motives other then need for positive self-evaluation as motivating self-oriented cognitions and other self-relevant behavior. One such motive is the need for self-consistency. The distinction between this motive and the need for positive self-evaluation, as made by Schwartz and Stryker (1970), is that between the motivation to create and maintain "stable, coherent identities" and the need to evaluate their identities positively. Although some have argued that the need for positive self-feelings (an ego drive) takes precedence over all other needs (Allport, 1961), and although evidence of an independently acting self-consistency motive is lacking (Jones, 1973; Wylie, 1979), according to some views, the process of conceiving the self is profoundly influenced by the self-consistency motive—that is, the need to create and maintain a consistent cognitive state with respect to one's evaluations of self (Jones, 1973). Various reasons are given for this cognitive tendency, including economy in the organizations of one's perceptions (Heider, 1958), the reduction of dissonance (Festinger, 1957), predictability in relationships with others (Newcomb, 1961; Secord & Backman, 1964), or the avoidance of cognitions with conflicting implications for action (Jones & Gerard, 1967).

Such a motive need not contradict the primacy of the self-evaluation motive. The maintenance of a stable, coherent identity may reflect the person's emotional investment in the particular self-concept as a basis for positive self-evaluation. Alternatively, the motive may reflect a need to maintain a stable, coherent identity toward the goal of facilitating the kinds of performances and eliciting the kinds of responses that, in the last analysis, will have self-enhancing implications. In this regard, the need for predictability in interacting with others appears to be among the more plausible explanations for the existence of a self-consistency motive to act in accordance, and to maintain the self-concept in the face of contradictory evidence (Gergen, 1971; Rosenberg, 1979), independent of the investment in a particular self-concept as the basis of positive self-evaluation. In the process of becoming socialized, the emergent self-concept might reflect the ways in which the person managed to negotiate reality. By knowing what he was, he knew what others might expect of him and was thus enabled to conform to their expectations, thereby reaping the rewards of social conformity. By a process of association, the individual might develop a need for self-consistency for its own sake. In short, the individual must maintain the self-concept because it had proved useful in negotiating self-ascribed and other-ascribed obligations, goals to which the individual was motivated to conform. In time, the utility of the stable self-concept became valued in its own right.

Although I favor the view that the self-consistency motive is functionally related to the need for positive self-evaluation, acceptance of this viewpoint is not a prerequisite to accepting the proposition that the need to maintain a stable, coherent picture of ourselves influences our self-referent cognitive responses, particularly in the direction of perceiving aspects of ourselves that are congruent and misperceiving aspects of ourselves that are not congruent with a stable identity. *Any motive that might be satisfied through particular self-referent cognitive responses may be expected to influence such responses.*

Need for Self-Acceptance. The motivation to conceive of ourselves in positive terms may influence us to recognize that we indeed possess personally and socially valued traits and that we normally perform valued behaviors. Conversely, the threat to our self-esteem posed by the recognition of our disvalued attributes or by the lack of valued attributes may lead us to contrary-to-fact perceptions of not possessing the disvalued attributes or of possessing the valued attributes. Thus, a male subject who is, in fact, highly dependent may come to see himself as independent because he needs to conform to what he accepts as the proper stereotype of his sex-based role. In short, as Wylie (1979) points out, many self-concept theorists argue that

> in order to maintain a favorable self-concept, persons use selective perception, interpretation, and memory of feedback regarding their characteristics. That is, theorists expect that unfavorable feedback will tend to be distorted, minimized, ignored, or forgotten to some degree, whereas favorable information will be exaggerated and remembered longer or more clearly. (p. 665)

Consistent with this expectation, Wylie (1979) notes "considerable consistency among the methodologically more adequate studies in showing trends toward self-favorability biases concerning evaluative characteristics" (p. 681).

Even positively valued traits or behaviors may evoke contary-to-fact self-perceptions if these pose a threat to the individual's self-esteem motive. Ordinarily, it might be expected that an individual who has a history of success would come to think of himself as being an effective person. However, this implies the expectation of a continuing high level of performance and a consequently greater risk of failure to reach the high standard (than if the expectation level were lower). Insofar as the person has a strong need to avoid experiences of failure, he may distort his self-perceptions by thinking of himself as one who possesses a low level of effectiveness (and, by implication, as one who should not be expected to succeed).

However, traits that are personally and socially disvalued may induce self-awareness of the traits in relatively undistorted form, if such awareness is in the service of the self-esteem motive. In short, positively and negatively valued traits or behaviors may or may not lead to subjective awareness of the traits or behaviors and may or may not lead to their conceptualization in relatively undistorted form, depending on their compatibility with the subject's need for self-acceptance.

How the self-esteem motive may influence the relationship between personal traits, behaviors, and experiences, on the one hand, and how people conceive of themselves, on the other hand, is illustrated by a consideration of positively and negatively valued social identities. With regard to *positively* valued social identities, research findings from samples of adolescents (Thomas *et al.*, 1974) suggest that positive valuation of specified social identities is a condition for these identities playing a prominent role in self-conceiving processes. Since Latin-American and Anglo-American societies were seen as differing in value configurations with regard to family, religion, and heterosexual relations, as well as in extent of industrialization–urbanization, the adolescent identities that developed in the two sociocultural contexts were expected to vary. Religious and family identities were expected to have greater importance in the more traditional societies in which more of the person's life revolves around these basic institutions. Thus, the frequency and importance of religious and family identities should be higher for Latin adolescents than for Anglo adolescents. Sex identities should predominate in those societies that accentuate sex-role differences, that is, Latin cultures. Peer groups were expected to increase in importance in American society, since religion and family have decreased in importance. In fact, these expectations were not consistently supported. The expectation that family identities would be more frequent self-designations for Latins was supported for male respondents. Anglo-Latin differences in frequency of sex identity were significant for male adolescents but not for female adolescents. The expectation that Anglos would have higher frequencies of peer identities was supported by the female respondents but not the male respondents. The findings on frequencies of religious identities were that Anglo females have significantly *higher* frequencies than Latin females.

One possible explanation for the uneven support of the hypotheses is that, for different social positions in the Latin-American and Anglo-

American societies, various social identities are differentially valued. If the self-esteem motive were operative, those identities that were positively valued and therefore contributed to the subject's self-acceptance would be more likely to prominently influence self-conception. Social identities that are culturally valued would be salient features of self-referent cognition when they are also personally valued. As expected, according to this reasoning, the hypotheses that Latin subjects would be more likely to express family, religious, and sex identities and Anglos would be more likely to express peer identities are supported when only positive evaluations of these identities are considered.

It is conceivable that the self-esteem motive conditions self-awareness and self-conception of *negative* identities as well. It has been observed that people are often labeled by others with a negative identity as a result of having been observed to deviate from consensual expectations (Becker, 1963; Kitsuse, 1962; Lemert, 1951; Scheff, 1966). As we noted earlier, such negative responses by others may lead directly to negative self-conceptions. Nevertheless, self-awareness and self-conceptualization in terms of the deviant identity might be facilitated by the operation of the self-esteem motive. First, the need for approval by others and for self-approval may increase the need to conform to the expectations of others. These expectations may be interpreted by the subject as including self-conceptualization in terms of the same labels applied to the subject by the significant others whose approval he needs. By adopting the same standards of rectitude as the other group members, he may hope to gain their approval. Second, the need for self-approval may induce the subject to affirm his identity as a means of gaining recognition from another (deviant) referent group and, at the same time, effectively rejecting the legitimacy of the membership group that labeled him with the negative identity. An extensive literature suggests that commitment to deviant patterns, in fact, serves such anticipated self-enhancing functions (Kaplan, 1975b, 1980). For example, Hammersmith and Weinberg (1973) provide data that are compatible with the model proposing that homosexual commitment (settling into a homosexual identity) leads to better psychological adjustment (as indicated by a more stable, positive self-image, fewer anxiety symptoms, and less depression).

The extent to which motivational process influences the relationship between personal traits, behaviors, and experiences, on the one hand, and self-cognition, on the other hand, is, in part, a function of the ambiguity of the traits, behaviors, and experiences and of the situational context in which they are presented. Certain personal characteristics are more visible, and for this and other reasons, their nature is unequivocal.

Hence, they will be recognized as having the same meanings that others would impute to the traits in similar situations. Other traits, behaviors, and experiences, however, are more ambiguous in their meaning. Therefore, in the former situation, it would be more difficult, and in the latter situation, it would be easier, to selectively perceive or otherwise to cognitively distort personal traits, behaviors, or experiences in accordance with one's self-evaluative needs. Empirical research has consistently demonstrated a self-favorability bias in self-descriptions in terms of evaluative characteristics, particularly with regard to those characteristics that are more open to distortion. The self-favorability bias, however, is less in evidence with respect to characteristics, such as grade-point average, that are less amenable to motivated perceptual distortion (Wylie, 1979). Similarly, self-perceptions, particularly regarding nonobservable qualities or behaviors, are facilitated by clarity of the situational context, not the least important components of which are the responses of others in the environment. When the situational context and, particularly, the responses of others are consistent and unambiguous, the personal characteristics implied by situational cues will more likely demand self-cognition in terms of those inferred attributes or behaviors. Conversely, when the situational context does not clearly imply specified attributes, behaviors, or experiences or when the personal attributes themselves are not clearly observable in unambiguous fashion, perceptual distortion in the service of the self-esteem motive is facilitated.

SOCIAL CONSEQUENCES OF SELF-CONCEIVING RESPONSES

The influence of self-conceiving responses on others' behaviors or outcomes is mediated by direct effects of self-referent cognitive responses on three classes of variables that either have already been discussed or will be considered in detail later. The three categories of variables are (1) personal traits, behaviors, and experiences; (2) self-evaluative behaviors; and (3) self-enhancing responses. Since they are discussed elsewhere in the volume, here we only briefly refer to these consequences. The social consequences of these variables are considered in the final chapter.

Personal Traits, Behaviors, and Experiences

The act of becoming aware of aspects of oneself, of holding certain beliefs about oneself, of conceiving oneself in particular ways is itself an exemplar of the more inclusive category of personal attributes, behaviors, and experiences. Responding to oneself cognitively may stimulate self-referent cognitions. If a person, in fact, conceives of himself in terms of particular social identities, the act of so conceiving himself may stimulate the self-cognition of being someone who thinks of himself in terms of particular social identities and, further, may be interpreted by the subject as an indicator of some other mode of self-cognition (as someone who is self-absorbed by particular group memberships). These consequences of self-referent cognitions are significant because they (as do all other cognitive responses to self) influence other self-referent responses, notably self-evaluative and self-enhancing responses.

Self-Evaluative Responses

Self-cognitions, in conjunction with the person's need-value system, elicit self-evaluative responses. Insofar as an individual becomes aware of; anticipates that he will possess certain properties; recalls or imagines that he is characterized by certain personal attributes, behaviors, or experiences that are highly valued in the context of his need-value system—he will come to evaluate himself positively. Insofar as the individual's cognitive responses to self reflect approximation to highly disvalued states or being distant from valued states, the individual will evaluate himself negatively.

Self-Enhancing Responses

We will discuss at some length in Chapter 5 the putative effects of level of and changes in negative self-feelings on the disposition to employ self-protective or self-enhancing mechanisms, at which point we will also explore in greater detail the proposition that the kind of patterns with which we respond to negative self-feelings or an increase in negative self-feelings are influenced by self-referent cognitions, that is, our beliefs about ourselves, as well as by our beliefs about the world in which we live. Among the self-referent cognitions that influence self-protection are the individual's beliefs in his ability to influence personal outcomes. Such beliefs are described in a variety of ways. However, all of them indicate a sense of self-efficacy. Individuals who perceive themselves in terms of a high degree of self-efficacy are moved more to respond in ways that will enhance their self-attitudes through manipulation of the external world than are individuals who perceive themselves as having a low degree of self-efficacy. If we believe that our actions will be effective, then we are more likely to behave in ways that are calculated to produce certain results. If, however, we believe that any action on our own part will be futile in bringing about desirable outcomes, then we are less likely to attempt it. In short, if we believe that we can change ourselves or the world in which we live in, and that such changes will be desirable, then we will attempt such changes. If we believe that we cannot change ourselves or the world we live in, as desirable as such changes might be, then we will be less likely to attempt such changes. This is not to say that we will not be moved to, and, in fact, attempt some self-protective responses but rather that the kinds of self-protective responses we will employ will be the outcome of our beliefs about ourselves and the world. Believing that we cannot change undesirable aspects of ourselves or the world we live in may lead, for example, to self-distorting or otherwise reality-distorting responses (interpretable as one form of withdrawal from an unacceptable reality) or to interpersonal withdrawal. Both, in the face of an immutable reality, accomplish self-enhancing goals by resulting in the perception of more self-relevant beneficent outcomes or the forestalling of self-devaluing experiences.

SUMMARY

How an individual responds to himself along any of a number of cognitive dimensions is influenced by the person's attributes, behaviors, and experiences in interaction with the situational context in which they appear, the system of concepts that the person has learned to use to structure stimuli, and motivation to evaluate himself positively. The person's traits, behaviors, and experiences (including the individual and collective responses of others that purposely or otherwise have an impact on the person's outcomes) are social in nature, both in the sense that their meanings are provided by the current situation and in the sense that they have their origins in the course of past social interactions.

The most direct route by which personal traits, behaviors, or experiences may influence self-referent cognitive responses is by immediately becoming objects of self-awareness. The personal traits, behaviors, and experiences of which one becomes aware may be conceived of in terms of their objectively given forms or in terms of other, perhaps unobserved or unobservable, personal traits, behaviors, or experiences that are suggested by the immediate object of awareness.

The person's traits, behaviors, and experiences are mutually influential, whether over a relatively long or short period of time. Therefore, any particular trait, behavior, or experience may have an indirect effect on self-referent cognition by, first, influencing others' personal traits, behaviors, or experiences that, in turn, directly stimulate self-awareness and self-conceiving responses. Traits, behaviors, and experiences vary to the extent to which they may directly stimulate self-conceiving responses as opposed to indirectly influencing such responses through their mediating effects on other influential traits, behaviors, and experiences.

The nature of the influence of personal traits, behaviors, and experiences on self-referent cognitive responses is moderated by the situational context, the person's system of concepts that he habitually uses to structure the world and himself, and the person's motivation to acquire self-enhancing experiences. The situational context provides symbolic cues that (1) specify the relevance of particular traits, behaviors, and experiences for the person's current life situation from among the many traits, behaviors, and experience in the person's repertoire and (2) provide a range and distribution of values along specific dimensions that allow and stimulate the person to discern the particular values that characterize himself along those dimensions. The person uses a relatively stable, more or less consensual system of concepts to guide the selective cognitive structuring of personal attributes—a system of concepts that is derived both from regularities in the person's responses and from the reinforcement value of (1) others' sanctions for the use of particular concepts and (2) the usefulness of the consensual concepts in anticipating others' responses to the person's behaviors. The person's need for positive self-evaluation motivates him to be sensitive to his own personal traits, behaviors, or experiences that are relevant to self-attitudes and to perceive and define them in ways that will enhance self-evaluation.

The extent to which the situational context and the person's system of concepts and need for positive self-evaluation will moderate the influence of personal traits, behaviors, and experiences on self-conceiving responses is a function of the ambiguity of the meaning of the person's traits, behaviors, and experiences and of the context in which they are presented.

Self-referent cognitive responses have direct consequences, both for the person's own traits, behaviors, and experiences and for other modes of self-referent response. The acts of responding to oneself cognitively in particular ways are themselves behaviors and may become personal attributes that, in turn, stimulate other self-referent cognitions. Self-cognitions, conjointly with the individual's need value system, influence self-evaluative responses and self-enhancing responses, particularly as self-cognition reflects beliefs about self-efficacy.

CHAPTER 3

Social Antecedents and Consequences of Self-Evaluation

In this volume, self-evaluative responses are differentiated both from self-referent cognitive responses and from self-feelings. Self-evaluation is differentiated from self-feeling, since the two reflect qualitiatively distinct processes: One is a cognitive function and the other is an affective function. The relationship between self-evaluation and self-cognition, however, is that of a less inclusive to a more inclusive category of cognitive responses. Self-evaluation may be thought of as a particular kind of self-referent cognition. A self-evaluative response is one that reflects the person's awareness and conceptualization of his own attributes, behaviors, and experiences *as more or less closely approximating relatively highly valued or disvalued states.*

From the social psychology perspective of self-referent behaviors, self-evaluative responses are significant as mediating the relationship between other kinds of self-referent cognitive responses and self-feelings. Thus, in the following pages, we will consider self-evaluative behaviors (1) as the conjoint influence of other (nonevaluative) modes of self-referent cognition and the person's need-value system and (2) as stimuli, together with the need to evaluate oneself positively, for self-feelings.

SOCIAL ANTECEDENTS OF SELF-EVALUATION

Self-evaluative responses are behaviors whereby the individual becomes aware of and conceptualizes himself or herself in terms of having attributes, performing behaviors, and being the objects of experiences that reflect more or less highly valued or disvalued states from the perspective of the individual's own need-value system. The individual's ascription of evaluative significance to personal traits, behaviors, or experiences presumes two conditions: (1) the person's awareness and conceptualization of the traits, behaviors, and experiences in nonevaluative terms (e.g., a person must conceive of himself in terms of sex before self-evaluation in terms of sex may proceed) and (2) the existence of a system of personal evaluative standards. Therefore, in order to understand the origins of self-evaluative responses, it is necessary to understand both the genesis of nonevaluative self-referent cognitive responses and the origins of the personal value system, in particular, those personal values that are applicable to self-evaluation. In Chapter 2, we considered influences on self-referent cognition. The person's traits, behaviors, and experiences were said to affect (moderated by the perceived situational context, the individual's personal system of concepts, and need for self-enhancing experiences) self-cognition. In this connection, we discussed the (in large measures, social) origins of the personal traits, behaviors, and experiences that, in general, stimulate self-awareness and self-conceptualization. It is the awareness and conceptualization of such attributes, behaviors, and experiences as these that are measured against the personal evaluative standards that comprise self-evaluative responses.

Self-awareness, in general, or self-awareness and self-conceptualization of particular traits, behaviors, or experiences, stimulates the *need* to evaluate oneself according to one's perception of what constitutes situationally applicable standards. Thus, the *onset* of self-evaluation is occasioned by the conjoint influence of self-awareness–self-conceptualization and the motivation to evaluate oneself. The *nature* of self-evaluative responses is a function of the self-conception of *particular* traits, behaviors, or experiences as approximating those evaluative standards that appear to be situationally applicable and of the salience of the self-evaluative standards in the personal hierarchy of values. Since the nature and determinants of self-referent cognition has already been considered, it remains to consider the motivation to evaluate oneself and the nature and origins of the personal value system, in order to comprehend the onset and nature of self-evaluative responses.

Self-Evaluation as Motivated Behavior

To understand the notion of self-evaluation as motivated behavior, that is, as behavior directed toward the achievement of a valued state or the avoidance of disvalued states, it is necessary to anticipate the discussion of the person's self-value system, since it will be argued that self-focused attention and, less directly, circumstances that facilitate self-focused attention, stimulate self-evaluation (Duval & Wicklund, 1972; Wicklund, 1979) because of the intrinsic value placed on self-evaluative responses by the subject.

The relationship between self-awareness and self-evaluation is asserted in several theoretical contexts but in none more explicitly than in objective self-awareness theory (Wicklund, 1975). This theory, as it has evolved, posits that the initial reaction to self-focused attention is self-evaluation, of a favorable or unfavorable variety depending on the nature of the salient within-self discrepancy between perceptions and standards. Generally, it is assumed that discrepancies are negative except when a standard of correctness (aspiration) has recently been exceeded. "If a person focuses on a negative discrepancy it appears even more negative, and positive discrepancies operate similarly" (p. 269) (Wicklund, 1975). Given salient negative discrepancies, the onset of self-focused attention will lead to attempts to avoid situations that increase objective self-awareness. If the self-focusing stimuli cannot be escaped, attempts will be made to effect discrepancy reduction.

However, in this theory, it is unclear as to why self-awareness should stimulate self-evaluation. In the present treatment, it is argued that because the person learns that self-evaluation functions to permit the person to so behave as to avoid disvalued life circumstances and to attain that which is valued, the self-evaluative act itself becomes intrinsically valued and becomes salient whenever self-awareness is present.

In the course of the socialization process, as we will note below, the person learns to need positive responses from others not only because these are intrinsically valued but also because they are instrumentally significant for the achievement of other goals and because they provide feedback about the person's unobservable characteristics. The responses of others to the person are contingent on the individual's traits, behaviors, and experiences at different times and in different situations. Since the person is motivated to receive positive responses from others, it is important that he know how others will respond to his present or anticipated characteristics or behaviors. Knowing this, he would be able to forestall or to remedy his own responses in order to maximize his chances of receiving desirable responses from others.

To this end, the person adopts the perspective of others in his environment and evaluates himself from their point of view. The person is thus able to imagine if others will respond favorably to particular traits or behaviors in particular situations and to vary his behavior so as to maximize the likelihood of receiving positive responses from others.

This is possible only because the individual has at his disposal the use of significant symbols (Mead, 1934), which he can employ and respond to as if he were the person to whom the symbols were addressed. In responding to the symbols as if he were the other person, he is taking on the attitude of the other toward his own gestures (i.e., symbols). In responding as another would to his own symbols, the individual has become aware of himself, conceived of himself, or otherwise objectified himself. He has become an object to his own conscious processes.

Insofar as the person successfully elicits the desired outcomes indirectly by evaluating himself from others' point of view, and adjusting his behavior accordingly, the individual is rewarded for evaluating himself and comes to intrinsically value what was once only instrumentally valued—the self-evaluative disposition. Over time, the tendency to evaluate oneself becomes a habitual response to self-awareness.

The tendency for self-cognition to stimulate self-evaluation may be facilitated by peculiarities of the self-cognition process. It has been argued that "when one is confronted by a complex stimulus whose aspects one cannot fully encode, one tends to notice selectively its more peculiar aspects" (p. 73) (McGuire & McGuire, 1982). If it is indeed the case that we tend to notice those aspects of the stimulus that are most peculiar, then it is reasonable to assume that they deviate from the norm in a positive or negative direction and, hence, stimulate a judgment to that effect. To the extent that the complex stimulus is ourselves in our current situation, we would tend to notice those aspects of ourselves that are most peculiar as well. Such perceptions, then, would evoke self-evaluations as being more or less deviant from what we perceived to be behavior, attributes, and experiences within the expected or appropriate range. McGuire and McGuire (1982) observed that

> the distinctiveness postulate is appropriately applied to one's self-perception because the self is a complex stimulus, the human individual being intrinsically complicated and one being relatively knowledgeable about the self. Hence, when suddenly asked to "Tell us about yourself," there has to be a great deal of selectivity in what comes to consciousness and is reported. The distinctiveness postulate predicts that when one is given the spontaneous self-concept probe, one describes the self in terms of a given individual-difference dimension to the extent that one's position on that dimension is peculiar in one's usual social environment. . . . Distinctiveness can also be affected by the momentary, as well as chronic, social environment. . . . Furthermore, by changing the person's social environment so that different characteristics become peculiar, we can change what is salient in his/her spontaneous self-concept. . . . In technical terms, we tend to notice aspects of ourselves to the extent that they have high information value (i.e., their atypicality makes them unpredictable). (p. 74)

Insofar as individuals do typically perceive the unique features of themselves, and these features, therefore, deviate from the expected and normative, the self-perception is likely to evoke judgments regarding whether the traits deviate in a more or less positive direction from the symbolic representation of the desirable states we call values.

Self-Evaluative Standards

As background to the discussion of the nature and social origins of the self-values that are the criteria for judging personal traits, behaviors, and experiences, we will consider the more general notions of values and value systems and then apply these to the personal value system and, more particularly, to that portion of the personal value system that encompasses self-values.

Values and Value Systems. Values are the symbolic expressions of more or less desirable experiential states. Values reflect more or less desirable states in the sense that the outcomes of approximating those states are distress-reducing and the outcomes of increased distance from the valued state are distress-inducing. To the extent that the distress-reducing–stress-inducing consequences are symbolically expressed in terms of other more or less desirable states, values can only be defined in terms of other values.

The desirable qualities or values in question may be conceptualized as continuous dimensions, such that they may be approximated to varying degrees. For example, a person may be more or less industrious or more or less beautiful. Alternatively, they may be conceptualized as discrete and mutually exclusive categories. For example, a person is either good or bad, either virtuous or not virtuous. The poles of the continuous dimensions or the discrete and mutually exclusive categories may be thought of in terms of opposite qualities, one defined as desirable, the other as undesirable (e.g., beautiful versus ugly, healthy versus diseased, moral versus immoral). Or, they may be thought of in terms of the presence or absence of a desirable or undesirable quality (e.g., beautiful versus nonbeautiful, healthy versus nonhealthy, moral versus nonmoral).

Ordinarily, the individual or group will conceive of numerous values that are more or less relevant, depending on the situational context. Certain values will be employed to judge particular attributes or behaviors in given situations, and other values will be used for judging other attributes and behaviors in other situations. Values of strength and beauty might be appropriate for judgments about physical characteristics; values of honesty and efficiency might be relevant for judging the performance of one who holds political office; and values of leadership potential and courage might be relevant to the evaluation of an army officer in the field.

Certain outcomes are considered intrinsically desirable, whereas other outcomes are valued only as instruments for achieving other intrinsically valued ends. Over time, because of their utility in this regard, what were once considered instrumental values may be intrinsically valued.

Values are ordered hierarchically so that, in a choice situation, one value is judged to have priority over another. For example, it might be more important to act for the public good and be disloyal to a friend than to be loyal to a friend at the cost of the public good. The totality of the values of a group or an individual organized in terms of such principles as situational applicability and ranked priority is a *value system*. A value system may be relatively stable but still may change slowly over time, both with regard to the trans-situational or situational applicability of values and with regard to the prioritization of values.

Value systems may be shared by more or less inclusive groups of individuals. Members of societies or identifiable groupings within societies may share value systems in the sense that they have common conceptions of the prioritization and applicability of values (including the social identities to which the values apply and the interpersonal situations in which they apply). These shared value systems may differ in some respects, but not in others, from the value systems shared by other societies or groupings. Universally, people value participation in a network of human beings. However, people do not universally value money, courage, or academic achievement.

Depending on the success of the socialization process, members of particular groups will internalize the shared values that are the basis for judgments of their physical and sociocultural environment (including other people) and of themselves. Because of processes of social change and multiple group memberships, a good deal of individual variability will be noted with regard to the adoption of a system of values. The system of values adopted by an individual according to which he judges his physical and sociocultural milieu, as well as his own personal traits, behaviors, or experiences, is the *personal value system*.

That aspect of the personal value system that the person regards as applicable to the judgments of the person's own traits, behaviors, and experiences will be referred to as the system of *self-values*—a set of values organized by priority and situational applicability, according to which the person judges his personal traits, behaviors, or experiences. It is the process of evaluating one's self as more or less approximating self-values that determines the extent to which the person perceives himself as approximating the most inclusive and overriding self-value of all, self-worth. The overall evaluation of self-worth is a function of the person's perception of the degree to which he approximates the relatively highly placed values in his hierarchy of values in a more or less consistent manner.

Self-Values System. The system of self-values is the normal outcome of the infant's early dependence on adults for physical need satisfaction. The infant associates the presence of adults with the satisfaction of his physical needs. As long as all the adults in the infant's environment are associated with noncontingent need satisfactions, the infant will come to *value the presence of* adults.

As the circle of people in the child's world widens, the child may note that need satisfaction is associated with certain persons and not with others. He may thus come to *value the traits and behaviors that are associated with those persons who satisfy his needs* and to disvalue the traits and behaviors that are associated with those persons who frustrate (or are irrelevant to) satisfaction of congenital or acquired values. Insofar as the persons who ordinarily facilitate the subject's satisfaction of needs on occasion fail to do so, the child will associate certain behaviors of caregivers with the occasions on which needs were satisfied and other behaviors of caregivers with the occasions on which he *failed* to have his needs satisfied. These behaviors (which will later be conceptualized as approving or disapproving attitudes), by virtue of their association with other valued responses, come to be valued in their own right. The subject has come to *value the positive and disvalue the negative attitudinal responses of others* and the forms in which the attitudes are expressed— physical punishment, disapproving words, failure to meet expectations.

Insofar as the attitudes of others are contingent on the attributes and behaviors of the subject, as they might be when such attributes or behaviors frustrate the achievement of the others' own values (in the most general sense, when they fail to conform to the expectations of others), the subject comes to *value the attributes and behaviors that were perceived as eliciting positive attitudinal responses* and to disvalue those that were perceived as eliciting negative attitudinal responses. Such behaviors and attributes, in the aggregate, constitute the range of normative expectations applied by others to the subject trans-situationally or in specific relational contexts. Those values that are given higher priority are the ones most closely associated with earlier satisfaction of significant needs.

Insofar as individuals are, by definition, moved to achieve these valued states, they will come to *value in their own right any behavior patterns, resources, or relationships that have been perceived as instrumental to the achievement of these valued states*. This includes the *disposition to evaluate oneself*. The satisfaction of the person's needs, in no small measure, depends on the responses of others. The responses of others, in turn, are frequently contingent on their evaluation of the person's traits and behaviors. Since the person is motivated to perceive himself as achieving valued states and as the object of positive responses by others, he adopts the perspective of others in his environment and evaluates himself from the point of view of these others. The person is thus able to imagine how he appears to others and to adjust his behavior in ways that would elicit positive responses from others. Since self-evaluation from the perspective of others (at first, particular others and, later, in addition, the "generalized other") is functional in obtaining gratifying responses from others, *the person comes to regard this pattern as intrinsically valuable* and, thus, to evaluate himself on occasions when he becomes self-aware. In the course of imagining how the other person responds (or would respond) to the subject evaluatively, the subject expresses an attitude toward himself that is the symbolic representation of the imagined attitudinal response of the other person and then responds to his own attitudinal expression as if the other person had actually expressed the attitude. Since the person is motivated to elicit positive evaluations from others (in their own right, and also because they signify achieving valued states), he responds to a favorable self-evaluation with positive self-feelings and to an unfavorable self-evaluation with distressful negative self-feelings. The subject's own attitudinal responses to himself thus become motivationally significant. Through their original association with the imagined attitudes of others, the subject's attitudinal expressions toward himself consistently tend to elicit relatively gratifying or distressing emotional experiences. The subject, at this point, may be said to have acquired the need to respond to himself in terms of positive evaluations and, thereby, to elicit further gratifying emotional experiences and to avoid responding to himself in terms of negative evaluations that would elicit other experiences of subjective distress. In short, the subject has come to *value positive self-evaluation* and to disvalue negative self-evaluations, a value that is the normal outcome of the human infant's early dependence on, and subsequent interaction with, other human beings in the context of stable social relationships.

Positive self-evaluation is the most inclusive value in the person's system of self-values, as negative self-evaluation is the most inclusive self-disvalued circumstance. The occasional or characteristic judgment of approximating the criterion of positive self-value depends on self-judgments of the degree to which the person approximates, of the frequency with which the individual approximates, and the duration during which the person approximates the relatively high priority values in the person's self-value system. Rosenberg and Kaplan (1982) observe that

> some dispositions are central to the individual's feelings of worth, whereas others are peripheral. Some people pride themselves on their attractiveness and care little about their literary skills; for others, the reverse is the case. It thus follows that if we are to understand what difference a particular self-concept component makes for one's global feeling of worth, we must know not simply how one evaluates oneself in that regard but also how much importance one attaches to it. (p. 177)

Among the self-evaluative criteria are the responses of specified others, social identities, and, generally, competence in dealing with the environment. The extent to which a person is loved, admired, and sought after may be, in itself, a basis for self-evaluation of personal worth, as when popularity among peers is a major criterion for self-evaluation among adolescent females. Because being liked by others is intrinsically important and occupies a high place in our hierarchy of values, if the others who like us are themselves worthy of being liked, it is likely to occupy an even higher place in the hierarchy. To be liked by well-liked people, to be admired by virtuous people, to be honored by those who are themselves held honorable, would be to provide a greater basis for positive self-evaluation, since they have achieved what in one's own hierarchy of values is an admirable outcome.

With regard to social identities such as those related to sex, it has been recognized that, in general, characteristics ascribed to the typical woman are less highly valued than characteristics ascribed to the typical man (Wylie, 1979). Insofar as the individual recognizes a social position as part of his own identity and incorporates into his own value system the salience of the position in question, the social position will contribute to his overall evaluation. This evaluation-relevant effect of social positions is independent of any other effects such positions might have by virtue of their evaluation-relevant correlates or consequences.

A high value may be placed on competence to deal with the requirements of the social and physical environment. A high sense of competence may contribute to one's overall feeling of self-worth (Covington & Beery, 1976). Indeed, discussions of self-efficacy have implied that, universally, self-esteem is based on a sense of competence, power, or efficacy (Gecas, 1982).

Regardless of the salience of the self-values, the criteria for self-evaluation depend on the social context and the person's social identities in social situations. If an individual becomes aware of his socioeconomic characteristics in his neighborhood, he may appropriately compare himself by neighborhood standards, whereas, in other situations, he may compare himself to the standards of achievement of the more inclusive society. Different standards are used for self-evaluation in the schoolroom, the family dining room, the restaurant when on a date, and the battlefield.

The person's social identities also serve to define the values that are subjectively applicable. Thus, girls were reported as being more concerned with interpersonal harmony and success, kindly virtues, and aesthetic appreciation than boys, who were more likely to value motor skills, physical courage, interpersonal dominance, etc. (Rosenberg, 1979). The nature of the standards individuals adopt for self-evaluation vary also, according to socioeconomic status. Asking which traits were important, Rosenberg (1965) reported that the percentage of boys who considered each of several traits to be among the most important was a direct function of socioeconomic level. These traits included being a good student in school; being intelligent, having a good mind; being a logical, reasonable type; being imaginative and original; and being well-respected and looked up to by others.

Other studies also suggest that different evaluative standards are appropriate for self-judgment, depending on sex. Men evaluate themselves by different standards than women. In one study, men and women were called on to compete at tasks the success on which was presumably sex-linked (Zanna, Goethals, & Hill, 1975). It was observed that the men tried to learn the scores of other men in order to evaluate their performance, while the women sought the scores of other women.

Apart from the socially defined situational contingencies, other personal contingencies will determine the salience of particular values in particular situations. To the extent that the person perceives no threat to higher-order values in a particular situation, he may attend more closely to a lower-order value, the approximation to which is problematic. The person may value popularity more than academic achievement. However, in a situation in which personal popularity is not at risk, the person may attend to those features of the situation that relate to academic performance (that is problematic), and evaluate himself according to the standards of academic excellence.

The prioritization of self-values, as well as the variable applicability of the standards, may make values vulnerable to change. Rokeach (1983) notes that

> because individual values are typically embedded in value hierarchies rather than existing in isolation, and also because different situations activate differ-

ent subsets of a person's total value hierarchy, he or she is continually forced in everyday life to compare the relative importance of any given value with others that might be activated by a given situation, or that might be activated by a larger change in the social milieu within which one is embedded. It is important to emphasize, to those who have always assumed that values, once formed, are stubbornly resistant to change, that it is such a process of continual comparison of the importance of one value with another that makes values, paradoxically, so vulnerable to change, that is, to change in priority. (p. 175)

We will consider motivated change in the self-value system in the service of positive self-evaluation in Chapter 5.

To summarize, the person is stimulated to evaluate himself on becoming aware of and conceptualizing himself. The disposition to evaluate oneself is learned in the course of the socialization process, when the person becomes aware of the functional value of self-evaluation from the perspective of others in securing gratifying outcomes. The person evaluates himself in terms of a hierarchy of situationally appropriate self-values that are learned and that are vulnerable to change in the course of the socialization process. The most inclusive value in the hierarchy is that of positive self-evaluation. Positive self-evaluation, as the most inclusive self-value, is defined in terms of the other, more or less salient and situationally appropriate self-values in the system. To evaluate oneself positively is to perceive oneself as meeting the general–specific demands made on one, as these demands (for behavior, attributes, experiences) are reflected in the person's more or less salient and situationally relevant values that comprise the hierarchy of values. The overall positive evaluation of self is a function of the person's perception of closely approximating the (in particular) relatively highly placed values in the system. Theoretically, the most positive self-evaluation is a function of perceiving oneself as meeting all situationally relevant self-imposed demands. Conversely, the most negative self-evaluation reflects the perceived failure to meet any of the self-imposed demands in a particular situation. The stability of positive self-evaluations depends on the constancy with which the individual perceives himself as meeting the situationally relevant demands made on him. Over time, if the individual fails to meet those demands, he will come to have a relatively stable, negative self-evaluation, reflected in the expectations of continued inability to meet what he regards as legitimate demands. If, however, over time, the individual consistently perceives himself as meeting the demands made on him (by self and others), he will come to develop a relatively stable positive self-evaluation, reflected in the expectation of continuing success in meeting these demands.

Empirical Findings

Self-evaluation is interpreted in terms of the self-awareness and self-conceptualization of personal traits, behaviors, or experiences as more or less closely approximating self-values. Self-referent cognition is expected to stimulate self-evaluative behavior. The nature of the self-evaluative response is said to be a function of the specific self-perceived and self-conceptualized traits, behaviors, and experiences, on the one hand, and the nature of the particular self-values according to which they are judged, on the other hand. Consequently, the relevant research literature falls into any of three categories.

The first of these categories relates to the stimulation of self-evaluative responses by general conditions facilitating self-cognition. Consistent with the premise that self-referent cognition stimulates the need to evaluate oneself, it was observed that, under conditions of presumed greater self-awareness, the presence of particular traits, behaviors, or experiences was more likely to be associated with self-evaluative responses.

The second category reports associations between self-perceptions (sometimes only assumed) of personal traits, behaviors, and experiences, on the one hand, and more or less positive self-evaluations, on the other hand. Implicit in these studies is the expectation that the personal traits, behaviors, and experiences reflect different degrees of approximation to salient personal evaluative standards.

The third category more explicitly considers the salience of the evaluative standard as a condition for observing an association between personal traits, behaviors, and experiences, on the one hand, and more or less positive self-evaluative responses, on the other hand. Each of the three categories of findings are considered in turn.

Self-Awareness. In support of the proposition that self-awareness stimulates self-evaluative responses are the results of a small number of studies. Data reported by Gibbons (1978) are consistent with the point of view that self-cognition influences the self-evaluative process. The data suggested that, under conditions facilitating self-awareness, an individual would tend to evaluate his behavior but that such evaluation would not occur under other conditions. Individuals who scored high on a sex guilt inventory (that I take as an index of the person's more or less negative evaluation of sex) tended to rate pornographic passages negatively, whereas those who scored low on the inventory tended to rate the passage more positively *under conditions in which self-awareness was stimulated* (confrontation with mirror image). However, in the absence of this condition, the self-evaluative response was absent. That is, there was virtually no association between the judgment of enjoyment of the sexual passage and the individual's score on the sex guilt inventory.

Also consistent with the hypothesized relationships is the observation of an association between self-focused attention on favorable attributes and positive self-evaluative responses in a study in which subjects were induced to write self-descriptive essays involving the marshaling of arguments designed to convey an extremely favorable impression of themselves (Mirels & McPeek, 1977). It was expected that the ideation involved in the preparation and organization of these arguments would facilitate enhancement of self-attitudes. In this experiment, in which half the subjects wrote about their personality attributes while the other half wrote about social issues, the subjects who wrote the self-laudatory essays subsequently rated themselves more positively than the control subjects who wrote in support of social issues. Since the experimental subjects were asked to focus on themselves (particularly on their positive attributes), the results are consistent with the proposition that self-recognition stimulates the readiness to conceive of one's self in terms of degree of approximation to more or less important values comprising one's system of values.

Less direct evidence for the hypothesis that self-evaluation is more likely to occur following an increase in the individual's self-awareness is provided by a series of studies that show that individuals act in ways that promote personal values under conditions that facilitate self-awareness (Carver, 1975).

Self-Perceptions of Personal Traits, Behaviors, and Experiences. A large number of studies report associations between self-perceptions of *presumably* valued attributes, behaviors, and experiences, on the one hand, and self-evaluations, on the other hand. For example, at different stages of the life cycle, associations have been observed between self-perceptions of various qualities or achievements and positive self-evaluation. At earlier stages, the influence of self-perceptions of more or less disvalued attributes on self-evaluation is reflected in a number of studies. The experimental induction of success on an IQ test has been related to an increase in overt self-ratings (Diller, 1954). Experimentally induced failure on an English grammar test has been related to reduced self-evaluations and to a reduction in the extent to which subjects believed they were valued by significant others in their lives (Gibby & Gibby, 1967). A longitudinal study of low-income black children revealed that teacher evaluation of academic performance in kindergarten is positively associated with self-esteem at grade six (Slaughter, 1977). Overachievers tended to be characterized in terms of higher self-esteem (Taylor, 1964).

Self-evaluations were observed to vary as expected in response to the experimental manipulation of ratings by a "visiting speech expert" of students' reading performance in introductory speech classes (Videbeck, 1960) and ratings by a "physical development expert" of male high school students' performance of physical tasks (Maehr, Mensing, & Nafzger, 1962).

In some studies many, but not all, of the expected relationships were observed. In the case of academic ability for both boys and girls and of athletic ability for boys, the path of causal influence appears to be from perception of the ability to self-esteem rather than vice versa (Bohnstedt & Felson, 1983). However, for being liked, the causal direction appeared to be in the opposite direction, with individuals with higher self-esteem being more likely to perceive themselves as well-liked, whatever their actual sociometric status. The investigators interpret the differences in the relationship, in part, in terms of the differential verifiability of the attributes (being liked is less verifiable) and, by implication, in terms of the feasibility of self-enhancing cognitive distortion. Alternatively, one might consider that the act of describing one's self in unfavorable or favorable terms itself has self-evaluative implications. Thus, the fact that perceptions of popularity did not appear to affect self-esteem (Bohrnstedt & Felson, 1983) may have reflected the need for individuals who were, in fact, popular not to describe themselves as popular (lest they appear to be bragging). Hence, a possible true relationship between the attribute (popularity) and self-cognition (by way of reflected appraisals) is confounded by the self-evaluative implications of the self-description process. However, subjects with higher self-esteem might have sufficient self-confidence to report their veridical perceptions of being liked, thus accounting for the observed causal direction from self-esteem to perceptions of being liked.

In any case, the weight of the evidence is in favor of the proposition that self-perceptions of favorable traits, behaviors, and outcomes are positively associated with self-evaluation. This is confirmed by studies at later stages in the life cycle as well, in which positive self-evaluation has been observed to be associated with such diverse phenomena as college grade point average (Bassis, 1977), successful adaptation to changing role demands (Morrison, 1977), organ donation (Fellner & Marshall, 1970), occupational prestige and employment status (Bachman & O'Malley, 1977; Bachman et al., 1978; Cohn, 1978), interpersonal influence (Archer, 1974), and winning or losing an election (Ziller & Golding, 1969). Thus, data from a longitudinal study reveal that among those who were employed at an earlier point in time, those who became unemployed at a later point in time, compared to those who remained employed, were significantly more dissatisfied, after adjusting for prior levels of self-satisfaction (Cohn, 1978). Ziller and Golding (1969), in a comparison of winning and losing political candidates, observed that those who were elected to office tended to gain in self-esteem, whereas those who were not elected were less likely to gain in self-esteem and, indeed, were more likely to show a decrease in self-esteem. Those candidates who gained in self-esteem, in spite of being defeated (all were nonincumbents), might have received gratification from the publicity associated with candidacy. Finally, Archer (1974), consistent with the idea that a person's relative power, dominance, or influence in the small group predicts the direction of change in self-concept the person experiences as a function of participation in the group, reported that members who were high in power were observed to change more toward a positive self-concept, whereas those low in power changed more toward a negative self-concept. These last findings are compatible with the hypothesis that self-perceptions of having valued qualities (such as the ability to influence others) influence positive self-evaluation. This is so whether the self-perceptions are interpreted as resulting from (a) subjects' contributions to group discussions, (b) group members' perceptions of the subject as influential, or (c) subjects' perceptions of receiving a disproportionate amount of attention from other group members.

As noted above, in these studies, the *presumption of salient evaluative standards* justifies the expected relationship. For example, Mackie (1983) explains that "because housewifery is devalued work and occupation an achieved status, housewives were hypothesized to have lower self-esteem than women in the labor force" (p. 348)—a prediction that, in this study at least, proved to be accurate.

Certain of these standards appear to be presumed more frequently than others in studies of the relationship between self-perception and self-evaluation. Among these are the extent to which one is the object of approving responses of others and the extent to which one can effect changes in one's environment. To the extent that the person experiences and, therefore, perceives himself as the object of approval by others and as an effective person, he is expected to evaluate himself as more or less closely approximating the standards of receiving approval by others and self-efficacy. The positive self-evaluations accompanying the perceptions of approximating the standards have been labeled (among other labels) by some as inner self-esteem (for approximating a standard of self-efficacy) and outer self-esteem (for approximating the standard of evoking positive responses from others). Franks and Marolla (1976) observe that

> one's sense of inner self-esteem derives from the experience of self as an active agent—of making things actually happen and realizing one's intents in an impartial world. . . . Input here is "inner" in the sense that it stems from

feelings of one's own capacity, competence, and potency. This feedback comes to us in terms of the consequences of our own actions upon the environment. . . . In contrast, outer self-esteem is bestowed by others, and the concern which makes such input meaningful is with the approval or acceptance of particular others. (p. 326)

Several studies have tested the expectation that experiences of approving responses from others and of successfully negotiating reality are associated with appropriate self-evaluations. With regard to perceived approving responses of others, a substantial literature, compatible with the hypothesis that self-perceptions of being the object of negative attitudes by others leads to negative self-evaluations, exists. Thus, Sears (1970) used measures of parental attitudes obtained from interviews with the subjects' mothers seven years earlier and concluded that parental warmth significantly influenced the child's self-esteem. Here I presume that the relationship is mediated by the child's perception of approving attitudes. Petersen and Kellam (1977) reported that quality and quantity of affectional resources in the family are related to self-esteem. Reports of parental punitiveness at the start of 10th grade showed an appreciable relationship with self-esteem measured at the end of high school (Bachman, 1982). Finally, Kaplan (1980) hypothesized and observed that seventh-graders who scored high on measures of perceived devaluation by peers, family, school, and membership groups, in general, and of perceived devaluation by others because of specified ascribed characteristics, compared to seventh-graders who scored low on these measures, manifested higher self-devaluation scores in the eighth grade and ninth grade and greater increases (or smaller decreases) between the seventh and eighth grade in residualized changes in self-derogation. Thus, the data support the expectation that subject perception of others' negative attitudes reflects the perceived failure to approximate the self-evaluative standard of securing approving responses from others, that is, it leads to negative self-evaluations.

With regard to the presumed self-evaluative standard of self-efficacy, individuals who are permitted the experience of competence are generally observed to evaluate themselves highly with regard to self-efficacy (or related criteria) or more general self-evaluative standards. Thus, the effect of self-perception of personal automony in the work place on self-judgment of personal competency is suggested by a panel study of male college graduates who were first studied in their undergraduate years and who were followed up ten years later in a mail survey (Mortimer & Lorence, 1979a). Consistent with this, Staples and his associates (1984) observed a significant effect of self-judgment of occupation-related self-efficacy on global self-esteem.

In another sphere in which individuals have varying degrees of success (dating), experiences of effectiveness were observed to be related to higher levels of positive self-evaluation. In one study, Haemmerlie and Montgomery (1982) randomly distributed males who were anxious about social interaction with females, and who dated infrequently, among either an experimental or a waiting-list control group. The experimental group was introduced to a "real" life, pleasant, prearranged social interaction with females. This intervention led to a significant change in self-perception concerning anxiety and an increase in self-confidence.

However, an individual is likely to evaluate himself as being less self-effective under circumstances in which he is most likely to be in a subordinate position and to perceive himself as being in a subordinate position (Gecas, 1982); and, as Helmreich (1972) proposes, "continued exposure to environmental stresses . . . serves to lower an individual's self-esteem by reducing his feelings of *competence . . .* in dealing with his physical and social environment" (p. 35) (italics added). The objective experiences of being unable to deal with the physical and social environment successfully is perceived by the individual in terms of low level of competence. This self-perception elicits negative self-evaluations.

To summarize, studies of the relationship between self-perceptions and self-evaluation tend to assume that the self-perceived traits, behaviors, or experiences are being measured against salient evaluative standards. We now turn to studies that more explicitly consider the salience of evaluative standards as moderating the relationship between self-perception and self-evaluation.

Salience of Evaluative Standards. A large number of studies are relevant to the issue of whether or not salience of personal evaluative standards moderates the relationship between self-referent cognitive and self-evaluative responses. In the most clearly relevant group of studies, the relationship between self-perceptions of personal traits, behaviors, or experiences, on the one hand, and self-evaluation, on the other hand, is compared under conditions in which applicable evaluative standards are more or less personally salient. In a second group of studies, the relationship between self-referent cognitions and self-evaluative responses are interpreted by the investigators in terms of differences or changes in salience of evaluative standards, or appear to permit such interpretations. We will consider representative studies from each group in turn.

Data from a longitudinal study of junior high school students (Kaplan, 1980) provide strong support for the proposition that self-perceptions of personal attributes, behaviors, or experiences influence self-evaluation consistently under conditions in which the traits, values, or experiences have high evaluative significance but not under conditions in which they do not have strong evaluative significance. Among subjects who judged particular qualities or behaviors to be important (e.g., I think it is important to be kind to others, . . . to be honest, . . . to have a lot of friends, . . . to be good at sports), those subjects who, in the seventh grade, indicated that they did not possess the important quality or perform the personally valued behavior tended to be significantly more self-rejecting one year and two years later and to display relatively greater residual increases in self-rejection between the seventh and eighth grade than subjects who had described themselves as possessing the quality or behavior in question. However, these relationships were not consistently observed where the subjects denied the importance of the attribute or behavior.

Consistent with the expectation that self-cognitions of personal attributes, behaviors, and experiences would lead to negative self-evaluations only under conditions in which the trait was of evaluative significance, Kaplan (1971b) observed, in a cross-sectional study of the adult population of Houston and Harris counties, that lower social class position is associated with higher levels of self-rejecting feelings under circumstances in which subjects were socialized to regard relative social class position as a personally relevant criterion. These circumstances are implied by the person having internalized the need to achieve as a child (reflected in being very much afraid of receiving a bad report card as a child) and in being socialized by a parent who had achieved higher levels of performance (reflected in having a more educated mother). Compatible with these findings, Rosenberg and Pearlin (1978) observed that the relationship of income to self-esteem was quite strong among adults who strongly agreed that one of the most important things about a person is the amount of money he makes but quite weak among adults who did not agree. Comparable results were observed with regard to the relationship between occupational prestige and self-esteem.

The influence of self-evaluation, considered as the convergence between self-cognition and personal values, on self-feelings is suggested by Rosen and Ross's (1968) report of a correlation of .52 between satisfaction with physical appearance and self-concept, a correlation that was appreciably higher (.62) when only those items that tended to be rated by the subjects as more important were considered.

Paradoxically, positive self-evaluation may depend on the individual failing at a task, if failure is defined as appropriate for a particular social identity. For example, in one study (Feather & Simon, 1975), females who failed on a masculinity-linked task were regarded more favorably by other females, whereas females who were successful were devalued by other females. In another study (Howe & Zanna, 1975), male and female subjects adjusted their performance (including doing less well) to conform to what they were led to believe were appropriate sex-related behaviors. That is, they worked harder at a task if they were told that it was appropriate for their sex and performed more poorly on the task (anagrams) if they were led to believe that it was more appropriate for the opposite sex to do well on the task. These data imply that the person evaluates himself according to appropriate standards. The adjustive behavior of the subjects suggests that the resulting, more or less positive self-evaluations influenced self-feelings that, in turn, motivated the adjustive behavior.

Frequently, self-perceptions relate to the attitudes of others toward the subject. The appropriate self-evaluative standard here is the extent to which one perceives oneself as the object of positive rather than negative responses. As is the case with other evaluative standards, the relationship between self-perception and self-evaluations depends on the personal significance of the standard. Thus, Rosenberg (1973) reports that the relationship between what a child perceived his mother as thinking of him and his own self-evaluation was relatively strong if he cared very much about the mother's opinion, but was much weaker if he cared little about the mother's opinion. Similar relationships were observed with regard to friends, siblings, classmates, teachers, and fathers.

Salience of the evaluative standard is apparent in circumstances other than the person's evaluation of the standard as important. It is also reflected in the direction to compare oneself to different standards presented in the situational context. As Brookover and Passalacqua (1981) state,

> self-concept or self-assessment at any particular time or situation varies from any other time or situation depending upon the social role the actor plays. Thus, the reference group to which he or she is referring in the self-assessment varies from one social context to another. This is well illustrated by the findings that the self-concept of academic ability of blind children varied with the comparison or reference group to which they were asked to respond— seeing children or other blind children. (p. 286)

When the direction to compare oneself to particular standards is not explicit, it is implicit in the situational presentation. Thus, Morse and Gergen (1970) described a study, in which "as one encountered others who were either highly desirable or undesirable in appearance, their own self-estimates changed." As Gergen (1981) comments, "when a desirable person was encountered, self-evaluation plummeted; when an undesirable appeared, self-estimates were often boosted" (p. 65).

That implicit situation-specific standards of comparison guide self-evaluation is apparent also in a study of underachievers in special education classes in several elementary schools. Rogers and associates (1978) observed that standardized ratings of students were positively related to self-esteem within classrooms but not across classrooms. This suggests that the salient evaluative standards are situation-specific. It is relative achievement that the person strives for and that influences positive self-evaluation. Along with this study, Rosenberg (1981) cites other studies that are compatible with this interpretation. In one study (Meadow, 1969), the self-esteem of deaf children with deaf parents tended to be higher than the self-esteem of deaf children with hearing parents. In another study (Craig, 1965), the self-esteem of deaf children in residential schools for the deaf was higher than that of deaf children in other schools. Although other interpretations are possible, these studies permit the interpretation that individuals evaluate themselves according to relative performance or attributes that reflect what is implicitly normative for the social environment.

The implicit situational applicability of evaluative standards may be reflected in studies of the effects on self-esteem of being consonant or dissonant with the racial–ethnic–religious distribution in the social setting. Rosenberg and Simmons (1971) found that blacks scored lower in self-esteem in the dissonant (predominantly white schools) contexts than in the consonant (predominantly black schools) contexts. These findings may suggest that, according to the evaluative standards in the consonant setting, the subject need not find himself wanting. However, these patterns were not observed for blacks by Simmons, Brown, Bush, and Blyth (1978). Variation in percent black had no impact on the self-evaluations of blacks or whites. Nor did Jensen, White, and Galliher (1982) observe the pattern for Chicanos. The failure to replicate the Rosenberg and Simmons study may have been the result of the extreme degrees of consonance and dissonance in their data (Jensen et al., 1982). Another possibility is that the failure to see a relationship between minority status (even in the presence of associated prejudicial and discriminatory behavior) and self-evaluation is accounted for in terms of a set of evaluative standards (that is, a democratic orientation) that preludes negative self-judgments on such grounds.

As Jensen and his associates (1982) observe,

> while perceived mistreatment or racial insults vary by ethnicity and/or by dissonance, such experiences do not, "of necessity," result in low self-esteem. . . . It may be that attacks based on ascribed characteristics are readily

"neutralized" among school children constantly exposed to an official ideology which stresses equality and condemns overt expressions of prejudice. (p. 238)

In a second group of studies, the existence of variable salience of evaluative standards is not explicit. However, the findings concerning the relationship between self-perception of personal traits, behaviors, and experiences, on the one hand, and self-evaluative responses, on the other hand, are interpreted or appear to be interpretable in terms of the variable salience of evaluative standards.

Bachman and his associates (1978) observed, for a panel of high school students, that the correlates of self-esteem change over time and they interpreted these changes in terms of shifts in the "centrality" of certain self-evaluative standards. They observed that

> factors of background, ability, and past school performance become less and less important for self-esteem as a young man continues through high school and beyond. . . . This pattern of declining importance for self-esteem appears with great consistency across a number of dimensions—family socioeconomic level, test scores, grade-point averages, rebellious and delinquent behaviors in school, and educational and occupational aspirations. . . .
>
> These declining correlations with self-esteem can be interpreted in terms of shifting centrality; those attributes of self-identity which have to do with conventional educational success had less centrality, and thus less impact on self-esteem, as young men moved through the final years of high school and go on to other experiences. (pp. 115–116)

Since, in a later analysis (O'Malley & Bachman, 1979), data for seniors in a nationwide sample of the high school class of 1977 revealed that the self-esteem of seniors was correlated with educationally relevant measures almost equally for males in the classes of 1969 and 1977, they interpreted the changes in centrality in terms of developmental rather than cultural change.

The influence of salience of evaluative standards on self-evaluation of perceived personal attributes, behaviors, and experiences is suggested by findings from a longitudinal analysis of the effect of job loss on self-satisfaction (Cohn, 1978). If it may be assumed that a person's self-perceptions leads to self-devaluation only if it deviates from expected standards, then we would expect self-perception of employment status to influence self-evaluation only to the extent that it reflected a deviation from the norm. Thus, in areas where unemployment was more prevalent, the individual's recognition of unemployment would be less likely to lead to self-dissatisfaction than in areas where the unemployment rate was low. In fact, this was observed. Self-dissatisfaction was significantly greater for the unemployed who lived in areas where the unemployment rate was low. Although these findings are interpretable in terms of the evaluative significance of employment, the findings are also interpretable (as, indeed, they have been interpreted) in terms of the extent to which the social situation facilitates attribution of blame to external rather than internal causes (Cohn, 1978).

The differential effects of the priority of evaluative standards on the impact of self-perception of disvalued circumstances on self-satisfaction is suggested also by other analyses in the same study. Reasoning that the occupational status of white-collar workers represents alternative standards for self-evaluation in the person's hierarchy of values, Cohn expected that loss of employment would have less of an impact on the white-collar workers than on the blue-collar workers. This was, in fact, observed. Although there was a significant difference in self-satisfaction between the unemployed and the employed among the blue-collar workers, no apparent effect of employment status change on self-satisfaction was observed among white-collar workers. Again, this is consistent with the hypothesis that the employment-status component is less important in the self-concept of white-collar workers relative to blue-collar workers (Cohn, 1978). In effect, white-collar workers may be unemployed, but at least they have the satisfaction of having been employed at a higher level in the occupational hierarchy. Similar effects were observed with regard to education. Among white-collar workers, those with a high school education or less show a significant decrease in self-satisfaction with job loss, although no difference in self-satisfaction associated with job loss was observed among white-collar workers with more than a high school education. Among blue-collar workers, however, no difference in the effect of job loss by educational attainment was observed.

A series of reports on a cross-sectional study of a representative sample of adults in Houston and Harris counties cite findings of associations between personal traits, behaviors, and experiences, on the one hand, and self-devaluation, on the other hand, that vary depending on the social identities (age, gender, race, socioeconomic status) of the person (Kaplan, 1970, 1971a,b, 1973; Kaplan & Pokorny, 1970a,b, 1972). The differences in associations are interpreted in terms of the differential salience of self-evaluative standards, depending on the person's range of identities.

For example, for women but not for men, reports of unusual expenses during the preceding year were significantly associated with higher self-derogation scores. If the primary economic responsibility of the woman was the allocation of available resources to meet the needs of the family, whereas the primary responsibility of the man was the provision of resources, then the findings are understandable. Unusual expenses would most challenge the allocative responsibility of the woman, thus posing a possible threat to her confidence in activities presumed to be part of her self-image. However, men were most self-derogatory in the face of events that affected their breadwinning role, such as losing money in business or changing jobs (events that were not associated with higher levels of self-devaluation in women) (Kaplan, 1970).

Further indications of the differential evaluative standards that people use to judge themselves, depending on social identity, are observations regarding the associations between self-perceptions of experiences and self-rejecting feelings that are unique to particular age groups. For adults below the age of 30, but not for other adults, current self-rejecting feelings were associated with reports that, during childhood, they were very much afraid of being punished by their parents, that they received poorer grades than most of the children they knew, and that they were not as good-looking as most of the children they knew (Kaplan & Pokorny, 1970a). Apparently at the age at which standards of self-evaluation relate to establishing independence, occupational achievement, and interpersonal attractiveness, the person's perception of having had experiences that impeded approximation of these standards are associated with self-rejecting feelings. If an individual had been excessively afraid of being punished by his parents and now expected himself to become independent, if an individual had expected to achieve occupationally but perceived himself as lacking the ability to compete with regard to the prerequisites for a good job, and if the individual expected himself to be attractive to his peers but perceived himself as being unattractive, then the negative self-evaluation would be expected to elicit distressful self-feelings. Subjects aged 40 to 50 tended to have self-derogative feelings in association with self-reports that the person did not do as well in life as his siblings. Perhaps it is during this decade that the individual defines his maximum level of achievement and evaluates himself against this standard. Subjects in the 50 to 59 decade tended to have high self-derogation scores if the subject had relatively few organizational affiliations and no children between the ages of 13 and 19 present in the home. These results suggest that the self-threatening aspects of the aging process may relate to the person's expectations of maintaining, while perceiving himself as losing, a number of social functions (Kaplan, 1971a).

Just as age may signal the applicability of some personal evaluative standards rather than others, so may the aging process itself reflect the deviation from self-evaluative standards. Thus, individuals who early in life learned the evaluative significance of earning the respect of others, of being in the company of others, of achieving, and of taking on responsibilities for others—as these are reflected in a fear of being laughed at by other children, a fear of being left alone, a fear of getting a bad report card, and being the oldest among sex siblings—on reaching an age when he is least able to achieve, to take on responsibility for others, to receive the respect of society, and to feel most strongly that he will be left alone, is likely to experience self-rejecting feelings as a consequence of perceived threats to the ability to meet the emotionally laden standards learned in childhood (Kaplan & Pokorny, 1970a). Conversely, aging should not be associated with higher levels of self-derogation but rather should be associated with lower levels of self-derogation when the subjects indicate approximation of personal evaluative standards. Aging was reported to be associated with lower self-derogation where the subjects (1) reported no recent life experiences requiring behavioral adaptations; (2) reported no disparity between their current and hoped-for standard of living; (3) reported that, as children, they were not afraid of being left alone; and (4) were living with their spouse in independent households (Kaplan & Pokorny, 1970b). To the extent that the individual did not receive any challenges to their expectations of adaptations, to the extent that their standard of living was as expected, to the extent that the likelihood of their being left alone did not violate standards in that regard, and to the extent that they were able to approximate their presumed expectations of personal independence, aging was not associated with self-rejecting feelings.

The self-evaluative significance of personal experience in different age groups is also apparent in other studies. For example, self-esteem was related to father's occupation among eighth-graders but not among fifth-graders. This suggests that social class is a basis for self-evaluation for the older children but not for the younger children (Demo & Savin-Williams, 1983).

The significance of this third group of findings is twofold. First, these findings suggest that for self-perception to be associated with self-evaluation, the object of the self-perception must be perceived to have evaluative significance. Second, they suggest that overall self-evaluation is a function of the extent to which the person perceives himself as approximating more specific self-evaluative standards that are more or less salient in the personal system of values.

To summarize the research findings relating to the association between self-referent cognitive responses and self-evaluative responses, general self-awareness or self-awareness and self-conceptualization of particular personal traits, behaviors, or experiences are associated with self-evaluative responses, whether expressed in terms of more specific (e.g., academic achievement) or general (global self-esteem) self-evaluative standards. The association between self-referent cognition and global self-evaluation is stronger when the more specific self-evaluative standards are judged to be more salient in the personal hierarchy of values.

As such, these findings are compatible with the conclusion that either general self-awareness, or self-conceptualization in terms of specific traits, behaviors, or experiences, stimulates the disposition to evaluate oneself according to situationally appropriate personal evaluative standards. The resulting self-evaluating responses, depending on their relevance for the personal hierarchy of self-values, contribute to the personal overall positive self-evaluation.

SOCIAL CONSEQUENCES OF SELF-EVALUATION

Self-evaluative responses directly influence personal traits, behaviors, and experiences and self-feelings.

Personal Traits, Behaviors, and Experiences

Self-evaluative responses, like self-referent cognitive behavior, become objects of self-awareness. Once the person evaluates himself, the self-evaluative behavior becomes part of the person's traits, behaviors, and experiences. As such it has the potential for stimulating self-awareness, and, by stimulating self-awareness and self-conceiving responses, it evokes self-evaluative responses. A person who perceives himself as one who evaluates his accomplishments highly may then evaluate himself in a way that contributes to his overall positive self-evaluation, insofar as pride in one's accomplishments is a salient self-value in the personal value system. Alternatively, self-conceptions *of evaluating oneself in these terms* may detract from positive self-evaluation to the extent that humility is a salient value in the person's system of self-values.

Self-Feelings

Values, as symbolic expressions of desirable states, are also the symbolic representation of the individual's needs. A need is reflected in the emotional excitation that accompanies the recognition of being more or less distant from socially desirable states. All self-referent value judgments contribute, to a greater or lesser extent, to overall feelings of self-worth. The contribution that each judgment makes to the overall judgment is reflected in the intensity of self-feelings that are evoked and in the consequent self-protective–self-enhancing responses of the person to the awareness of those feelings.

In Chapter 4, we consider the influence of self-evaluation on self-feelings. In Chapter 5, we consider the person's self-protective–self-enhancing responses stimulated by self-feelings.

SUMMARY

Self-evaluative responses are personal judgments of the extent to which the person approximates desirable states. The *initiation* of a self-evaluative response is a function of the person's self-awareness, in general, or of self-awareness and self-conceptualization, in particular, and of the person's learned disposition to evaluate himself when becoming aware of himself. The nature (content) of the self-evaluative response is a function of the nature of the person's self-perceptions and of the personal system of evaluative standards (in particular, that aspect of the personal value system that encompasses self-values), according to which he judges that which he perceives in or about himself. The specific self-perception, in conjunction with social situational cues, stimulates self-judgments with reference to the situationally applicable personal evaluative standards. The most inclusive self-value in the person's system of self-values is positive self-evaluation. The person's overall self-evaluation is a function of self-perceptions of approximating specific self-evaluative standards that are more or less salient (central, important) in the personal hierarchy of values.

A number of research reports support these conclusions by suggesting that (1) conditions facilitating self-awareness are associated with self-evaluation; (2) self-perceptions of particular traits, behaviors, or experiences are associated with self-evaluations, in terms of specific and global self-evaluative standards; and (3) the association between self-perceived traits, behaviors, and experiences, on the one hand, and global positive self-evaluation, on the other hand, is stronger under conditions in which the more specific self-evaluative standards are judged to be more salient in the person's hierarchy of self-values.

The person's self-evaluative responses become objects of self-awareness and objects of self-evaluation, more or less contributing to positive self-evaluation, depending on the nature of the self-value system.

Depending on the degree to which the person judges himself to be distant from positive self-evaluation, he will experience more or less negative self-feelings that motivate him to behave in ways that appear to reduce the likelihood of negative self-feelings and to maximize the probability of experiencing more positive self-feelings.

CHAPTER 4

Social Antecedents and Consequences of Self-Feelings

In this chapter, we consider the social antecedents and consequences of self-feelings. In general, self-feelings will be treated as mediating the relationship between self-evaluative responses and self-protective–self-enhancing responses. Self-feelings will be viewed as the direct consequences of self-evaluative responses and as the antecedents of self-protective–self-enhancing responses.

SELF-EVALUATION AND SELF-FEELINGS

The relationship between self-evaluative responses and consequent self-feelings presumes the existence of a relatively stable system of personal needs and self-values. Depending on the nature of the need-value system, self-evaluative responses, as the judgments of being more or less proximate to self-values, stimulate some forms of self-feelings that express the preexisting needs and motivate the person to behave in ways that will satisfy these needs.

Self-Values and Needs

Self-values are the symbolic expressions of personal needs, as needs are internalized self-values (Kaplan, 1983).

Self-Values. Self-values are the symbolic representation of personal goals and, at the same time, the standards against which we perceive ourselves as more or less approximating those goals. To the extent that we perceive ourselves as approximating a particular value, we evaluate ourselves as high on that value. If we value the possession of certain facial features or particular kinds of physiques and perceive ourselves as possessing those features or physiques, we evaluate ourselves positively (that is, as handsome or having a good build) according to those criteria. The values may reflect, in addition to physical attributes, the ability to elicit certain kinds of responses from other people (such as liking, deference, attraction), to possess certain talents (skills in woodworking, mathematical ability, problem solving skills) or other accomplishments (getting good grades in school, understanding social etiquette), or to approximate an abstract moral code (being honorable, dependable, faithful, moral). By definition, each of these is of value. However, the individual ranks these so that some are of greater value than others. To the extent that an individual perceives himself as approximating more important values, his overall evaluation of self-worth (the most inclusive value) will be relatively high.

Needs. Needs are internalized values. Values are internalized by processes leading to the subjective association of particular attributes, behaviors, or experiences, or the symbolic representations of these, with more or less distressing and pleasurable experiences. When the person internalizes a value, he is conditioned to respond affectively (that is, with feeling) to the awareness and conceptualization of being more or less distant from the desirable state symbolized by the value. This process is described by Reis (1981) with regard to individuals' internalization of the values of distributive justice (being rewarded for just behavior and punished for injustice):

> Through operant and classical conditioning, as well as observational learning, they learn which behaviors are acceptable and which are not. Fairness becomes a label attached to acceptable activities, at first by mere association with rewarded behaviors and then by acquiring secondary reinforcing properties of its own. Within this perspective, internalization entails learning these reinforcement contingencies and then reproducing them on one's own through anticipated rewards and sanctions, or self-generated reinforcement, without the intervention or presence of others. These motivational constructs are typically referred to as guilt, anger or tension. (p. 284)

As noted in Chapter 3, it is through such processes that the person comes to value and need the presence of others, positive evaluations by others, and positive self-evaluations. The infant's subjective association of the presence of adults with satisfaction of his physical needs influences the acquisition of a need for the presence of adults (independent of their physical need-satisfying function) and a sensitivity to the range of adult behaviors. The infant's perception of an association of satisfaction or frustration of his physical needs with specific adult behavior leads to the acquisition of a need to behave in a way that will evoke the kinds of adult responses earlier associated with need-satisfaction and to avoid the kinds of adult responses earlier associated with need-frustration. These adult behaviors are conceptualized as an expression of positive or negative attitudes toward the subject. In order to maximize the satisfaction of the acquired need to evoke expressions of positive attitudes (and to avoid the expression of negative attitudes) from others, the child adopts the role of others and perceives, evaluates, and expresses attitudes toward himself from their point of view in order to provide guides for his own behaviors that (based on past experience) he imagines will elicit positive attitudes from others. The child then responds to his own *imagined* expressions of attitudes toward himself as if they were, in fact, the expressed attitudes of others, *with positive or negative affect*. In this way, through the symbolic association of the imagined responses of others with his own attitudinal responses to himself, the child acquires the need to behave in a way that will maximize the experience of positive, and minimize the experience of negative, self-evaluations. The child has thus acquired the self-esteem motive.

Values and needs, then, cannot be understood except with reference to each other. As Rokeach (1983) argues, values ("conceptions of the desirable" or "prescriptive-proscriptive" beliefs about desirable end-states and desirable modes of behavior")

> become internalized as standards for judging one's own and others' competence and morality. We thus see that values serve a dual purpose: on the one hand, they are the *cognitive representations of societal demands* for competence and morality; on the other, they are the cognitive representations of individual needs. (p. 175)

Self-Evaluation and Stimulation of Need

A need, as part of a relatively stable personal system, is a disposition or readiness to respond in ways that will approximate valued states and distance oneself from disvalued states. The need disposition is stimulated by the personal recognition of being more or less distant from (dis)valued states. This *recognition* takes the form of self-evaluative responses, whereby the person judges himself to be more or less distant from relatively important specific, or general, self-values. The *stimulation of the need disposition* takes the form of *self-feelings* that, in turn, motivate the responses that are calculated to achieve the valued ends that satisfy the person's needs. Jones (1973), for example, observes that in "self-esteem" (as opposed to self-consistency) theories,

> the self-esteem need is viewed as responsive to evaluative information the individual gains from his own behavior and comparative or reflected appraisals from other people. Coping effectively with the tasks and problems

one encounters in his physical and social environment as well as gaining information from others that he is liked and respected or that his actions or characteristics are highly evaluated produce satisfaction for his self-esteem need. (pp. 186–187)

Self-feelings, then, reflect the contemporary exacerbation of a need disposition stimulated by current self-evaluative responses. The experience of positive self-feelings (associated with the perception or expectation of approximating personally and situationally relevant self-values) and the experience of negative self-feelings (associated with the perception or expectation of being distant from personally and situationally relevant self-values or of approximating disvalued states) reflect the preexisting needs to approximate desirable and to distance oneself from undesirable states. In short, the stimulation of need dispositions by self-evaluative responses is experienced as self-feelings.

Self-Feelings as Responses to Self-Evaluation

Self-feelings are the affective or emotional experiences individuals experience on the occasions of stimulation of need dispositions by self-evaluative responses. The person perceives, recalls, imagines, or anticipates personal traits, behaviors, or experiences. These self-referent cognitive responses stimulate self-evaluations of the association of the objects of the self-referent cognitions with the person's self-values that are internalized as need dispositions. The self-evaluations stimulate the need dispositions. The stimulation of the need dispositions are experienced as self-feelings. The experiences of self-feelings, then, as reflections of stimulated needs, are excited by self-evaluative responses.

Theoretical Contexts. The conceptualization of self-feelings as affective or emotional responses by a person to self-evaluations of personal, traits, behaviors, and experiences has surfaced in a variety of theoretical contexts. This notion is apparent in the early discussion by Charles Horton Cooley (1902), where he distinguished among the three components of "a self-idea": the subject's imagination of how he appears to another person, the subject's imagination of the other person's judgment of that appearance, and "some sort of self-feeling." Implicit in these distinctions are assertions that how we appear to others and how we imagine they respond to our appearance will influence the kinds of feelings we have about ourselves. By the examples given (pride, mortification), it is clear that "self-feelings" are affective rather than ideational. It is the imagined judgments of others that evokes our self-feelings.

More recent statements have focused on the same theme. For example, Jourard (1957) viewed compatibility between real-self and ideal-self as influencing the nature of self-cathexis or self-feeling (that is, affective investment in self). In self-awareness theory, subjective discomfort occurs insofar as a "negative within-self discrepancy is the salient aspect of the self-awareness" (p. 223) (Wicklund, 1982).

The equating of self-feelings with the felt needs that are the consequences of subjectively perceived distance from high priority, more or less general, personally applicable values has been expressed by others in similar terms. Rollo May (1980) notes:

> The distinctive quality of human anxiety arises from the fact that man is a valuing animal, who interprets his life and world in terms of symbols and meanings. It is the threat to these values—specifically, to some value that the individual holds essential to his existence as a self—that causes anxiety. (p. 241)

Finally, the conceptualization of self-feeling as affect evoked by self-evaluation and (less directly) by self-cognition (Kaplan, 1972b, 1975b, 1980) is consistent with Denzin's (1983) equation of emotion to self-feeling. From this perspective *"emotions are temporally embodied self-feelings which arise from emotional social acts persons direct to self or have directed toward them by others"* p. 404. This last perspective implies that there are no emotions that do not reflect self-feelings and that any stimulus that excites emotion reflects perception of degrees of approximation to self-evaluative standards that elicit self-feelings. It is problematic, however, as to whether all emotional states derive exclusively from stimuli that have self-evaluative significance—that is, whether all stimuli that elicit any emotional state are interpretable in terms of self-evaluative significance.

Dimensions of Self-Feelings. Self-feelings vary simultaneously along several dimensions. Self-feelings differ with regard to quality, polarity, generality, intensity, and stability.

With regard to *quality,* it is, perhaps, of little practical significance for our purpose as to whether self-feeling is a unitary affective state (varying in polarity and intensity over time) that is variously labeled depending on circumstances or whether self-feeling is a general term for qualitatively distinct affective states. In any case, the differentiation among a large number of self-feelings is made frequently, as by Denzin (1983):

> It is my thesis that all the emotional terms used in everyday language, including being angry, resentful, sad, fearful, joyful, depressed, hostile, enraged, ashamed, proud, affectionate, friendly, embarrassed, rejected, guilty, or in pain, refer to embodied feelings, mental states, interactional experiences, and judgments of others (real and imagined) that persons feel and direct (or have directed) toward self. (pp. 404–405)

Various labels are applied to the self-feeling, depending on any of a number of situational variables. Thus, embarrassment has been characterized, for example, by Modigliani (1971) as a

> special, short-lived, but often acute, loss of self-esteem. More specifically, because this loss of esteem is always related to some ongoing social situation, we shall say that embarrassment reflects a loss of *situational self-esteem*. (p. 16)

The most important defining characteristic of the qualitatively distinct self-feelings is the nature of the valued states that are the standards for self-evaluation in the situation. Specifically, personally valued states might include the related experiences of being part of a social network, eliciting good opinions from valued others, doing what is expected of one, and achieving occupational goals. The perceived frustration of the need to be part of an interpersonal network may be experienced as the self-feeling of loneliness or alienation. The failure to approximate the desire to evoke positive responses from others may be experienced as shame. The subject's inability to satisfy his felt need to meet what he regards as others' legitimate expectations of him may be experienced as feelings of guilt. The person's achievement of valued occupational goals may be experienced as the self-feeling of pride.

Another defining characteristic of the qualitatively distinct self-feeling is the temporal relationship between the object of the self-evaluation and the self-evaluation. Thus, distressful self-feelings that result from self-evaluations of anticipated *future* failure maybe labeled anxiety, whereas recollection of *past* failures may be labeled guilt.

Emotional responses to self-evaluative responses vary according to *polarity*, ranging from positive (pleasurable) to negative (distressful). The person's more global or his specific self-evaluations elicit appropriate self-feelings, depending on the person's perception of being close to or distant from more or less important values. To the extent that the person perceives himself as approximating a very important standard, he will feel great pride, whereas self-perceptions of being distant from the same standard will elicit feelings of strong disappointment. If a person feels that he is quite distant from the value of being well liked, he may feel ashamed, whereas to experience a sense of being well liked is to have feelings of self-pride. If the individual perceives himself as approximating things he values most, he will have a general sense of well-being that he might conceptualize as personal liking or esteem. A self-judgment of having failed to achieve salient values might be experienced as feelings of self-contempt.

In describing a person's self-feelings, one also must consider the *generality* of the self-feeling. Is the person said to be emotionally responding to specific self-evaluations or to more global self-evaluations? The most general self-feeling experienced by the person is that which is the consequence of perceived proximity or distance to the goal of general positive self-evaluation. The general self-evaluation of approximating valued states is the ultimate value in the person's hierarchy of values. The person needs to think of himself positively—that is, as having valued attributes and performing valued behaviors, and as the object of valued outcomes of social and other environmental processes. The extent to which the person evaluates himself positively in these regards, that is, as experiencing attributes, behaviors, and outcomes that reflect high priority values, influences, in large measure, the more or less intense experience of the general self-feelings that are reflected as self-derogation of self-hate, when the self-evaluation is negative, and as self-acceptance or self-love, when the self-evaluation is positive.

The *intensity* with which self-feelings are experienced depends on the salience of the valued states and the perceived degree of distance between the person and the valued states. The individual will experience a need more intensely if a more salient value is threatened than if a less salient value is threatened. The person will experience a greater sense of need if he conceives himself as being more distant from a desirable state or too close to an undesirable state. If it is important to a person to receive good grades, then the person's needs are more likely to be stimulated by self-conceptions relating to the achievement of or the failure to achieve good grades. If the individual has few artistic aspirations, then the self-conception of having produced a more or less worthy artifact will have little influence on the person's needs. In any case, the sense of need will be greater if the threat to the achievement or the promise of achievement of a particularly valued state is imminent. The expectation of imminent success or failure or the recent experience of success or failure will have greater impact on the urgency of one's need to receive good grades than if the threat or promise of success or failure in this regard is more remote in time. The sense of urgency of the needs elicited by the self-judgment of having achieved or failed to achieve a valued state or the expectation of achieving or failing to achieve a valued state is reflected in more or less intense positive or negative self-feelings.

Finally, self-feelings may be considered with regard to their *stability*. Self-feelings may be characteristic of the individual or they may be situationally circumscribed. They are characteristic of the individual in that, on a day-to-day basis, personal self-evaluations tend to elicit, for example, negative self-feelings. Over a long period of time, the quotidian self-evaluations of the person lead to feelings of self-reproach, shame, guilt, or self-derogation. In contrast to these durable self-rejecting feelings are occasional ephemeral experiences of positive self-feelings. Conversely, in a particular situation, the person may so behave that he perceives himself as violating an important norm in his personal system of values. The result may be a momentary, and certainly time-limited, expression of self-rejecting feelings that has little lasting impact on the person's characteristic experience of positive self-feelings. After a period of time, the characteristic positive self-feelings may again predominate in the person's reflexive affective life.

The person's characteristic self-feeling is a function of his history of past self-evaluations and concomitant self-feelings. As a result of past experiences, the individual develops what might be called an affective expectancy set. The individual anticipates self-devaluing experiences and consequent self-rejecting feelings. The significance of any particular current self-devaluation assumes a greater importance for the self-rejecting individual, since it confirms the expectations of self-rejecting feelings and exacerbates a persistent need for self-accepting responses. For self-rejecting individuals, a self-devaluing circumstance has a greater effect on the self-esteem motive than a similar experience on a characteristically self-accepting individual. Consequently, the self-rejecting individual is more likely to undertake more marked self-protective–self-enhancing responses in response to the self-rejecting feelings.

Practically, it is difficult to describe a person's characteristic self-feelings. Over a period of time, an individual expresses a large number and a wide range of self-feelings. If it were possible to draw a representative sample of instants within that time span and then describe the quality, polarity, generality, and intensity of the person's self-attitudes (if any) expressed at those points in time, his "characteristic self-attitude" would be said to be a function of the frequency with which the observed self-attitudes of varying quality, polarity, generality, and intensity were expressed.

Research Findings

The conclusion that self-evaluative responses induce self-feelings appears warranted in light of four groups of studies.

Psychophysiological Studies. A number of studies report relationships between personal experiences and psychophysiological indices under conditions in which the individual experiences may be presumed to have self-evaluative relevance. The psychophysiological responses are interpreted here as reflecting affective significance (whether of a positive or a negative polarity) of the personal experiences. The observation of an association between personal experiences and psychophysiological responses when the experiences appear to reflect degrees of approximation to self-values, then, is interpretable as compatible with the conclusion that self-evaluation influences self-directed affect or feelings.

In one study (Kaplan, 1972a; Kaplan, Burch, Bloom, & Edelberg, 1963), individuals' behaviors toward people in small groups whom they liked or disliked tended to be correlated with their own physiological (galvanic skin response) activity to a significantly greater extent than when behaviors were directed toward people they neither liked or disliked. To the extent that the galvanic skin response is interpretable as an index of emotional significance or physiological arousal, these findings lend themselves to the interpretation that, with increasing evaluative significance of interpersonal behavior, the probability of self-feelings being aroused is significantly increased.

This conclusion appears warranted, again, when the results of a study of 29 pairs of subjects is considered (Kaplan, Burch, Bedner, and Trenda, 1965). In ten of the pairs, each member expressed a liking for the other person. In eight of the pairs, each person disliked the other person. In eleven of the pairs, each member neither liked nor disliked the other person. The pairs met for two consecutive 20-minute sessions during which they discussed topics previously determined to be of equally strong interest to both persons. For each session, the galvanic skin response was recorded. Following each session, the pair members responded to an instrument consisting of statements characterizing social behavior. Each subject ranked the ten statements according to degree to which she perceived the statement to be characteristic of her behavior during the preceding discussion and then ranked the same statements according to the degree to which she judged each behavior to be characteristic of her partner during the session.

The results are compatible with the conclusion that those occurrences during the session that were most threatening to the consensual values of the participants were most likely to elicit physiological responses. Among the pairs in which the members expressed a dislike for each other, high physiological activity was associated with members' self–other descriptions relating to the expression of negative affect. This suggests that a major need for members of the negative group is the management of affect expression, their concern with this problem being reflected in the association between physiological response and descriptions relating to socioemotional parameters (I was eager and agressive, I was irritated, I was not especially warm and friendly to my partner). Among the members of pairs in which each partner liked the other, physiological activity was significantly associated with the members' self–other descriptions relating to disruption of the task process (not trying to get the partner in the discussion, suggestions being frequently off the point). Apparently, the management of negative emotional expression was not a serious problem for positive group members. Rather, the tensions aroused in these subjects related to task fulfillment. It is expected that positive pair members would be more highly motivated to accomplish the task (and, therefore, more prone to evaluate themselves in terms of task accomplishment) than negative or neutral pair members and that, in view of the existing close personal relationships, too much time spent in positive socioemotional activity might impede task fulfillment. Given a high task motivation, it would be expected that disruption of the task process would be accompanied by a physiological response. For pairs in which neither person liked or disliked the other person, physiological response was most closely related to descriptions of active attempts at interpersonal influence as opposed to mutual passive withdrawal. In view of the relatively low task involvement in such groups, one would expect that under a condition of withdrawal by mutual consent, the pair members would experience a minimum of tension but that when one member tried actively to influence the other, the consequent resistance would engender high tension levels, which would be reflected in more physiological activity.

Other studies also suggest that the evaluative significance of perceived experiences are reflected in distressful self-feelings, as these are indicated by physiological changes. Thus, higher subject diastolic blood pressure has been reported when the interviewer showed a warm and interactive as opposed to a neutral and noninteractive style (Williams, Kimball, & Williard, 1972), and significantly greater rises in plasma free fatty acid level were observed when the experimental induction suggested that the task was important rather than unimportant (Back & Bogdonoff, 1964). When self-evaluative standards are salient, social situations reflecting degrees of approximation to the standards are more likely to elicit affective (reflected in psychophysiological) responses directed toward oneself than when self-evaluative standards are not salient.

An interesting set of studies lend themselves to the interpretation that self-feelings are associated with the performance of particular social roles that are defined in terms of salient social standards and under conditions in which the appropriate level of role performance is problematic. The roles in question are those in which the social identity requires the *acceptance of responsibility for the safety of others*. Generally, these studies suggest that individuals whose ability to fulfill the demands made on them in the situation is in question will experience intensified self-feelings, as these are reflected in psychophysiological activation. Presumably, the individuals are evaluating themselves according to the certainty with which they are able to fulfill the expectations made on them in the identities they now accept. For example, student aviators attempting their first aircraft-carrier landings had higher mean serum cortisol levels and higher levels of urinary excretion of cortisol and 17-OHCS (-hydroxycorticosteroid) metabolites than the radar intercept officers in the rear cockpit, who had no flight control and had to rely completely on the pilot's skill (Rubin, 1974). In an earlier study, the only men in a special combat unit in Vietnam anticipating enemy attack who showed elevated levels of 17-OHCS were the two officers and the radio operator (Bourne, Coli, & Datel, 1968). Kiritz and Moos (1974) discuss studies in which the results reflect higher heart rates in pilots than in copilots, a difference that reverses itself when the individuals change positions; a positive association between responsibility for other individuals and diastolic blood pressure; a greater amplitude of gastric contractions in subjects who are able to press a button to avoid strong auditory stimulus to both members of the pair than in the passive members of the pair; highest levels of 17-OHCS secretion in aircraft *commanders;* and sharp increases in heart rate of key NASA personnel when suddenly given additional responsibility. In short, when the self-evaluative standard may be presumed to be important, and when the approximation of the standard is problematic, the person will experience exacerbation of self-feelings, as these are reflected in psychophysiological activation.

   Global Self-Evaluation and Subjective Distress. Data from longitudinal studies demonstrate that antecedent indices of negative self-evaluation anticipate self-reports of negative self-feelings after controlling for reports of negative self-feelings at an earlier point in time. The data were from a panel study of several thousand seventh-grade students interviewed annually, up to three times, during their junior high school years. A measure of self-rejection in the seventh grade was related to subsequent self-reports of indices of negative self-feelings in the ninth grade among students who denied the presence of the symptom in the eighth grade. The negative self-feelings were expressed variously in terms of depressive affect, self-distress, and a wide variety of psychophysiological manifestations of anxiety (Kaplan, 1980). Subjects who, in the seventh grade, were characterized by higher levels of self-derogation were, two years later, significantly and appreciably more likely to report being bothered by nervousness, getting angry or annoyed or upset, and having trouble sitting still for a long time. Similarly, individuals who were relatively more self-devaluing in the seventh grade were more likely by the ninth grade to report wishing they could be as happy as others seemed to be, not being in good spirits most of the time, feeling downcast and rejected, not getting a lot of fun out of life, and, on the whole, not being fairly happy. For example, of the subjects who denied feeling downcast and dejected in the eighth grade, 24 percent of the subjects whose self-devaluation levels were high in the seventh grade, compared with only 16 percent of those with medium levels of self-devaluation and 10 percent of those with low levels of self-devaluation, reported such feelings in the ninth grade.

The influence of self-evaluation on self-rejecting feelings has been observed over quite long periods of time. Individuals who displayed higher scores on a measure of self-derogation in 1971, as junior high school students, were significantly more likely to display higher scores on an index of psychological distress administered over ten years later when they were young adults (Kaplan, Robbins, & Martin, 1983).

Consistent with the hypothesized effect of global self-evaluation on self-feeling, regression analyses reveal that, for male and female college students, a tendency to overgeneralize a single failure more broadly to the self-concept accounted for an appreciable (17.5 percent) portion of the variance in depression (Carver & Ganellen, 1983).

Specific Self-Evaluations and Self-Feelings. The influence of more specific self-judgments on self-feelings is apparent in a number of empirical studies reporting relationships between awareness of discrepancies of personal characteristics from evaluative standards, on the one hand, and physiological indicators of affect or subject assessment of emotional states, on the other hand. Noteworthy among these are studies of the influence of experiences related to one's occupation and subsequent experiences suggestive of more or less negative self-feelings. Generally, success or failure in one's occupation reflected in the prestige associated with the position, extrinsic rewards, and upward, or downward, mobility has been associated with self-reports of self-attitudes (Bachman *et al.*, 1978; Cohn, 1978) or of conditions that are interpretable as sequelae or concomitants of distressful self-feelings such as physical and psychological distress (Kasl, Gore, & Cobb, 1975; Pearlin & Lieberman, 1979). Responses to self-report instruments also suggest that people who are paid appropriately for their work reported themselves to be more contented than people who were overpaid or underpaid, conditions that might be expected to lead to negative self-evaluations (Austin & Walster, 1974).

With regard to other characteristics, self-evaluation was observed to be associated with self-feelings. This relationship is implicit in findings regarding the relationship between apparent judgments of personal inefficacy ("learned helplessness"), on the one hand, and depressive or phobic responses, on the other hand (Seligman, 1975; Bandura, 1977). In addition, the influence of self-devaluing experiences on self-feelings was observed in a study reported by Burish and Houston (1979), in which the circumstances of being told that one was taking a very important achievement test, and then being informed that they performed more poorly than expected, were associated with increases in reported anxiety, depression, and anger.

Changes in Self-Evaluation and Self-Feelings. Also consistent with the premise that self-evaluation stimulates need dispositions that are experienced as self-feelings are studies that implicate changes in self-evaluative standards in processes of changes in negative self-feelings. A case in point is a study in which subjects who compared themselves with people who were worse off on self-devaluing characteristics (i.e., subjects who evaluated themselves more positively relative to others) experienced a reduction in feeling upset (Hakmiller, 1966). In the study, female college students in groups were given a personality test and were informed that the measured traits reflected either extreme maladjustment or maturity and responsibility. As part of the study, the subjects rated their feelings of upset following information regarding their own personality score and later, after learning the score they had chosen to see which, as part of the experimental induction, was more unfavorable than the person's own score. Individuals who were informed that the trait indicated maladjustment manifested a significant decrease in anxiety after they received information regarding the other person's score.

The influence of reconstruction of the personal value system in response to self-rejecting feelings on controlling negative self-feelings is also suggested by data reported by Burish and Houston (1979). Experimental subjects who were informed that they performed more poorly on an important achievement test than they had expected, and who were given the opportunity to estimate how poorly their friends would have scored on the test had they taken it and not performed well on it, experienced a smaller increase in anxiety than subjects who did not estimate how their friends would have done. Similar results were not observed with regard to increases in depression or anger, however. Thus, the findings suggest that the establishment of reference group norms appear to be effective in controlling at least one manifestation of distress. The investigators (Burish & Houston, 1979), speculating on possible reasons why feelings of anxiety but not feelings of depression or anger were influenced by the experimental condition ("similarity projection," i.e. encouraging subjects to estimate how poorly their friends would have scored on the test had they taken it and not performed well on it), comment as follows:

It may be that similarity projection reduced anxiety because, as Bramel (1962) suggested, it enabled subjects to convince themselves that they did not deviate from the persons with whom they ordinarily compare themselves, but failed to reduce depression or anger because it was not adequate to alleviate subjects' concerns over the possible causes of their behavior. That is, while concerns about the acceptability of one's behavior may be alleviated by believing that one's peers would have behaved similarly, concerns about the causes of one's behavior may not be affected by such a comparison process. (p. 68)

In summary, the research literature suggests that circumstances having self-evaluative implications are associated with exacerbation of self-feelings, as these are expressed in physiological responses. Although these studies have no necessary implications for the nature, particularly with regard to the positive or negative aspects, of affective responses, other studies do report relationships between more or less positive self-evaluations and more or less distressful self-feelings. The studies used both more and less global indicators of self-evaluation and demonstrated associations of these with appropriate self-feelings over longer and shorter periods of time. Further, changes in self-evaluative standards appear to be associated with appropriate reductions in distressful self-feelings.

SOCIAL CONSEQUENCES OF SELF-FEELINGS

The major consequences of self-feelings are with regard to (1) the personal system of traits, behaviors, and experiences and (2) the initiation of self-protective–self-enhancing responses.

Personal Traits, Behaviors, and Experiences

Once the person experiences self-feelings, they become part of the system of personal traits, behaviors, and experiences that further stimulate self-referent responses. As Denzin (1983) points out, we become aware of our own feeling states:

The feelings that a person feels have a threefold structure: (1) a sense of the feeling in terms of awareness and definitions; (2) a sense of the self feeling the feeling; (3) a revealing of the moral or feeling self through this experience. . . . The feeling person, the person in emotional consciousness, feels his or her self in emotion. (p. 404)

The self-feelings of which the person becomes aware, in turn, have implications for how the individual evaluates and feels about himself. Gordon (1981) points out that

our self-image in a situation reflects the appropriateness of our feeling; we feel proud or guilty about feeling a certain way. Helen Merrill Lynd (1958) noted that the incongruity between a trifling event and a deep sense of shame can evoke a "double shame: we are ashamed because of the original episode and shamed because we feel so deeply about something so slight that a sensible person would not pay any attention to it." (p. 588)

Self-Protective–Self-Enhancing Responses

Self-feelings reflect the activation of need dispositions (the most inclusive of which is the need for positive self-evaluation) occasioned by self-evaluative responses. As such, self-feelings stimulate the person to behave in ways that their system of expectation about themselves and reality lead them to believe will have consequences that will be perceived and evaluated as desirable (valued) outcomes and will assuage the needs reflected in distressful self-feelings. The self-protective–self-enhancing responses, as these behaviors stimulated by self-feelings are conceptualized, are reflected in changes in (1) self-referent cognitive responses, both directly, by sensitizing the person to be self-aware in particular regards and by distorting self-awareness, and indirectly, by influencing changes in the person of which he becomes aware; (2) the personal need-value system, which, in turn, influences self-referent cognitions, the nature of the self-evaluative response, and the choice of particular self-protective–self-enhancing responses; and (3) personal traits, behaviors, and experiences, in addition to those relating to the need-value system, that will be recognized and evaluated as more or less proximate to the person's self-values. The antecedents and forms of the self-protective–self-enhancing responses are considered in detail in Chapter 5.

SUMMARY

Self-feelings reflect the activation of need dispositions that are stimulated by the person's self-evaluative responses, that is, by self-judgments of being more or less distant from valued or disvalued states. Need dispositions are internalizations of self-values and reflect the readiness to behave in ways that will permit approximation of valued, and distancing from disvalued, states. Self-feelings as the experience of needs stimulated by self-evaluative responses are experienced as more or less intense and more or less durable affective or emotional responses to self-evaluative responses. The feelings are experienced as more or less distressful, depending on the self-evaluations of being more or less distant from the valued or disvalued states and the certainty and immediacy of approaching these states. The most inclusive of the needs is the need for positive self-evaluation. The stimulation of this need is a function of the more or less salient self-evaluative responses to more specific personal traits, behaviors, or experiences and of the corresponding, more specific self-feelings that are evoked by self-referent evaluative responses to personal traits, behaviors, or experiences.

The research literature is compatible with the expectation that, under value-relevant circumstances, the person will experience exacerbation of self-feelings and that more or less distressful self-feelings, whether more or less inclusive, will be associated with the person's success or failure in approximating salient self-values. To the extent that a revision of evaluative self-standards permits a person to evaluate himself more favorably, the person experiences a reduction in distressful self-feelings.

Affective or emotional responses to self-evaluation (i.e., self-feelings) become part of the repertoire of personal traits, behaviors, and experiences. As such, they stimulate self-awareness and self-conceptualization, and, thereby, stimulate self-evaluative responses relating to the propriety of the self-feelings.

Self-feelings, the experience of need, stimulates the person to behave in ways that will permit the person to satisfy his needs. These needs relate to the approximation of self-values, the most inclusive of which is overall positive self-evaluation. In view of this, the responses oriented to the satisfaction of needs, stimulated by self-values and expressed as self-feelings, are collectively considered to be self-protective–self-enhancing responses. These responses to self-feeling take the form of changes in self-referent cognition; the person's need-value system; and other personal traits, behaviors, and experiences that have self-evaluative significance.

Nature and Antecedents of Self-Protective–Self-Enhancing Responses

The final category of self-referent responses to be considered is that of self-protective–self-enhancing responses. The essential nature and forms of the responses are both considered, as well as the variability of responses in each formal category with regard to their deviation from or conformity to normative expectations. Following this, the influences on self-enhancing–self-protective mechanisms are discussed. These patterns, in their variable form and degree of approximation to normative standards, are interpreted as the outcome of three major influences. First, self-protective–self-enhancing responses are viewed as stimulated by self-feelings. The precise form of the response is profoundly influenced by the position of the self-feelings on their different dimensions. In addition, the nature of self-protective–self-enhancing responses is influenced by the person's self-referent cognitions, including beliefs about the person's relationships to the environment, and the person's need-value system that provides criteria for self-evaluation, including standards relating to the use of certain self-protective–self-enhancing mechanisms.

NATURE, FORM, AND FUNCTION

We will consider, in turn, the definition of self-protective–self-enhancing patterns, their major forms, and their variable implications with regard to their approximation of normative standards.

Definition, Origins, and Continuity

Definition. Self-protective–self-enhancing responses are behaviors by the person that are oriented, more or less consciously, to (1) forestalling the occurrence, recognition, or evaluation of personal traits, behaviors, and experiences that detract from positive self-evaluation, and consequent positive self-feelings (self-protective responses), or (2) facilitating the occurrence, recognition, or evaluation of personal traits, behaviors, or experiences that contribute to positive self-evaluation and consequent positive self-feelings (self-enhancing responses).

Self-protective responses are nicely described by Zimbardo (1982) with reference to avoidance of self-devaluing interpersonal transactions by the shy person:

> At the core of shyness is basic anxiety over rejection by others, ontological insecurity and loss of identity. Such anxiety is both a cause and a consequence of the individual's inability to accept himself or herself as a worthy, lovable, competent, self-regulating, and autonomous person. Three fundamental fears flow from this core anxiety: fear of being socially inappropriate (one's unacceptable differences from others will be publicly exposed); fear of failure (one's incompetence will be publicly exposed); and fear of intimacy (one's real private self will prove vulnerable to criticism or indifference when publicly exposed).
>
> The defensive posture of shyness is designed to minimize the daily stresses engendered by having to cope regularly with these fears. The chronically shy person inhibits, withdraws, avoids, and escapes. Possibility for social evaluation is minimized by not affiliating with others. When it is not possible to avoid social contact, the shy person may still present such a low profile as not to be noticed (deindividuating) or not to initiate action. (pp. 467–468)

Self-protective strategies are also detailed by Covington and Beery. In his discussion of strategies for maintaining self-esteem in the classroom, in particular, Gecas (1981) cites Covington and Berry (1976), who describe two patterns of achievement motivation in response to school pressure; one pattern is oriented toward success, the other is oriented toward avoiding failure (i.e., self-protection):

> It is the latter that is considered to be a major obstacle to school achievement. The reason why it is adopted, of course, is to protect one's self-esteem. There are several strategies that students use to avoid failure. The most common are non-participation (if you do not participate, you cannot fail); if forced to participate, putting in a minimum of effort; and procrastination, or putting things off until it is too late to do a good job. The objective in these strategies is to disassociate one's performance from one's ability, and certainly to deny that it reflects one's worth. It is a form of role distance, the separation of self from the behaviors required of a role occupant. Failure, then, can be attributed to lack of effort or to various external circumstances, and not to one's

lack of ability. In a sense, this is viewed as "failure with honor." The irony of these failure-avoiding strategies, as Covington and Beery point out, is that they are self-defeating. In their attempt to avoid *feelings* of failure these students, by their actions, increase the probability of actual failure. (p. 183)

In contrast to self-protective mechanisms that aim to forestall the negative, self-enhancing mechanisms affirm positive aspects of the self and expend effort to achieve outcomes the recognition of which elicits positive self-evaluation.

The definition of self-protective–self-enhancing responses, by recognizing variable degrees of self-consciousness of goal-orientation, encompasses what others have differentiated as coping activity and automatized adaptive behavior. According to Lazarus and Folkman (1984),

coping implies effort, whereas automatized adaptive behaviors do not. . . . Many behaviors are originally effortful and hence reflect coping, but become automatized through learning processes. (p. 140)

Origins. Self-protective–self-enhancing patterns may be learned by the individual as part of a process whereby the initial purposive or nonpurposive response has serendipitous positive outcomes and so reinforces the response. Alternatively, the person, whether by social observation or direct instruction, learns the pattern in the course of social interaction. Indeed, the group may collectively evolve self-protective–self-enhancing patterns in response to common threats.

The adoption of shared self-protective mechanisms in response to common threats to self-evaluation has been observed in a variety of contexts. Kaplan, Boyd, and Bloom (1964) documented the nature of self-protective patterns employed by patients on a psychiatric ward. Two major threats to the person's self-evaluation were noted. These concerned the essential nature of the therapeutic process and the public and institutional image of the mentally ill. With regard to the former, the nature of standard methods of psychodynamic therapy involves the uncovering and interpreting of the characterological defenses of the patient—the modes of adaptation, which, as imperfect as they may be, constitute the means whereby the patient maintains an acceptable identity. In an attempt to maintain the defensive patterns, which they utilize to maintain an acceptable self-image, while submitting to psychotherapeutic necessity, the patients effectively employed unique self-referent cognitions for each of two mutually exclusive parts of their life space, namely, the therapeutic and nontherapeutic spheres. These individuals perceive themselves as appropriately submitting to therapeutic incursions in situations, when staff members were present, that occurred within the confines of group therapy rooms and that involved interaction among members of the same therapy group. However, in all other situations it was considered appropriate to maintain their characteristic defenses.

Interpatient confrontations, in which devaluation was attempted, led to a pattern whereby the patient perceived himself as blameless and defined the attempts by the other patient to devalue the subject in terms of the other person's illness.

The patients' perceived negative attitudes toward the mentally ill (on the part of both the public and institutional personnel) were responded to with both cognitive and evaluative mechanisms. In the former case, the individual would confine their self-perceptions to present situations and would avoid considering the past or posthospital experiences. Evaluative reformulations related to devaluation of the staff and public, whom they saw as devaluing them, and selecting a reference group with standards by which they might favorably evaluate themselves. Thus, they would evolve a common understanding that everybody has problems, they would favorably compare themselves with the situation of less privileged patient groups, and they would ridicule the characteristics of the institutional staff and representatives of the public at large who visited the hospital.

Continuity. Initially, the person may not be conscious of the self-enhancing–self-protective function of the pattern. At a below-conscious level, however, successful outcomes reinforce use of the pattern. Over time, the response is invoked automatically, stimulated by value-relevant cues. When the individual is aware, initially, of the self-enhancing function, the person comes to value the pattern as instrumental to the achievement of gratifying outcomes. Over time, the association of the pattern with gratifying outcomes invokes an intrinsic valuation of the behavior. With frequent use, the response becomes habitual, being invoked by stimuli below the conscious level of awareness.

Although all self-protective mechanisms will tend to continue, depending on such factors as the net personal gratifications they elicit, certain other mechanisms are likely to continue because, by their very nature, they preclude extinction. Bandura (1977) observes that,

> once established, self-protective behavior is difficult to eliminate even though the hazards no longer exist. This is because consistent avoidance prevents a person from learning that the real-life conditions have changed. Hence, the nonoccurrence of anticipated hazards reinforces the expectations that the defensive maneuvers forestall them. (p. 209)

The person may be unaware not only that conditions have changed but also that other, more effective mechanisms are available.

When the automatic responses that have been learned in the past fail to protect or enhance self-feelings, the individual, at conscious or unconscious levels, will be motivated to initiate effortful self-protective–self-enhancing responses. Any new circumstances that lead to negative self-evaluation or the anticipation of negative self-evaluation, such as the requirement that one respond successfully to novel demands or other threatening requirements, lead to the need for new self-protective–self-enhancing behaviors. As Bandura (1977) notes, until effective coping behaviors are achieved, perceived threats will produce high emotional arousal and various defensive maneuvers:

> But after people become adept at self-protective behaviors, they perform them in potentially threatening situations without having to be frightened (Notterman, Schoenfeld and Bersh, 1952). Should their habitual coping devices fail, they experience heightened arousal until new defensive learning reduces their vulnerability. (p. 209)

Whether they succeed in learning new patterns and whether the patterns will serve self-protective–self-enhancing functions is problematic. In any case, for such reasons as have been noted above, there will be a tendency for the patterns already learned to persist even when they are limited in forestalling self-devaluing experiences and enhancing self-attitudes.

Forms of Self-Protective–Self-Enhancing Responses

We will not here consider the consequences *for the individual* of self-referent behavior with regard to self-protective–self-enhancing responses. Self-protective/self-enhancing responses have no meaning apart from their formal manifestations as consequences for changes in self-referent cognition; the personal need-value system; and other personal traits, behaviors, and experiences. These consequences *are* the self-protective–self-enhancing mechanisms. In considering their formal manifestations, at the same time, the consequences for the person of self-protective/self-enhancing responses are considered necessarily. However, these personal self-protective–self-enhancing responses do have consequences for the socioenvironmental system. These consequences will be considered in Chapter 6.

The notion of self-protective mechanisms (and kindred concepts), although referred to by various terms, has appeared in discussions stemming from various theoretical systems including Freudian theory, Heider's balance theory, and Festinger's theory of cognitive consistency; social perception theory; and the symbolic interactionist tradition, among others (Rosenberg & Kaplan, 1982). A good deal of space has been devoted to describing these mechanisms, which have been interpreted as means for defending and protecting the self-concept (Murphy, 1947; Hilgard, 1949; Allport, 1961). Among those who have described patterns of self-protection or self-defense are Sykes and Matza (1957), Scott and Lyman (1968), Hewitt and Stokes (1975), and Kaplan (1975b). The self-protective–self-enhancing responses have been called *protective attitudes,* which are defined as "a constellation of related ideas by means of which the individual maintains, enhances, and defends the self" (p. 851) (Washburn, 1962); *controls and defenses,* which "refer to the individual's capacity to define an event filled with negative implications and consequences in such a way that it does not detract from his sense of worthiness, ability, or power" (p. 37) (Coopersmith, 1967); and *coping behavior,* defined as "constantly changing cognitive and behavioral efforts to manage specific external or internal demands that are appraised as taxing or exceeding the resources of the person" (p. 178) (Lazarus & Folkman, 1984).

Although the range of patterns encompassed by these terms have been variously categorized, I find it useful to consider three formal categories.

Self-protective–self-enhancing activities fall under three rubrics. These relate variously to direct effects on self-cognition; personal value systems; and personal attributes, behaviors, and experiences. Direct effects on self-cognition concern the changing awareness and conceptualization of one's attributes, behaviors, and experiences that have self-evaluative significance and, therefore, eventuate in more or less positive self-feelings. Effects relating to personal value systems permit the reordering of values by which personal traits, attributes, and experiences are evaluated by the person and elicit more or less positive self-feelings. Direct effects on personal attributes, behaviors, and experiences are accomplished through patterns that facilitate or forestall the attainment of attributes, the performance of behaviors, and experiences that, when recognized and conceptualized, lead to more or less favorable self-evaluations and, subsequently, more or less positive self-feelings. Patterns that influence self-cognition, for example, may permit individuals to structure their perception of self as not being causally involved in adverse outcomes or of possessing valued attributes when, in fact, the person does not possess those attributes. Patterns that influence the personal value system might permit the individual to devalue standards that would result in negative self-evaluations and to attribute greater salience to standards that would elicit positive self-evaluations. Self-protective–self-enhancing patterns that influence the experience of personal attributes, behaviors, and experiences may take the form of mechanisms that influence changes in the person or the environment the result of which is to foster self-cognitions that are positively valued and elicit positive self-feelings or to forestall attributes, behaviors, and experiences the self-recognition of which would lead to negative self-evaluations and negative self-feelings.

A fourth mode of self-protective–self-enhancing mechanism could be suggested. It might be argued that certain mechanisms directly impinge on the experience of self-feelings. That is, self-rejecting feelings are repressed, or certain drugs produce euphoric feelings or mask dysphoric feelings. For the most part, however, these mechanisms may be interpreted in terms of their effects on self-cognition (e.g., the perceptual distortion facilitated by the use of drugs), personal value systems (whereby the person focuses on more immediate experiences as being the basis of self-evaluation), and on personal attributes, behaviors, and experiences (e.g., by permitting withdrawal from the interpersonal world that is the basis for self-devaluing experiences). Hence, we will consider only three forms of self-protective–self-enhancing responses.

These three analytically distinct forms of self-protective–self-enhancing mechanisms may represent diverse outcomes of common antecedents. The same behavior by the person may variously have implications for *perceiving* himself as having valued attributes; for selecting *self-evaluative standards*, according to which he would judge himself positively; and for eliciting *favorable outcomes*. A case in point are these diverse outcomes of impression management, that is, "any behavior by a person that has the purpose of controlling or manipulating the attributions and impressions formed of that person by others" (p. 3) (Tedeschi & Riess, 1981). A person's self-presentation for impression management purposes creates favorable changes in self-referent cognition in a number of ways. For example, once a person presents himself to others as having a particular social identity he, in effect, assigns to them a complementary social position. By communicating to them his identity, the person at the same time requires that they identify themselves in relationship to him and conform to the role expectations incumbent on them in that complementary position when acting toward the subject. The consequences for favorable self-referent cognition are twofold. First, the complementary responses of others to the self-presentation functions confirm the possession or performance of a valued identity. Others are granting the person's right to the identity. Second, the subject may need the complementary responses of others in order to fulfill the prized identity. Not only does the deferential response of the other validate the subject's leadership role, it is also instrumental to the performance of the leadership role. The subject requires people to accept direction from him if he is to exercise a directive function. In either case, the complementary role facilitates the subject's self-conception as a leader, a self-conception that elicits positive self-evaluation and, consequently, positive self-feelings.

In the same way, by managing how he appears to others, the person may structure the interactive situation so that the social interaction is viewed by the other party in terms of one rather than another social, relational context. Thus, one rather than another set of evaluative standards is appropriate in the situation. The self-presentation becomes a self-protective–self-enhancing response insofar as the values that are thus selected allow the individual to make favorable self-evaluative judgments and to preclude recourse to evaluative standards by which the individual would find himself wanting. If the person has a desirable position in the social class structure but lacks athletic ability, for example, he may structure a chance encounter at a country club in a way that requires that the other person judge him in terms of social standing.

Finally, the person may create a particular impression in order to create outcomes (changes in the person's traits, behaviors, or experiences) the self-awareness of which will lead to positive self-evaluations. The impression that the person creates may or may not reflect the person's true qualities. In any case, the person may succeed in eliciting positive responses from others. The responses may be intrinsically valued. That is, the individual perceives himself as the object of certain responses, and by being the object of these responses, he is able to evaluate himself positively. He values being the object of, for example, approving responses by others. Or he intrinsically values his ability to influence others' responses. By perceiving himself as an object of such responses, then, the person is able to evaluate himself positively.

In sum, the same behaviors may reflect all three modes of self-protective–self-enhancing responses. We now consider each in greater detail in terms of their putative functions for forestalling negative and enhancing positive self-feelings. At the same time, however, these very responses become part of the personal system of behavior that stimulates other self-referent cognitive, evaluative, affective, and protective–enhancing responses. For example, the individual becomes aware of how he behaves in response to more or less positive self-feelings. The self-awareness of these responses will lead to more or less positive self-evaluation, depending on the value relevance of these responses vis-à-vis the person's value system.

Self-Referent Cognition. Self-protective–self-enhancing responses involving self-referent cognitions has long been recognized within the context of self-theory and related theoretical frameworks. Perhaps the most noteworthy discussions of the ways in which individuals distort self-perceptions of self and of self in relationship to the environment have occurred in the context of considerations of defense mechanisms (Allport, 1943; Murphy, 1947). More recent statements continue in this tradition. Thus, Norem-Hebeisen (1981) argued that "persons have a tendency to process information and to behave in a way that is most enhancing to self-concept" (p. 140), and Combs (1981) asserts,

> perception is determined by need. Perception, including perception of self, is no haphazard event. The process of perception is always directed toward fulfillment of personal need. Perceptual psychologists have called this need the maintenance and enhancement of self, personal adequacy, self-actualization, or self-fulfillment. By whatever name, the person's fundamental need exerts selective effects upon perception of events in the world, the self, and the relationships of those to each other. (p. 12)

Within the context of attribution research, self-protective–self-enhancing functions are suggested in the form of attributing the responsibility of beneficent outcomes to oneself while attributing responsibility for maleficent consequences to forces beyond the self (Arkin, Appelman, & Burger, 1980; Bradley, 1978). Further, a competing theoretical stance, cognitive dissonance, has slowly evolved so that "the psychological character of the motivation for cognitive change can be interpreted, in recent statements of the theory, as a need to preserve self-esteem rather than a need to maintain logic-like consistency among cognitions" (p. 53) (Greenwald & Ronis, 1978).

Self-protective or self-enhancing functions or both are reflected in self-referent cognitive responses in each of the following ways.

First the person may distort his perception of reality such that he fails to correctly perceive his disvalued attributes or performances or fails to correctly perceive the negative attitudes expressed toward him by valued others. The distortion may or may not be facilitated by the use of drugs or by structuring the interpersonal environment to preclude negative feedback from others. In a related fashion, the person may define an outcome as something for which he is not blameworthy, since it was a result of forces beyond his control. The explanation of failure is found in such external circumstances as the intrinsic difficulty of a task, insufficient instrumentation necessary to complete the task, or chance factors beyond the control of the individual. Indeed, the person might induce the circumstances in which achievement would be remarkable and failure would be acceptable. The individual, in the event of failure, thus would not perceive himself as responsible for the failure (Jones & Pittman, 1982). Rather, the failure would be accounted for by the person's incapacitation by alcohol or his persecution by society, circumstances that the person invited.

The pattern of denying disvalued circumstances or one's culpability for the circumstances may have competing effects on self-evaluation. Thus, the selection of such defenses as denial that the person possesses disvalued attributes leads to self-perceptions of not possessing disvalued attributes, which increases the likelihood of positive self-evaluation and positive self-feelings. However, denial precludes taking action so as to achieve the personally valued attributes and behaviors, which indirectly decreases the likelihood of positive self-evaluation.

Second, the person's self-protective–self-enhancing responses may take the form of perceiving himself in terms of positive qualities. The self-perception may reflect selective awareness of qualities that, in fact, characterize the person, or it may reflect distorted views of the person's qualities. With regard to selective perception, Gergen (1981) observes that,

> given the fundamental subjectivity of social definition, the individual is free to select those forms of self-understanding or self-conception that yield positive as opposed to negative outcomes. Self-conception can essentially be viewed as a matter of desire, need, taste, or purpose. (p. 71)

The selective perception may focus on identifications with individuals, groups, or other social entities that are highly valued. The person may thus perceive himself as extensions of these individuals or gorups and, therefore, of value. The selective perception of positive qualities may be facilitated by selecting arenas for social interaction and by social conventions that inhibit negative feedback.

However, the person may incorrectly perceive himself as possessing valued attributes and performing valued behaviors or incorrectly perceive the expression of positive attitudes toward him by valued others. These contrary-to-fact self-perceptions may be facilitated by the intentional creation of situational ambiguity that permits the individual to perceive himself in terms that are most self-enhancing. Alternatively, the person may manage others' impressions of him in ways that contribute to his self-deception regarding positive attributes. The person behaves so as to secure others' recognition of the person's apparent attributes. That is, the individual behaves in a way that will elicit responses from others that seem to indicate that the others believe the person is intelligent, attractive, or sincere. Such responses on the part of others may facilitate the person's distorted self-perception of his own qualities. Although the individual may have realistic doubts about possessing such desirable qualities, the manipulation of others' responses to indicate that the person does, in fact, possess such qualities may enable the individual to "fool himself" into thinking he does have those qualities. The self-deception, presumably in the service of the self-esteem motive, leads to positive self-evaluation and consequent positive self-feelings.

Third, regardless of whether a person perceives himself in a positive or negative manner, for purposes of self-protection–self-enhancement, it very often is imperative that he perceive himself *correctly* in order that he may then behave in ways that will elicit self-perceptions leading to positive self-evaluations and positive self-feelings. He may, for example, seek feedback from others in order to know how he may properly perceive himself, as a guide to future behavior. He may become particularly sensitive to the effects he has on other individuals, and then use these observed effects as indices of his own qualities. The need to be sensitive to his own value-relevant characteristics and capabilities is heightened under conditions in which his own identities are ambiguous and the situation is novel, carrying with it no visible cues to guide either the appropriateness of behavior or the likely consequences of it. Those environmental cues that in the past were associated with frustration or achievement of salient self-values are most likely to incite the person's sensitivity. The disposition to be sensitive to the nature of the self in relationship to environment varies somewhat. Snyder (1974) observes that

> Individuals differ in the extent to which they monitor (observe and control) their expressive behavior and self-presentation. Out of a concern for social appropriateness, the self-monitoring individual is particularly sensitive to the expression and self-presentation of others in social situations and uses these cues as guidelines for monitoring and managing his own self-presentation and expressive behavior. In contrast, the nonself-monitoring person has little concern for the appropriateness of his presentation and expression, pays less attention to the expression of others, and monitors and controls his presentation to a lesser extent. (p. 536)

It is possible that pervasive and continuous self-rejecting feelings may lead the individual to become extremely sensitive to potentially threatening aspects of the environment or of aspects of the self that have self-devaluing implications. Presumably, the person with a history of self-devaluing experiences is more likely to be sensitive to the potential threats in the environment than individuals who have little reason to anticipate such self-devaluing threats.

Fourth, self-protective–self-enhancing responses are reflected in the perceptual distortion of lacking *valued* as well as disvalued attributes. On the one hand, self-perceptions of possessing favorable attributes may lead to positive self-evaluations and positive self-feelings. However, such self-perceptions may also imply to the individual the expectation by self and others of continued good performance or superior performance. In view of the situational demands for such performance, this would pose a risk to the individual's future self-evaluations and self-feelings. Hence, it might appear to the person to be a better strategy for maintaining self-accepting attitudes to deny that the individual is a superior performer. Although he would then be unable to perceive himself as a superior performer, he would also be less vulnerable to future failure, according to the standards of high performance. Here the assumption is that the person is doing more than communicating to others a basis for lower expectations. It is presumed that the individual has distorted his self-cognitions to such an extent that he believes himself incapable of that which he is indeed capable.

Fifth, changes in self-referent cognition that result from purposive changes in the person and the person–environment relationships reflect self-protective–self-enhancing motivation. The person strives to approximate self-values. To the extent that the person is successful in approximating the self-values (and in distancing himself from disvalued states), he is able to perceive himself accordingly and, thereby, stimulate positive self-evaluation and positive self-feelings.

The Need-Value System. A second mode of self-protective–self-enhancing response relates to changes in the person's system of self-values that comprise the more or less salient criteria for self-evaluation. The recognition of this mode of self-protective–self-enhancing responses is recognized in a number of theoretical systems, including Rokeach's (1983) belief system theory:

> We proceed on the assumption that a person will voluntarily undergo lasting changes in values, and in value-related attitudes and behavior, and, moreover, that he or she will resist such changes for identical reasons, namely to maintain or to enhance self-esteem. Maintenance implies a motivation not to lose whatever level of self-esteem one presently has, and enhancement implies the presence of a less-than-altogether-satisfying existing level of self-esteem about one's competence or morality, and thus a motivation to improve upon it, in order to reach some higher level of self-esteem. (p. 172)

In a sense, the development of the person's value system is the end result of his need to protect or enhance himself. The person learns to need and value certain outcomes and then to value other outcomes that are associated with the earlier developed ones. From a contemporary, as well as a developmental point of view, changes in the value system are a function of self-protective–self-enhancing responses.

In effect, individuals choose bases of comparison that are most likely to have self-enhancing consequences. The basis of comparison may be other people or groups, ideal levels of performance or being, past levels of performance or being, anticipation of future levels, etc. The stronger the need for self-enhancement (i.e., the lower the level of current self-esteem), the more the individual is likely to vary his aspirations in ways that will maximize the likelihood of success by changing the standards against which he measures himself. If he is unlikely to achieve the standard of other individuals or groups, he will cease to refer to these groups for standards.

The major distinctions to be made are whether the person changes his values or changes the evaluation of those who share the values and whether the change reflects the assignment of higher priority to the values or the reduction of salience of the values or both.

The reordering of the value system, then, permits an individual to (1) give higher priority to, or adopt, values that allow the person to evaluate existing attributes and behaviors positively (a good athlete chooses to define athletic ability as a highly valued trait); (2) give lower priority to, or reject, values by which the person whould necessarily evaluate himself negatively (the person who receives bad grades at school revises his evaluation of good grades downward); (3) come to value more positively than previously groups or individuals perceived by the person as positively evaluating him (the person seeks out the company of a particular clique of students whose company he did not previously value, since he now perceives that they admire him or would admire him if they became acquainted with him); or (4) come to more negatively value that previously individuals or groups who are per-ceived as negatively evaluating him (the person rejects a group of stu-dents to whom he had previously been attracted and the standard of these students because he perceives himself as being rejected by them). The more precise description of revisions of the need-value system will be considered as special mainfestations of these four types that are con-sidered in turn.

First, self-protective–self-enhancing functions are served by assign-ing a higher priority to certain self-values whether on a temporary or more permanent basis. The temporary reordering reflects the goal of favorable self-evaluation. The same self-perception that, by other eval-uative standards, would necessarily be judged negative is, in effect, reevaluated in a way that may lead to positive self-feelings. If a person "snitches" on another person, to evaluate himself by the standard of loyalty he must be found wanting and reject himself accordingly. How-ever, by invoking the standard of community responsibility, he might legitimately inform to the police, judging that the norm of community responsibility takes precedence over the loyalty to the delinquent group. The same self-perception, when evaluated by different standards, results in different self-judgments and consequent self-feelings. If a person perceives himself as possessing an attribute, performing a behavior, or as the object of an experience that, by some applicable standard, would eventuate in negative self-evaluation and consequent negative self-feelings, the person may well select another conceivably applicable evaluative standard as taking precedence over this standard—adopting a standard that would justifiably lead to a positive self-judgment and self-accepting feelings.

In effect, the individual justifies his own traits, behaviors, or experiences. In justifying one's behaviors, "the actor admits personal responsibility for the action and its attendant consequences, but denies that the consequences are negative, bad, wrong, inappropriate, unwelcome, or untoward in any other sense" (p. 7) (Tedeschi & Reiss, 1981). Classifications of justifications have been offered by a number of individuals (Sykes & Matza, 1957; Scott & Lyman, 1968; Jellison, 1977). Tedeschi and Riess (1981) cite their own codification of types of justification and refer to their implications for the application of evaluative standards:

> Many of these types of justifications relate the action in question to some socially acceptable rule or norm of conduct. Thus, appeals to higher authority, including superiors, officials, organizational rules, or supernatural and extraterrestrial beings; appeals to ideology, including nationalism, revolutionary goals, and the promotion of a religion; norms of self-defense; relational norms of loyalty; standards of justice; and appeals to humanistic values of love, peace, truth, or beauty are used to realign the action to some acceptable value, rule, norm, or law. In this way an action that may have been perceived as negative may actually bring credit and approval to the actor, or at least the degree of negative reaction by observers may be mitigated. (p. 8)

Although these writers refer to the process by which justification in the eyes of others is obtained, the same process may be thought of as operating with reference to self-justification. That is, the individual is able to evaluate himself positively in his own eyes by applying certain evaluative standards rather than others according to which the person's behavior or attributes would have been self-disvalued. The person justifies himself to himself (self-justification) as well as to others.

In order to establish the legitimacy of the reordered values, the person presents himself in certain ways to signal the appropriateness of the values. To the extent that the person can create situations in which one set of standards, or one standard within a set of standards, is particularly applicable, the person can selectively apply those values that (given the person's self-perceptions of attributes, behaviors, and experiences) appropriately lead to positive self-evaluation. By presenting himself in certain ways, the person manipulates the situation to ensure that the performance in certain identities is appropriate. Of course, the social identities that are emphasized are those that the individual feels confident about with regard to conforming to the social demands made on people who have that identity. By conforming to the expectations that he and others share of himself while in that identity, he is able to perceive himself, and to evaluate himself, positively, thus earning the experience of positive self-feelings. Thus, impression management permits the person to create situations in which he can, on the one hand, display personal attributes, perform behaviors, and be the object of experiences, the self-perception of which leads to positive self-evaluation and positive self-feeling, and, on the other hand, define the applicability of evaluative standards according to which the individual will be able to evaluate himself positively.

As was noted in another context, the person may present himself in a way that signals (to himself as well as to others) that he is handicapped. At the same time that a person creates situations in which he is or appears to be handicapped in his ability to perform valued behaviors or gain valued attributes, the individual defines another set of standards as applicable for self-evaluation in the current situation. In effect, the establishment of salutary self-evaluative standards is achieved by self-handicapping strategies (Jones & Berglas, 1978), in which such roles as the alcoholic or drug abuser or underachiever are adopted. In so doing, the person communicates to self and other that normal standards of self-judgment would be inappropriate. Rather, the person should be judged according to standards that recognize the limitations imposed by the alcoholic state (Not bad for a drunk, huh?). More generally, if the proper standards of evaluation are applied (taking into account mitigating circumstances or recognizing that other issues are relevant), the person need not devalue himself but rather, by alternative standards, may recognize himself as conforming to situationally appropriate standards.

The self-enhancing mechanism of reordering self-value to permit favorable self-evaluation may be reflected in the processes by which a person derogates others and accepts deviant labels.

The processes by which a person devalues others necessarily implicates the selective application of evaluative standards. If an individual perceives himself as possessing more of a desirable characteristic than others, or fewer undesirable characteristics than others, he will, relative to applicable standards, evaluate himself somewhat positively. Among the self-protective mechanisms that are activated by the experience of self-rejecting feelings are those behaviors that lead an individual to perceive himself in this fashion and to accordingly evaluate himself as relatively more favored. To these ends, the person may select those values for self-judgment according to which he is favored relative to others in his social environment. Or, regardless of the evaluative criterion, he may perceive himself (correctly or incorrectly) as relatively more favored than others. Finally, he may take actions that increase the likelihood that he will be favored relative to others either by taking actions that derogate and harm others or by associating with others that are less fortunate. In either case, the person may perceive himself appropriately as relatively more favored. As Wills (1981) observes:

> A basic fact about human life is that people experience frustration, failure, or misfortune. The theory of downward comparison elucidates the fact that a way to make one's self feel better . . . is to compare oneself with other persons who are equally unfortunate or more unfortunate. Put differently, people who are unhappy like to see others who are unhappy. They may not necessarily go out of their way to produce unhappiness in others, but sometimes they do. (p. 268)

The derogation of minority groups is an example of this pattern. Rejection of a minority group implies invocation of the evaluative criterion of being in a more favored group, a standard that the person perceives himself as approximating. Therefore, the person merits positive self-evaluation.

The acceptance of a stigmatized label provides another example of this self-enhancing pattern. Once individuals commit themselves to particular behaviors, they tend to enhance their evaluation of that which they have committed themselves to and tend to devalue alternative responses. In effect, they tend to select evaluative standards according to which self-perceived attributes, behaviors, and experiences eventuate in positive self-evaluation. If a person, because of violation of certain normative expectations, is labeled as a deviant, the need for self-approval may require that he justify the label by identifying with it and positively valuing it.

In short, individuals who experience self-rejecting feelings tend to adopt or increase the salience of self-evaluative frameworks that permit them to judge themselves as more closely approximating desirable states and as becoming increasingly distant from undesirable states. Those evaluative standards that are selected permit favorable self-evaluations.

Second, in addition to selecting or granting higher priority to certain values, the rejection of certain values (according to which the person would necessarily devalue himself) serves self-protective or self-enhancing functions or both. In essence, individuals who experience self-derogation are increasingly likely to either ignore or to attack the validity of standards by which they devalue themselves, at the same time that they adopt, or increase the salience of, evaluative standards by which they are able to evaluate themselves positively. If the person is unlikely to achieve expected past levels, he will cease to view them as applicable to his present state. If he becomes increasingly distant from his ideal values, he will change his ideals. And, on the basis of his past performance, if he is unlikely to achieve high levels of future performance, he will lower these expectations. The subject's protective attitudes permit him to effect changes in his evaluations such that what was once considered a desirable trait, behavior, or response from others is now evaluated as undesirable or less desirable relative to other traits, behaviors, and others' responses to him.

The self-protective mechanism of reducing the salience of personal values is reflected in Pearlin's (1980) discussion of the reevaluation of the salience of various social roles:

> The control of meaning typically relies heavily on the selective use of socially valued goals and activities . . . if a man is exposed to intense strain in his work, he may avoid distress by relegating work to a marginal place in his life, committing himself instead, for example, to being a good husband or father. Thus, adults not infrequently will move those roles in which there is a painful experience to the periphery of importance, making more central those that are comparatively free of hardship. In rearranging their priorities, people temper stress by demeaning the importance of areas in which failure and conflict are occurring. (p. 185)

Third, self-protective–self-enhancing functions are served by coming to value, more positively than previously, groups or individuals who are perceived by the subject as positively evaluating him.

When an individual suffers from comparison with those with greater wealth and power, the person may frequently avoid or assuage self-rejecting feelings consequent on negative self-evaluations by changing the self-evaluative frame of reference. He may do this either by accepting the legitimacy of the institutionalized inequality and comparing himself only with those within his own class or by rejecting the legitimacy of the system and finding a basis for self-worth in the mechanism through which he rejects the system.

Consistent with the former device, Della Fave (1980) argues that

> those possessing greater wealth and power in a society will tend to be perceived as having more of a whole range of other positive characteristics than those less fortunate or powerful. Through the status attribution process, those possessing greater amounts of primary resources come to be seen as actually being superior. At this point, the principle of equity takes over, and people believe that those who appear to be superior deserve to be more richly rewarded. . . .
>
> Of course, the attribution of superior characteristics to those with greater wealth and power implies that those lower in the stratification system will

attribute to themselves relatively inferior characteristics, through comparison. . . . Thus, if they are, in relevant ways, inferior, then they deserve
to have lesser wealth and power. (pp. 962–963)

Because the differences are legitimated, people will tend to compare
themselves with members of their own stratum rather than with members of strata that are obviously better off or worse off than their own.

The latter type of comparison is meaningless precisely because those persons
substantially higher or lower than one's self are obviously deserving of corre-
spondingly greater or lesser rewards. The differences are simply taken for
granted. It is the relatively small differences in rewards between one's self
and those similar to self that excite feelings of deprivation. (p. 963)

Just as individuals may feel deprived relative to the standards of
expectations of one's class, so may one feel of positive value according to
the same standards by possessing in greater abundance what is valued
in that class.

Related to the process of selecting others as standards of evaluation
because they permit reality-based favorable comparisons is the process
of misattributing characteristics to more or less valued others in order
that the person may either feel that the individual's own disvalued traits
are more acceptable because they are the norm or that the person's
"disvalued" trait is not really disvalued at all, since it characterizes a
respectable group (Bramel, 1962). The process "by which a person attributes to other persons behaviors or personality characteristics which
are similar to his/her own" (p. 58) (Burish & Houston, 1979) is similar to
a mechanism that has been called similarity projection (Burish & Houston, 1979), sometimes called "supplementary" or "classical" Projection
in psychoanalysis.

The attraction to a group for purposes of enhancing oneself is generally accomplished because the person perceives that he or she is able
to approximate the norms of the group. Frequently, however, the basis
for self-acceptance is acceptance by a group, according to the standards
of which the person would be disvalued. Here the problem is to approximate the standards, since the person, presumably, is unwilling or unable to reject the group as a basis for self-acceptance. The self-enhancing–self-protective mechanisms by which the person successfully
approximates the self-values is the subject of the third mode of self-
protective–self-enhancing responses to be considered below.

Fourth, self-protective–self-enhancing functions are served by the
avoidance or rejection of groups or individuals whose rejection of the
person contributes to the person's self-devaluation (since acceptance of
the group or person was a salient self-value). By rejecting the others as

legitimate bases for self-evaluation, the person becomes more estimable in his own eyes. The rejection of the others may range from a drastic reduction of the value placed on previously valued people or normative standards to more overtly hostile responses by the individual, up to and including physical aggression against the group members and material representations of the group's normative structure that symbolizes the basis of the group's rejection of the person.

To summarize, the second mode of self-protective–self-enhancing responses related to revisions of the person's need-value system. The person comes to adopt self-values that he views himself as approximating or that he shows promise of approximating. Since acceptance by others frequently is a significant basis of self-acceptance, as well as an indication of approximating other shared values, the person comes to value those others who give evidence of accepting, or who offer promise of accepting, the person. At the same time, the person comes to reject those values that he views as beyond his ability to approximate. Insofar as rejection by others is a basis for self-evaluation, as well as an indication of failure to achieve shared values, the person will tend to become less attracted to and will reject those others who fail to accept the person, in part because of his failure to approximate shared values. These revisions in the person's need-value system forestall further self-devaluing and facilitate self-enhancing responses.

Approximating Self-Values. The third mode of self-protective–self-enhancing responses consists of behaviors that increase the likelihood of approximating and decrease the likelihood of failing to approximate self-values. The person behaves in ways the self-perception of which will be viewed as approximating salient standards of self-evaluation. If attaining a certain skill, being accepted by specified others, or behaving in a certain way is a salient criterion for self-evaluation, the person will attempt to attain the skill, behave so as to be accepted by others, and behave, in general, in those ways that will earn self-acceptance. At the same time, the person so behaves as to avoid the experiences of failing to approximate the self-evaluative standards. This mode of self-enhancing or self-protective responses is distinguished from the first two categories in that the person's veridical perceptions and the existence of one or another system of personal values are taken as given. Given the self-values, the person will behave in ways that will allow him to perceive realistically that he is approximating self-values or that he is not failing to approximate the values.

Purposive attempts to approximate self-values are more or less specific, depending on the nature of the salient self-evaluative standards. If the person values scholarship, he will study hard, seek out scholarly companions, and otherwise behave in ways that will permit him to evaluate himself positively by this standard. If conformity to the expectations of a particular social identity (e.g., male) is a salient basis for self-evaluation, he will strive to conform to what he perceives as the expectations of males in his group. More generally, the person may evaluate himself in terms of his self-perceptions of conforming to others' expectations.

Associated with the need to conform to others' expectations are the needs to elicit certain responses from others. I have argued that the person is motivated to behave in ways that will reflect positively valued attributes, behaviors, and experiences. These attributes, behaviors, and experiences, as the individual becomes aware of them, permit positive self-evaluations and, subsequently, self-accepting feelings. An important class of these behaviors are those that the person more or less consciously undertakes to elicit intrinsically valued responses from others or responses from others that are prerequisite to the achievement of value-relevant outcomes.

The more or less purposive attempts to elicit responses from others have been treated from a variety of (somewhat overlapping) perspectives in the literature: in terms of self-presentation (Goffman, 1959; Jones & Pittman, 1982), self-disclosure (Jourard, 1964; Cozby, 1973), and impression management (Tedeschi, 1981). The individual behaves in ways that will elicit positive responses from others that are valued for their own sake or responses from others that are instrumental to the achievement of other valued goals. In the former case, being the object of positive responses from others is itself valued. The individual wishes to perceive himself as liked or respected by others. In the latter case, such responses, whether they are also intrinsically valued, aid the individual to reach other valued goals. If the individual behaves in ways that elicit positive responses from others, they may offer goods and services that permit the individual to achieve such other valued attributes as upward social mobility.

For example, an individual may take credit for something that he may or may not have had anything to do with in order that his employer will reward him (perhaps by promotion). The motive here is not to perceive himself as having done something (which, in fact, he might not deserve credit for), but, rather, to achieve the promotion. The self-perception of the promotion is positively valued and will lead to an enhancement of the person's global self-evaluation and, consequently, to positive self-feelings. Although the person might not be able to positively value himself for outcomes that he knows he was not responsible for, he may be able to evaluate himself positively for possessing something that is of value (a better position in his firm).

For various reasons, an individual may wish to present himself to others as likeable, dangerous, competent, morally worthy, or dependent (Jones & Pittman, 1982). If the person is successful, others will attribute these characteristics to him and respond with the desired expressions of affection, fear, respect, guilt, or nurturance. These attitudes, as noted above, may be intrinsically valued or may be regarded by the person as instrumental to the achievement of other valued ends.

Paradoxically, a self-presentation of self-abasement may be intended to serve self-enhancing functions. To the extent that the person is motivated to be accepted by a group that rejects him, by abasing himself the person may be attempting (with greater or lesser degrees of success) to curry favor with those who reject him—to evoke the expression of positive attitudes toward himself from valued others by adopting attitudes that are similar to those held by the valued others *including rejecting attitudes toward the person*. In related fashion, the person may overtly devalue his own deviant behavior in order to demonstrate to others that he shares their value system and, that, consequently, he merits their respect.

Purposive self-presentation does not necessarily imply a false communication to others of the person's real self. It may well be to the advantage of the person to properly communicate to others his own true social identities, attributes, or behavioral dispositions, as well as his expectations of others. However, he may be motivated to communicate a false impression of himself either to elicit salutary responses from others or to permit distorted self-referent cognitions toward the goal of positive self-evaluation and the experience of self-accepting feelings.

Frequently, self-presentational behavior in response to the need for positive self-feelings is automatic. The person unconsciously fulfills the demands of those social identities that are the basis for self-acceptance. The person conforms to the normative prescriptions that define one or another social identity and, in presenting himself to others, is, in effect, realizing self-cognitions that merit positive self-evaluation and, consequently, positive self-feelings.

So prevalent are self-presentational strategies that it is difficult to determine whether or not these processes are implicated in other modes of self-enhancing strategies. Thus, we argued above that one manifestation of self-referent cognitive distortion is the tendency to attribute to oneself responsibility for benign outcomes and to attribute to external forces responsibility for maleficent outcomes. However, the attribution of personal responsibility for positive outcomes and the attribution of external causation for negative outcomes may be interpreted either in terms of self-serving distortion of self-referent cognitions or in terms of self-serving self-presentation. In both cases, the self-protective–self-enhancing mechanism affects self-cognition. In the one case, through perceptual distortion, the individual believes himself to be the effective agent of positive outcomes and, therefore, evaluates himself positively. In the other instance, the individual is able to present himself to others as the effective agent of positive outcomes (whether he privately believes that this is the case). As a result of presenting himself in this way, the person elicits positive responses from others and is able to perceive himself as the object of positive responses by others. He, thus, evaluates himself positively, as one who elicits positive responses from others.

In addition, people frequently do not attribute positive outcomes to themselves and negative outcomes to external causes. These cases are particularly amenable to the interpretation that individuals will sometimes deny responsibility for positive outcomes and accept responsibility for negative outcomes when, by so doing, they will elicit positive responses or avoid negative responses from others. For example, if the individual is led to believe that he will be evaluated as humble or generous by denying personal responsibility for positive outcomes, or as a responsible person for accepting responsibility for negative outcomes, or that he will be found out and criticized for accepting responsibility for positive outcomes when he was, in fact, not responsible, then the individual will, in fact, deny responsibility for the positive outcomes and accept responsibility for the negative outcomes. In so doing, the individual effectively enhances himself by eliciting positive responses from others, thus enabling himself to perceive himself as the object of admiration from valued others. To the extent that he values such responses, the individual will enjoy positive self-feelings, feelings that ultimately have no intrinsic relationship to the outcomes for which he did or did not accept responsibility.

The attempts to approximate self-values (one important class of which relates to obtaining desirable responses from others) may be more or less closely related to the particular self-evaluations that stimulated the self-enhancing–self-protective responses. On the one hand, the self-evaluation may lead to efforts to approximate a particular value that the person judges himself to be distant from. For example, self-judgments of academic failure might prompt the self-enhancing response of studying harder and getting better grades. Alternatively, the person's self-judgment of academic failure might lead to attempts to achieve alternative self-values (athletic ability, courageousness, altruism) that might serve higher-order or equivalent self-values within the more or inclusive value system (when such attempts do not reflect the rejection of one set of standards in favor of an alternative more achievable system of standards). The attempt to compensate for failure according to some values, with attempts to succeed according to others, sometimes takes the form of altruistic behavior, such as offering to help others. Observations of prosocial behavior following the person's violation of personal values are interpretable in terms of either attempts to achieve alternative values or in terms of alternate routes to the same value—approval of others (Tedeschi & Riordan, 1981). In either case, the attempts may be thought of as attempts to conform to self-values to restore positive self-evaluation. As Jones and Pittman (1982) state,

> the desire for self-validating approval may become especially strong when events conspire to threaten cherished features of the phenomenal self. Thus, the rejected suitor may try especially hard to be charming and likeable around his female friends; the solid citizen arrested for speeding might decide to increase his community service work. In such cases threats to the phenomenal self lead to self-presentations designed to secure restorative feedback. To the extent that the threatened actor sustains his counteractive behavior or to the extent that the counteractive behavior involves effortful and costly commitments, social confirmation will have the restorative power sought. (pp. 255–256)

The purposive behavior of individuals toward the goal of approximating self-values may involve taking action that will create outcomes for other individuals. If a person evaluates himself in terms of being *relatively* more powerful than others or richer than others, then the goal of positive self-evaluation in these regards can be served as well by actions that cause others to be weaker and poorer as by actions that cause the person to be stronger and richer.

Up to this point, I have been describing responses by individuals that attempt to approximate self-values and, thereby, enhance overall positive self-evaluation. However, individuals also act to prevent situations in which they will fail to achieve self-values. Thus, Norem-Hebeisen (1981) observes that

> as persons mature, they tend to insulate themselves from tasks and relationships that they experience as denigrating. They select life-styles that minimize chronic feelings of unease and become more adept at identifying and circumventing derogating events. (p. 143)

For example, they may avoid expressing extreme attitudes, regardless of their true feelings, on some subjects in order to avoid reproving responses by others. The relevance of these behaviors for self-feelings is that the person avoids perceiving himself as the object of negative responses by others, when to be the object of negative responses by others is a highly disvalued circumstance. The person so behaves not only to avoid intrinsically disvalued disapproving responses by others, or to avoid, thereby, the loss of resources that these others might provide toward the goal of achieving other intrinsically valued goals, but also to avoid experiences that would be perceived by the person as otherwise disvalued. Thus, the person might avoid competitive situations, since it increases the probability of failure. Or, the person may avoid interaction with people whose personal attributes and accomplishments are such that the person would suffer badly by invidious comparisons.

Just as purposive self-presentational strategies represent an important class of mechanisms whereby individuals approximate self-values, so do these mechanisms serve to forestall the occurrence of self-devaluing circumstances associated with the person's perception of obtaining unwelcome responses from others. The person adopts a "protective self-presentation" style that reflects the individual's wish to avoid disapproval rather than the wish for approval. The person creates an image that is unlikely to attract such disapproval. As Arkin (1981) observes, with regard to the attempt to avoid disapproval by using protective self-presentation, that

> the most common and diverse expression of a protective, conservative orientation is composed of behaviors that serve either to foretall challenges from others or to proactively create an impression that is unassailable. . . . Highly modest portrayals of one's personal characteristics, behavior, and accomplishments may serve to forestall challenges from others. Neutral, uncertain, or qualified expressions of some judgements render them relatively unassailable. Conformity and compliance are entirely safe and defensible, requiring no explanation or justification, and so on. In still other cases the process may be more complex, involving the structuring of a situation so that others will themselves spontaneously make the desired inference. (pp. 316–317)

Purposive presentation of self as a self-protective device permits a person to structure the situation so that he elicits only those responses, which, when perceived, will eventuate in positive self-evaluations and self-feelings. The individual, by creating certain impressions, defines the situation for those who participate in the situation with him. He places restrictions on the range of behaviors by others that would be considered appropriate by them. Thus, the individual is able to prescribe the range of behaviors with which he would feel comfortable. In effect, the person is able to forestall the occurrence of unwelcome experiences. For example, a person who feels threatened by intimate relationships, believing that they will eventuate in rejection of him, may structure the situation as an impersonal one. He may define the situation for the person with whom he is interacting as an employer–employee relationship. Although he may achieve intrinsically gratifying deferential responses from others by creating the illusion of being in authority, at the same time he precludes any more intimate overtures that might threaten his future self-esteem.

To summarize, the third mode of self-enhancing–self-protective responses consists of behaviors that are oriented toward the approximation of more or less salient self-values. The approximation of these values stimulates self-awareness and self-evaluation of approximating the self-evaluative criteria. A significant category of such behaviors comprises self-presentational responses whereby the person elicits positive responses from others, responses that are salient criteria of self-evaluation or are instrumental to the approximation of salient self-evaluative criteria. Responses oriented toward the approximation of self-values may attempt (1) to approximate a particular self-value that the person perceives himself as being distant from or (2) to approximate higher-order or equivalent values within the same value system, where the person does not choose to approximate values in newly adopted alternative systems of values. The purposive behavior that is oriented to the approximation of self-values may involve affecting the outcomes of other people insofar as the criteria for self-evaluation are defined in terms of the status of the person relative to that of others.

Purposive behaviors that are oriented to approximation of self-values may also involve the forestalling of failure as well as the achievement of success with regard to approximation of self-values. A number of behaviors in the person's repertoire of responses (including self-presentational strategies) are oriented toward protecting against self-devaluing circumstances as well as attaining self-values.

Deviant Modes

The response patterns that comprise the three modes of self-enhancing–self-protective responses described above may be socially countenanced or socially defined as deviant. At one extreme, the patterns may be positively valued, and social structures may be provided that facilitate the utilization of these mechanisms. At the other extreme, the mechanisms may be socially condemned, and a variety of social control mechanisms may be institutionalized that would not sanction the patterns. For example, giving a false impression may be judged to be hypocritical in certain circumstances and acceptable in others. The changing of value systems may be facilitated by the multiplicity of interest groups that are available to an individual in a complex society. However, affiliation with a delinquent subculture toward the goal of adopting self-enhancing standards would be negatively sanctioned. To some degree, fooling one's self about one's abilities might be deemed acceptable, but severe reality distortion might be judged to be a psychiatric disorder, or otherwise negatively sanctioned. The achievement of personal attributes, behaviors, or experiences that are socially valued through legitimate means would elicit appropriate social rewards. However, the same goals achieved through illegitimate means (e.g., theft) would be condemned. Fulfilling one's obligations would be regarded as laudable, but too much of that might be regarded as slavish conformity to the demands of others.

Normally, conventionally approved self-protective–self-enhancing mechanisms function to maintain personally acceptable levels of self-approval. Normative self-protective–self-enhancing responses (stimulated by the need for positive self-feelings), however, may be frustrated by a number of circumstances. To the extent that the consistent and clear feedback of members of one's social group are unambiguous, for example, the individual will find it more difficult to distort self-perceptions. To the extent that situational demand characteristics are so obvious and social consensus on the applicability of evaluative standards to the individual in a particular situation is apparent, the individual will be unable to reorder his system of values or adopt a different identity to redefine the personal applicability of particular evaluative standards. Normative self-protective–self-enhancing responses relating to acquiring attributes, performing behaviors, and being the object of benign experiences presume the ability of the individual to adapt to normatively defined and personally subscribed to environmental demands. In addition, these mechanisms presume the ability of the person, within personally and socially defined bounds of acceptability, to change the environment to make it more congruent with the person's need-value system. However, although the individual may be motivated to so behave as to attain the personal attributes, perform the behaviors, and become the object of socially desirable responses, he might be unable to do so as a result of any or all of a number of more or less longstanding circumstances: socially ascribed or constitutionally given deficits; the inability to conform to multiple sets of applicable but conflicting expectations; ignorance of which normative expectations are situationally applicable, either because of the absence of visual cues or inadequate socialization; lack of resources; and deviant responses by others in the person's social relational framework (Kaplan, 1983).

The frustration of the normative self-protective–self-enhancing responses increases the experience of self-devaluation. Nevertheless, the person's outcomes are so intimately tied to the conventional order that the individual continues to be emotionally invested in conventional socializing agents and the evaluative standards internalized in the course of the socialization experience, including those that define the acceptability of self-enhancing–self-protective mechanisms. However, should the individual's experience of self-rejecting feelings be so intense, continuous, and pervasive in the person's current life space because the range of normative responses proves to be ineffective in either reducing the experience of self-rejection or in forestalling the continuation of self-rejecting feelings, the definition of what constitutes acceptable self-protective–self-enhancing responses may change. The range of responses within the individual's limits of acceptability (and, at the same time, within the socially defined limits of acceptability) that have proved to be ineffective in the past and threaten to be futile in the future with regard to restoring the experience of positive self-feelings and reducing the experience of negative self-feelings, ceases to be attractive to the individual. The individual, consciously or unconsciously, seeks and becomes aware of alternative mechanisms that fall beyond the limits of what were once personally acceptable standards of behavior, that offer the promise of reducing the experience of self-rejecting feelings (Kaplan, 1984).

These alternative deviant responses parallel the modes of conventional self-protective–self-enhancing responses. That is, they represent adjustments in self-perceptions, involve reordering of the system of values, and reflect attempts to secure attributes and experiences or perform behaviors that would lead to self-perceptions of having valued attributes. However, these responses now exceed the limits of what had been personal standards of acceptable behavior and continue to be social standards of conventional behavior. Whereas the individual previously might have taken advantage of situational ambiguity to perceive himself in a more favorable light, or might have rationalized his behavior as being beyond his control, the individual now so seriously distorts his self-perceptions that he, for all practical purposes, ceases to be a functioning member of conventional society. Whereas the individual may have selectively perceived certain values to be situationally applicable in order to be able to approve of his behavior, the individual now rejects the value system and becomes attracted to an alternative system of deviant values that permit him to perceive himself as approximating group standards. Whereas the individual once behaved so as to secure the approval of conventional others and to perceive himself as possessing conventionally valued attributes, he now behaves in ways intended to secure the approval of outlaws or to perceive himself as having attributes and performing behaviors that are admirable from the evaluative stance of outlaws. In short, having failed to assuage self-rejecting feelings, and having little expectation of being able to forestall self-rejecting feelings through the use of response patterns that were previously personally valued and continue to be socially endorsed, the individual adopts deviant responses (cognitive, evaluative, and conative) in the hope of attaining or restoring positive self-feelings or reducing and forestalling the experience of negative self-feelings.

To illustrate the deviant manifestations of the self-protective patterns, the use of hallucinogens allows drug users to "feel through perceptual distortions that they have become in reality what they believe they are in imagination" (p. 192) (Sharoff, 1969). Further, to the extent that adoption of drug abuse patterns is accompanied by rejecting attitudes on the part of society, the individual is able to perceive his own failure as justified by blaming it on such societal attitudes toward the addict. In the face of the obstacles imposed by these attitudes, the addict can justifiably, in his own eyes, cease to struggle further for achievement. In short, drug use facilitates self-referent cognitive responses that serve self-enhancing functions.

With regard to changing the salience of self-evaluative criteria, Sharoff (1969) argues that the abuse of narcotics, in part, depresses the intensity of the demands for achievement made by the individual's superego. The need for achievement simply seems relatively unimportant under the influence of drugs. The individual is permitted "to withdraw from his conflicts without struggle or self-condemnation" (p. 189).

With regard to the use of deviant responses to approximate self-values, the responses may serve self-enhancing functions in either of two ways. First, the person may use delinquent responses to approximate conventional values (Kaplan, 1984). Delinquent behavior may provide, for example, opportunities to engage in leadership behavior or to demonstrate daring. The self-values are not in themselves deviant. Rather, the means of approximating the self-values are contranormative. Alternatively, the self-protective responses resulting in changes in personal attributes, behaviors, and experiences may result in favorable self-cognitions only when measured against the standards of a deviant value system. Becoming a competent thief or engaging in substance abuse may allow the individual to perceive himself in a favorable light only when measured against the standards of a criminal subculture or a substance-abusing membership group. Thus, Leon (1969), in discussing excessively cruel crimes, suggests that the person perceives aggressive behavior as a vehicle for self-enhancement by evoking approving responses from others. In this connection, he notes that the criminals were frequently boastful about their aggressive ability and occasionally enjoyed great prestige. The criminal atrocities may function

> as a form of self-assertion and achieving distinction. The criminal in this way
> gains notoriety and steps out of the limbo of mediocrity and anonymity in

which he feels immersed. This accounts to achieving self-assertion through outdoing others in cruelty. (p. 1572)

Just as conventional mechanisms serve self-protective as well as self-enhancing functions, so deviant responses permit the person to forestall self-devaluation. For example, Arieti (1967) asserts that many psychological defenses are ways of protecting the self, and provides several examples:

The detached or schizoid person decreases his emotional or actual participation in life in order not to feel inadequate and injure his self-image. The hypochondriacal person protects his self by blaming only his body for his difficulties. (p. 732)

Delinquent behavior has been conceptualized as a form of ego restriction, "as a way of avoiding situations which endanger self-esteem and of engaging in experiences that promise a form of self-enhancement" (p. 292) (Gold, 1978). Obsessions and phobias have been interpreted as avoidance methods that arise by way of defending against threats to self-esteem (Salzman, 1965).

The adoption of socially disvalued deviant behavior patterns serves to assert the person's separation from a world in which he is not valued. Further, the negative reactions of others to his deviant acts lead to the exclusion of the subject from active group participation and membership and, hence, from the very self-devaluing experiences associated with the genesis of the person's characteristic self-rejection. The effect, as well as the conscious or unconscious intent of the deviant behavior, thus might serve avoidance functions.

In short, the same forms of self-protective–self-enhancing responses may fall within or outside of the limits of conventional acceptability. Whether the person adopts deviant patterns will depend largely on the effectiveness of conventional patterns in forestalling self-devaluing experiences and facilitating self-enhancing experiences.

DETERMINANTS OF SELF-PROTECTIVE–SELF-ENHANCING RESPONSES

The occurrence and nature of a person's self-protective–self-enhancing responses are influenced by (1) the nature of the person's self-feelings; (2) the person's self-referent cognitive responses, including beliefs about the person in relationship to the physical and sociocultural environment; and (3) the person's evaluation of the self-protective–self-enhancing mechanisms.

Self-Feelings

The assertion that self-feelings profoundly influence self-protective–self-enhancing responses is implicit in the earlier discussion of the
self-evaluative process. Values are internalized by processes leading to
the subjective association of particular attributes, behaviors, or experiences, or the symbolic representations of these, with more or less distressing and pleasurable experiences. The person becomes motivated to
approximate those desirable states and to distance himself from undesirable states in order to approximate positive feelings and to avoid distressful ones. The person's experience of affective responses to the expectation or perception of failing to approximate valued states or of
approximating disvalued states (that is, to self-evaluative processes) are
referred to as self-feelings. The experience of positive self-feelings associated with the perception or expectation of approximating personally
and situationally relevant self-values, and the experience of negative
self-feelings associated with the perception or expectation of being distant from personally and situationally relevant self-values or of approximating disvalued states, reflects the *need* to approximate desirable states
and to distance one's self from undesirable states. These needs, in turn,
motivate the individual to behave in ways that will result in the approximation of the desirable and the avoidance of the undesirable states that
are associated with positive and negative self-feelings, respectively.

The recognition of self-feelings as motivating self-protective–self-
enhancing responses is apparent in the context of a number of theoretical systems. Rokeach (1983) for example, asserts that

> humans continually assess whatever they do or say in their everyday lives for
> its implication about their own sense of competence and morality. . . . De-
> pending on the nature of the information provided, the person will experi-
> ence varying degrees of feelings of satisfaction or dissatisfaction with himself
> or herself. A *change* in belief systems and behavior is expected to come about
> to the extent that the information provided to the person (about what one
> believes, values, or does) leads him or her to become dissatisfied with self.
> Self-dissatisfaction is a noxious state and should set into motion a sequence
> of cognitive reorganization and behavioral changes that should lead to the
> alleviation or reduction of such feelings of self-dissatisfaction. Conversely,
> stability, or the constancy of belief systems and behavior, can result when the
> salient information provided to a person about one's competence or morality
> leads him or her to feel gratified. (p. 176)

In a similar vein, Norem-Hebeisen (1981) notes that a negative self-
concept "is often accompanied by feelings of inadequacy which serve as
a signal that the individual must make some kind of action in defense of
or in assertion of his or her well-being" (p. 142). Indeed, it would be

difficult to identify a position that would be at odds with Pepitone's (1968) observation that "the striving toward higher self-esteem and status (or avoidance of loss of esteem and status) must surely be counted as the most powerful and pervasive motivations in man's repertoire" (p. 349). It is this self-esteem motive that "is postulated to energize and structure self-processes" (p. 54) (Wells & Marwell, 1976).

As is apparent from the preceding discussion, the overall more or less positive self-feelings that the person momentarily or characteristically experience and that motivate self-protective–self-enhancing responses is frequently referred to by such terms as *self-esteem*. In the traditional literature dealing with the relationship between self-feelings, on the one hand, and self-protective–self-enhancing responses, on the other hand, the resolution of needs expressed in diverse self-feelings is expressed primarily through what has been called the self-esteem motive. I have avoided use of this term *self-esteem*, however, since self-esteem connotes both evaluative and affective-feeling responses, an ambiguity I wish to avoid.

The occurrence and nature of the self-protective or self-enhancing responses that are motivated by self-feelings will depend on the quality, polarity, generality, intensity, and stability of the self-feelings. These dimensions were discussed in Chapter 4. I consider, in turn, the influence of self-feelings in its various manifestations on each of the three major forms of self-protective–self-enhancing responses and on the extent to which specific responses in each formal category reflect deviation from or conformity to conventional standards.

Self-Referent Cognitive Responses. A very rich research literature addresses the relationship between self-feelings and self-referent cognitive responses. One category of findings relates to the tendency of distressful self-feelings to elicit *perceptual denial or avoidance* of self-devaluing attributes or circumstances, particularly when the threatened self-values are highly salient in the personal system of self-values. Under conditions implying more favorable self-feelings, the individual is more likely to permit self-perceptions of personal traits, behaviors, and experiences.

Data from panel studies, the experimental literature, and cross-sectional analyses suggest that individuals with self-rejecting feelings tend to deny culpability for disvalued attributes, as well as any other threats to their self-esteem. The influence of degree of self-rejecting feelings on self-protective attitudes appears to be confirmed by relationships observed by Kaplan (1980) in a panel study of junior high school students. Increasingly greater levels of self-derogation, at an earlier point in time, were apparently related to the adoption of responses that reflect the individual's self-perceptions of being victims of forces beyond his control. Considering only subjects who had denied each of several self-justifying statements in the eighth grade, it was observed that seventh-grade students with higher levels of self-derogation were significantly more likely than those with lower levels of self-derogation to affirm in the ninth grade, for example, that it was mostly luck if one succeeded or failed, that they would do better if society did not have the cards stacked against them, that their families could not give them the chance to succeed that most kids had, that when they did something wrong it was almost as if someone else were doing it, that the law is against the ordinary guy, that people often talked about them behind their backs, that they were unfairly punished as children, and that people frequently put them down because their families were poor or because of their religion. Self-rejecting feelings at an earlier point in time also anticipated responses indicative of avoidance of self-perceptions of environmental demands at a later point in time. The tendency to deny the reality of obligations applicable to them is reflected in the observed tendency of increasingly more self-rejecting persons in the seventh grade to affirm in the ninth grade (after denying at an intermediate time) that they sometimes wish they were little kids again, that they would like to travel with a circus or carnival, and that they spend a lot of time daydreaming.

Wicklund (1975) concluded that

> finally, there are two possible reactions to self-focused attention to the initial reaction of self-evaluation. The first is of the nature of an avoidance or approach response. If the discrepancy in focus is positive, the person will welcome stimuli that bring on the objective state, and will tend to seek out self-focusing circumstances. If the salient discrepancy is negative, there will be an active avoidance of such stimuli, including efforts to create distractions. Further, and only in the case of negative discrepancies, an inescapable self-awareness will result in attempted discrepancy reduction. (p. 238)

Using cross-sectional data, Washburn (1962) observed that negative self-feelings are associated with the use of retreating defenses, marked by the avoidance of coming to grips with problems or by the denial of reality, as these were indicated by a Reality Rejection Subtest reflecting the attempt to detach one's self from potentially threatening situations by refusing to accept and face existing circumstances. Retreating defenses included suppression, regression, withdrawal, and negativism. The influence of self-protective–self-enhancing motivation on self-cognition is also reflected in the association of negative self-feelings with hostile defenses (marked by critical, suspicious behavior and lack of identification with others). Hostile defenses were indicated by a Self-

Other Distortion Subtest and reflected both exaggeration of threats in the external environment and the use of symptoms of physical illness to excuse the person's behavior. Among the hostile defenses are projection, displacement of hostility, substitution, and conversion.

Generally, negative affect–negative self-esteem, anger, depression, anxiety, and interpersonal sensitivity—is associated with the use of defense-like responses, defined as behavior intended to change perceptions of the fit between personal behavior and environmental demands. In another study, indices of defense-like behavior included responses that, in my terms, involve cognitive distortion of reality (trying to forget failure, avoidance of situations in which one might perceive negatively-valued responses, interpreting experiences as beyond one's control) and changes in the personal value system (expressions of dissatisfaction with the system of evaluation and the evaluative process, and reducing level of aspirations) (Caplan, Naidu, & Tripathi, 1984). Similar results were found in other studies (Felton et al., 1984; Billings & Moos, 1981; Pearlin & Schooler, 1978).

These tendencies appear to be exacerbated in circumstances in which the negative self-feelings are more intense, that is, in which the threatened self-value is very important to the individual. Strong support for the proposition that self-feelings motivate the individual to distort self-referent cognitions, particularly with regard to attributing responsibility for positive outcomes to one's own efforts, is provided by the results of a study in which ego involvement was varied (Miller, 1976). Following administration of a test on social perceptiveness, the subjects were instructed either that the test was valid and correlated positively with desirable characteristics (high ego involvement condition) or that it was not validated (low ego involvement condition). The subject was later informed that he had performed either well or poorly. In general, successful outcomes were attributed by the subject to internal factors (effort, ability) and unsuccessful outcomes were attributed more to external factors (luck). For present purposes, however, the most significant feature of the study was that these self-protective–self-enhancing tendencies were greater under conditions of high rather than low ego involvement. Under conditions of high ego involvement, subjects who were informed that they did poorly on the task were more likely to attribute their failure to bad luck and were less likely to attribute it to low ability and effort than low-involvement subjects who were informed that they did poorly on the task. Subjects who believed that they did well on the task under high-involvement conditions were more likely to attribute their performance to personal ability than under the low-involvement condition. As noted, however, it should be recognized that such findings may reflect a tendency to present oneself favorably rather than a change in self-cognition. Bradley (1978) notes, "while an individual may publicly deny responsibility for his own negative outcomes, we do not know whether he also privately denies such responsibility; that is, we do not know whether his public and private self-attribution correspond" (p. 67).

The influence of threats to salient self-values is also reflected in studies of achievement motivation in which, under conditions of a strong need to avoid failure, individuals will structure the situation in ways that will permit them to ignore their self-awareness of their own ability. According to Arkin (1981),

> it has been axiomatic in social psychology that people are eager to receive accurate and reliable information concerning their capacity to act on the environment. However, within the context of achievement motivation, it has been shown that this is only true of persons high in need achievement; by contrast, persons high in test anxiety (fear of failure) prefer tasks *low* in diagnostic informational value concerning their ability (e.g., very easy and very difficult tasks, and tasks with very low population variance). (p. 321)

Conversely, under conditions in which the threat to salient self-values is not apparent, the person appears to be open to and, indeed, prefers to perceive himself veridically. This conclusion is consistent with findings from a number of studies. In these studies, discussed by Wicklund (1982), individuals who learned they were attractive to the opposite sex (Gibbons & Wicklund, 1976) or who were asked to engage in behaviors that were in conformity to their own opinions on women's rights (Greenberg & Musham, 1981), respectively, tended to express a preference for hearing their own voice as opposed to the voice of another male and to choose to sit before a mirror rather than away from a mirror. Of course, these findings also permit the conclusion that, rather than reflecting a condition of permitting realistic self-perceptions, these outcomes merely reflect self-approving responses to self-perceptions of desirable characteristics.

A second set of studies involves the relationship between self-feelings and the *distortion* of self-perceptions *in a favorable direction*. Generally, the research literature suggests that there is a prevalent tendency toward a self-favorability bias, a direct relationship between positive self-feelings and the self-favorability bias (particularly under conditions implying perceptual ambiguity), but a direct relationship between situationally induced threats to self-values, reflected in negative self-feelings, and self-perceptual distortions in a favorable direction.

In general, a given population will overwhelmingly tend to endorse socially desirable self-descriptions and deny socially disvalued self-descriptions. As Wylie (1979) notes,

> unless the need to maintain a favorable self-concept . . . is counteracted by some other typically rarer or weaker need (e.g., the need to reduce purely cognitive dissonance, or the need to expiate guilt through self-punishment, or the need to use self-denigration to avoid threatening an important other person), one would expect the need for self-enhancement to lead to a favorability bias in the self-concept and the corresponding self-reports. Thus a trend toward self-favorability would be expected to hold true for groups of persons. (p. 665)

For example, Bachman and his associates (1978) reported that

> most people tend to think of themselves as better than average, rather than below average. In fact, over 80% of our 1966 respondents rated themselves as better than average in school ability. In the absence of an "average point" on the response scale, the great majority with near average ability chose to rate themselves as being slightly above average. (p. 45)

The normal tendency is for individuals characterized by more positive self-feelings to distort self-perceptions in a self-favorable direction.

Several studies report that positive self-attitudes are related to such measures of defensiveness as the K scale of the MMPI (Wylie, 1974)—said to indicate a disposition to deny, among other things, feelings of inferiority *and to look at others and oneself through rose-tinted glasses* (Marks & Seeman, 1963). Lewinsohn and Mischel (1980), cited by Gecas (1982), consistent with these studies, observed that normal control group subjects were more likely to engage in self-enhancing distortions then were clinically depressed patients, who are more realistic in self-perception as measured by the compatibility between self-ratings and observer ratings on a variety of social competencies. Felson (1981) reported a study in which college football players evaluated themselves on seven types of athletic ability. Further, coaches rated their players on the same abilities and, in addition, on how much self-confidence the players had. Some of the attributes in question were more ambiguous than others. Whether a player has speed, size, and strength was less ambiguous than ratings of "mental toughness," "quick reactions," or "football sense." It was hypothesized and observed that players' self-confidence would be a better predictor of self-ratings for the ambiguous abilities than the unambiguous abilities. Data reported by Bohrnstedt and Felson (1983) suggest that individuals who are higher in self-esteem were more likely to perceive themselves as well-liked, whatever their actual sociometric status, which suggests that individuals need to perceive themselves positively in terms of traits that are for them salient features of self-evaluation. Since this distortion was observed for being liked but not for athletic ability or academic ability, it might be presumed that the capability for distorting self-perceptions depends on the degree to which possession of the attributes in question are verifiable. Possibly it is easier to verify academic and athletic ability than popularity.

The relationship between positive self-feelings and the bias toward favorable self-perceptions may not reflect a causal process whereby favorable self-feelings influence the favorable self-perceptions. It may be the case that the ability to distort self-perceptions in a favorable direction is a prerequisite to the experience of positive self-feelings. This interpretation of the findings might account for the apparently paradoxical circumstance whereby, in the studies cited immediately above, subjects with more favorable self-attitudes are more likely to manifest favorable self-distortions, and, in other studies (discussed earlier), the more self-rejecting subjects are more likely to display tendencies toward defensive distortion. Perhaps the former studies reflect a causal process whereby self-deception permits the person to maintain positive self-feelings, whereas the latter studies reflect exacerbation of the *need* (indicated by negative self-feelings) to restore positive self-feeling and the consequent defensively distorted self-perceiving responses.

Consistent with the hypothesized effect of self-rejecting feelings on the tendency to distort self-perceptions in a favorable direction are observations of reconceptualization of self in terms of favorable ego-extensions and defensive attributional processes, *under conditions suggesting ego-threat*. Thus, the tendency to bask in reflected glory (e.g., to conceive of one's self as associated with a winning athletic team) was more pronounced following an experimentally induced failure (failing a "knowledge of campus events" test) (Cialdini, Borden, Thorne, Walker, Freeman, & Sloane, 1976).

Alternative evaluations and interpretations of the relevant literature notwithstanding (Miller & Ross, 1975), a number of studies may be cited that are compatible with the notion that individuals perceive themselves as having greater responsibility for success than for failure in response to a personal need to experience positive self-feelings. Bradley (1978) examines such studies and also considers data apparently inconsistent with the idea of defensive attributional processes in terms of a "broadened self-serving bias formulation" (p. 57). In one type of study that bears on the hypothesis of motivational bases for the attribution process, subjects are instructed to deliver therapeutic instructions that are expected to produce more or less positive effects or changes in the patient's condition (e.g., a minor phobia). In one particularly interesting study following such a paradigm, Federoff and Harvey (1976) varied the influence of (1) objective self-awareness, presumed to stimulate self-evaluation processes (Duval & Wicklund, 1972), and (2) expected and observed (more or less negative) therapeutic outcomes on causal attributions. The presence or absence of a camera serves to indicate conditions of high or low objective self-awareness. The investigators observed that, under conditions of high objective self-awareness (presumably stimulating the need for positive self-feelings), the individuals attributed the outcomes to their own efforts more for positive than for negative observed therapeutic outcomes. Under conditions of low objective self-awareness, however, self-attributions did not vary with either expected or observed outcomes.

Summarizing the results of this investigation and other studies, Bradley (1978) concluded that these studies

> all provided results consistent with the proposition that under certain conditions, people do make self-serving attributions. In general, these investigations indicated that when concerns for self-esteem were likely to be aroused (e.g., public performance, high perceived choice, unexpected negative outcomes), individuals tended to accept responsibility for positive outcomes and, *when possible,* to deny responsibility for negative outcomes. . . . It seems unlikely . . . that prior experiences, expectations, or the perceived covariation between response and outcome could account for the pattern of results provided by these . . . studies. (pp. 59–60)

Again, it is unclear as to whether the self-serving attributions reflect self-referent cognitive distortion or self-presentational strategies in response to threats to self-esteem (i.e., to negative self-feelings).

A third group of studies report findings that are relevant to the *sensitivity* of subjects to self-threatening communications. Generally, the normal response of individuals is to be aware of those aspects of self that constitute important self-evaluative criteria. Individuals who are chronically self-rejecting, however, tend to perceive themselves as more vulnerable to ego-threat and are more likely to be sensitive to an even broader range of potential threats to self-evaluation.

Individuals tend to perceive those aspects of themselves that are most relevant to self-evaluation. The sensitivity to selective aspects of self may be reflected in the individual's spontaneous self-descriptions. Women are more likely to mention marital status and parenthood status as well as household work, in spontaneous self-descriptions (Mackie, 1983). Men, however, are more likely to mention work-related characteristics. Rand and Hall (1983) focus on the evaluative significance of attractiveness for females as opposed to males in our culture in interpreting their findings that the positive correlations between self-ratings and judges' ratings of the subjects' photograph with regard to attractiveness was significant only for the female subjects. This would suggest that either females were less likely to distort their self-perceptions than males with regard to physical attractiveness (a conclusion that does not fit perceptions of the significance of physical attractiveness to females in our culture) or that females were perhaps more sensitive to the significance of physical attractiveness and, hence, were likely to be aware of their objective status with regard to physical attractiveness. These authors state,

> We believe that our findings reflect the differential significance of physical appearance in the lives of men and women. . . .
> Women in our culture probably learn early to take stock of the strengths and weaknesses of their appearance up to established standards . . ... Constant awareness and practice, therefore, may make women more accurate judges of their own physical attractiveness than men.
> Men's self-assessments of attractiveness may be less accurate because the stereotype does not put as much emphasis on male attractiveness as on female. (p. 362)

Apparently, under normal conditions (that generally imply accepting self-feelings), the person will be attuned to aspects of himself and the environment that are particularly relevant to self-evaluation. However, more self-rejecting individuals tend to be more broadly sensitive to a range of potentially threatening stimuli. Thus, Rosenberg (1965) reports that low self-esteem subjects are more likely to score high on a "sensitivity to criticism" scale and are more likely to be described by others as "touchy and easily hurt."

Self-rejecting subjects tend to deny more specific bases of self-devaluation but also generalize their self-disaffection. Tippett and Silber (1966) report findings from a study of college students in which subjects were exposed to fictitious research staff evaluations involving the alteration of subject self-ratings on selected items in a "less favorable but plausible direction." Those students who were evaluated as having *high self-esteem*, less psychopathology, and more autonomous behavior with parents tended to change in the direction of the fictitious unfavorable ratings *more* than the subjects assessed as having *low* self-esteem, more psychopathology, and oppositional behavior with parents. The latter subjects were said to be less open to influence—a resistance apparently "based more on negativism than on considered reflection" (p. 384) (Tippett & Silber, 1966). This is consistent with the findings reported earlier in which more self-rejecting subjects were more likely to deny or avoid highly self-devaluing circumstances. However, here, the low self-esteem subjects tended to change more in an unfavorable direction on the *unaltered* items. As Tippett and Silber (1966) speculate: "It is as though being challenged in one area leads to a more generalized disturbance in their function of self-evaluation" (p. 384).

It appears, then, that self-rejecting feelings stimulate self-protective responses in the form of a broad sensitivity to potential threats to self-evaluation, in addition to responses in the form of denial of self-devaluing experiences and self-cognitions of positive qualities.

Self-protective responses, as noted, may directly affect self-referent cognitions by permitting individuals to deny or distort perceptions about themselves. Self-protective responses may influence self-cognition also in less direct ways. Self-protective–self-enhancing responses may influence the individual's attributes, behaviors, and experiences that become the basis for self-cognition. That is, the person, for example, exercises in order to build up his muscles and so perceives himself as having muscles. Or, the individual may orchestrate the kinds of experiences he has that more or less permit him to perceive himself in certain ways. That is, they may behave in ways that increase or decrease the amount of interaction they have with others, they may purposely elicit other people's opinions about themselves, and so forth. By so behaving, they influence the kinds of cues that stimulate self-referent cognitive responses. The self-protective–self-enhancing functions of changes in person attributes, behaviors, and experiences is suggested by, for example, Shrauger and Schoeneman (1979):

> If, for instance, an individual were evaluated as being self-centered but didn't like that attribute, he or she might expend a special effort to be more altruistic and accordingly to strengthen this perception of altruism. It has been shown that when subjects are told that they are making shorter or slower responses than those of other individuals they lengthen and speed up their subsequent responses (Burnstein & Zajonc, 1965; Kleinke, 1975). (p. 568)

In extreme forms, self-protective patterns that involve distortion in self-cognition achieve deviant proportions. Thus, Fitts (1981) observes that

> People who are suffering with paranoid schizophrenia or extreme manic states often report the most positive self-concepts of anyone. However, the measures of defensiveness, apart from their other deviant behavior, usually suggests that their grandiose level of self-perception is unreal and defensively distorted. (pp. 266–267)

In support of this conclusion is Fitt's (1981) study of graduate students:

> Self-concept measures at the beginning and end of the year first seem to indicate substantial gains in self-esteem. They had weathered a year of

stress, demonstrated their competence, and elevated their self-regard. Closer inspection, however, indicated that these were artificial gains which in turn were clouded over and apparently accounted for by marked increases in defensiveness. Subjective exploration of this phenomenon led us to conclude that the extremely stressful year, characterized by inordinate work demands, cutthroat competition, and strife within the faculty, have simply made the students more paranoid. (p. 267)

Frequently, favorable self-cognitions can only be achieved by pro-scribed patterns, such as substance abuse. The use of chemical sub-stances to permit favorable self-cognition is suggested by findings re-ported by Berg (1971). These results were interpretable as indicating that, for alcoholic subjects, intoxication represents a favored technique for enhancing self-esteem or defending against self-rejection. Five days after being given tests by which self-attitudes were measured, male subjects who were psychiatrically diagnosed as alcoholic and were resi-dent in the alcoholism unit of a psychiatric hospital for at least two weeks submitted to an intoxication procedure during which they drank a mixture of rye whiskey and orange juice. Following this, the self-attitude tests were again administered. The comparison of the self-at-titude scores in the sober and intoxicated condition revealed that "when intoxicated the alcoholic showed more favorable and less derogatory self-concepts than when sober" (p. 448) (Berg, 1971). However, the self-enhancing effects held only for those who had a history of heavy drink-ing and a dependence on alcohol. When similar procedures were used for a group of social drinkers, intoxication was observed to have an *adverse* effect on self-attitudes.

The favorable effect on self-cognition of alcohol abuse may also be inferred by observing the effects of withdrawal. Data gathered from male members of Alcoholics Anonymous (AA) revealed a gradual de-crease in self-cathexis scores for subjects reporting sobriety (White and Gaier, 1965).Similarly, White and Porter (1966) reported, for hospi-talized male alcoholics participating in the AA Program at a state hospi-tal, a negative correlation between length of time sober and an index of favorability of self-concepts, and a positive correlation between sobriety interval and responses interpreted as indicating self-defeat, guilt, and fear.

Need-Value System. Self-protective–self-enhancing responses that are stimulated by self-feelings frequently take the form of reordering the system of self-values and interpersonal affiliations that comprise the bases for self-evaluative responses. One of the modal patterns in which these self-protective–self-enhancing responses are manifested is the se-lection of, assignment of higher priority to, or the attraction to new self-values that the person uses to evaluate his worth. More self-rejecting subjects are more highly motivated to change their evaluative standards in directions that will permit themselves to judge themselves more favorably.

Consistent with the expectation that negative self-feelings would lead to changes in the personal value system are the results of a number of studies reported by Rokeach (1983). The basic paradigm for all these studies involves the arousal of a state of self-dissatisfaction by providing experimental subjects with feedback intended to increase self-awareness about their own and others' values and how these values are related to specified attitudes and behaviors. In nine experimental studies, Rokeach asked respondents to indicate, following experimental feedback of information about their own and others' values, attitudes, and behaviors, whether they were satisfied or dissatisfied with the rankings on values that they had given prior to the treatment.

> Without exception, all nine studies showed larger, statistically significant value changes, measured weeks and months subsequent to treatment, among those who were "dissatisfied" than among those "satisfied" with their rankings given to target values. (p. 184)

The adoption of new values as a self-protective–self-enhancing response to self-rejecting feelings is suggested also by the following relationships observed in a longitudinal study of junior high school students (Kaplan, 1980). Considering only subjects who denied in the eighth grade that specified talents were important, self-rejecting feelings at an earlier point in time were associated with later affirmation of the importance of the talent. Among subjects who denied in the eighth grade that these talents were important, subjects with increasingly greater levels of self-derogation in the seventh grade were increasingly likely to report in the ninth grade that they thought it was important to be good at drawing or painting, to get good grades, and to be good at sports. These relationships are consistent with the interpretation that people with a greater need for positive self-feelings will be more likely to adopt new values that offer greater promise of self-enhancement, either because their values may more easily be approximated by the person or because there is an increased likelihood of evoking positive responses from those who endorse the values. Thus, for his adolescent subjects, Rosenberg (1965) found that those subjects who perceive themselves as possessing specific qualities were more likely to value those qualities than those who perceive themselves as not possessing the qualities. Self-values were selected in a way that permitted the individual to evaluate himself positively.

Further support for the proposition that the stimulation of the need for positive self-feelings leads to self-protective–self-enhancing responses, including those relating to the reconceptualization of one's personal value system, is provided by a study in which college students who were given false feedback as having a low level of "latent creativity" were compared with a control group. Subjects in the failure condition tended to rate their own university higher and to downgrade a rival university to a greater extent than the subjects in the control group (Cialdini & Richardson, 1980). Although these data permit alternative interpretations, they are also consistent with the notion that exacerbation of the need for positive self-feelings leads the individual to revise his personal value system in ways that permit him to experience more positive self-judgments (in this case, as being associated with a more highly valued educational institution). The tendency to upgrade one's own institution and to downgrade a rival institution was a function of the degree to which one might presume the experience of negative self-feelings. Subjects rated their home university most positively following feedback of being low in creativity, somewhat less positively after receiving feedback of being average in creativity, and least positively following the no-feedback condition. Similarly, subjects rated the rival university most negatively following the failure condition, less negatively following the feedback of being average on the trait, and least negatively following the no-feedback condition.

The selection of favorable standards for self-evaluation may be reflected also in downward comparison processes. The frequently observed effect whereby individuals who are derogated, derogate other persons who are unrelated to their own devaluing experiences (Wills, 1981) suggests that individuals in ego-threatening circumstances selectively evaluate themselves according to standards that permit positive self-judgments. Thus, studies of the relationship between self-esteem and prejudicial attitudes (Ehrlich, 1973; Stephan & Rosenfield, 1978) suggest that negative self-feelings leads to the rejection of others, a finding that is interpretable in terms of the selective self-evaluation of individuals by standards that would increase the positive nature of self-evaluations. Presumably, the selection of evaluative standards relating to race or ethnicity permit the otherwise self-derogating individual to evaluate himself positively by current standards regarding evaluation of race and ethnicity. Also consistent with this interpretation are observations that individuals who are themselves lower in the prestige scale of society tend to compare themselves with those who have even lower ranking in the scale. Wills (1981) notes that the persistent finding of prejudice among persons of lower social status continues to be replicated in current literature (Smedley & Bayton, 1978; Taylor, Sheatsley, & Greeley, 1978; Brewer & Campbell, 1976).

The literature on projection (Holmes, 1978) whereby individuals under conditions of ego-threat attribute unfavorable personality characteristics to others is also interpretable in terms of reevaluation of personal characteristics. By attributing undesirable characteristics to others, the person perceives the attributed characteristics as new standards against which he evaluates his own more desirable personal characteristics.

In general, then, individuals will select for purposes of self-evaluation standards that permit them to evaluate themselves more positively, particularly when their need for positive self-feelings has been aroused. As Arkin (1981) comments on the relevant literature,

> Wilson and Benner (1971) found considerable "defensive avoidance" of comparison with the highest ranking other when the comparison was explicitly public, presumably so that subjects could avoid appearing inferior. *Defensive social comparison was greater among low self-esteem males, especially those relatively more certain of their actual inferiority.* Likewise, Friend and Gilbert (1973) found that persons persuaded of their inadequacy were less likely to compare with the best-off other, more likely to compare with worse-off others, and that these tendencies were most prominent for persons scoring high in fear of negative evaluation. (p. 327, italics added)

In view of the foregoing comments, it would not be surprising to see individuals with characteristic self-rejecting feelings, or who feel momentarily threatened, to create situations that would permit them to affiliate with individuals who have been characterized in terms of unfavorable characteristics relative to the person. Such situations would permit the person to perceive himself as relatively more highly placed according to an evaluative dimension.

Since the self-values an individual uses to value himself include his relative standings in a group along a number of dimensions, it is to be expected that the person who experiences self-rejecting feelings will be motivated to orient himself to groups in which he will be able to evaluate himself relatively more favorably. Such groups are those that appear to have the same disvalued experiences as the person's. Thus, under conditions of negative self-feelings, people affiliate with others who share a common threat. In effect, the individual is adopting standards to which he can accommodate without suffering from comparison with those who share the same expectations. The ego-threatening situation becomes the norm. Rather than having to devalue himself, the individual is able to judge himself to be quite normal with regard to his attributes, behaviors, or aversive experiences. This tendency to affiliate under threatening conditions has been well documented (Cottrell & Epley,

1977). For example, in one study, subjects who were relatively depressed compared with those who were relatively happy were more likely to indicate a preference for working with a person who is in an unhappy mood rather than one who is in a neutral or happy mood (Bell, 1978).

This process was used earlier to account for a number of seemingly paradoxical observations in the attitude-change literature. These observations refer, in particular, to the inverse relationship between conditions of stress, self-rejection, or deviant status, on the one hand, and persuasibility by low credibility communicators, on the other hand.

Helmreich (1972) notes that a general finding of stress research has been that high stress influences increases in dependency needs and in reliance on authority figures. In view of this, it was hypothesized that the influence of the credibility of the communicator would be increased by external threat. However, results in the program of study were consistently different from this hypothesized outcome. The normal pattern of credibility effects observed under low stress is either eliminated or reversed under high stress. In one study, Navy recruits under conditions of high stress (anticipating tear gas) were more influenced by the same communication when it was believed to come from a student or a fellow recruit than when it was believed to come from an admiral. Similarly, college students awaiting electric shock were more influenced by a communication about drugs when the speaker was thought to be postal clerk than when he was thought to be a distinguished researcher in the field of drug effects. In contrast, under a low stress condition, the scientist produced more attitude change than the postal clerk. In yet another study, a videotaped message on the effects of television violence produced more attitude change when the speaker was thought to be a media expert than when the identical message was thought to come from a fellow student. Under high stress, however, the peer was more influential.

In related studies of social comparison processes, an increased desire to associate with similar peers under conditions of high threat was reported, and subjects who were induced to feel deviant from their peers were more influenced by communication from a peer than from a more authoritative source (Helmreich, 1972).

Helmreich finds these results understandable if one proceeds from the central assumption that psychologically stressful situations threaten a person's self-esteem. The feelings of low self-esteem motivate the individual to behave in ways that will restore his self-esteem. Thus,

> the individual with low self-esteem counts on others to provide him with normative data on the correct and acceptable response to novel situations

and ideas. The individual whose self-esteem is temporarily lowered by situational factors is likely to perceive himself as different or deviant from his peers and should be highly motivated to enhance his self-concept, to return to his normal state of perceived competence. Indeed, the individual who has received a temporary blow to his self-esteem should be much more strongly motivated to gain a sense of acceptance and normality than the person with chronic feelings of unworthiness. This desire to restore self-esteem should be reflected in strong needs for social comparison with peers who can provide information on normative behavior and attitudes. (p. 41)

The most appropriate models for social comparison would be people who are akin to the person in emotional state or ability, that is, that person's peers. Under conditions of lowered self-esteem, Helmreich (1972) notes that

the individual's need to minimize his perceived noncomparability with or deviation from others of "normal" or average competence should cause him to see the "normative" response as being that of a peer or other low status individual. Agreeing with a peer may bolster the self-concept by decreasing feelings of difference and augmenting feelings of being part of a "normal" group. (p. 41)

To agree with an authority, however, is not relevant to the person's need to appear typical. In fact, feelings of being different may be accentuated if the authority is seen as holding views that differ from the views of the peer reference group. Under conditions of lowered self-esteem, "even an authority towards whom one displays greater dependency may be a less potent referent for determination of attitudes than a peer or status equal who can define a 'normative' response" (p. 41) (Helmreich, 1972). It is likely that a person will resolve a conflict between loyalty to the group and loyalty to the leader in favor of the former.

The self-enhancing consequences of affiliating with others who share the person's fate may account for the observation that, although people who are devalued tend to derogate others under individual circumstances, when the individual as a member of a group is derogated, the derogation of others is not apparent (Wills, 1981). Perhaps under conditions of shared devaluation, the individual is permitted to redefine personal standards and define himself as approximating those standards relative to the achievements of the other group members. When individuals share a common fate, to recognize the sameness of one's achievements or failures is to define one's self as having performed according to group standards.

Just as negative self-feelings stimulate the selection of values or affiliations that serve as standards for favorable self-evaluations, so do distressful self-feelings lead to the rejection of standards and affiliations by which one necessarily devalues oneself. One manifestation of this is a lowering of aspirations. When a person has failed to achieve personally valued attributes or to approximate a personally accepted standard of performance, he may be expected to lower his aspirations and thus increase the probability of subjectively defined success and decrease the probability of self-reproach at failure to attain the earlier (higher) standards.

Longitudinal data from a panel study of junior high school students (Kaplan, 1980) strongly support the idea that individuals characterized by negative self-feelings would subsequently revise their expectations downward. The tendency for more highly self-derogating subjects in the seventh grade to revise their expectations of themselves downward (presumably to forestall occasions for self-devaluation) by the ninth grade was reflected in the observation that subjects having increasingly greater levels of self-derogation in the seventh grade were increasingly likely, two years later, to agree that they expected too much of themselves, doubt that they would get ahead in life as far as they would like, and say that if they could not get what they wanted they would try for something just as good, which was easier to get. Only subjects who disagreed with these statements during an intervening time (eighth grade) were included in the analyses. Thus, it is unlikely that the relationship is spuriously accounted for by seventh-grade levels of aspiration.

A similar process appears to be operating in another study (Kiesler & Baral, 1970), where it was reported that low self-esteem subjects acted more romantically toward a moderately attractive confederate than toward a more attractive one, whereas high self-esteem subjects behaved more romantically toward the very attractive confederate than toward the moderately attractive one. Cross-sectional survey results regarding the positive relationship between low self-feelings and lowered level of aspirations are suggested by Rosenberg's findings (1965) that adolescents with lower self-esteem were more likely to report lower expectations of success in work, getting ahead in life, being as successful as most people seem to be, or going into the business or profession they would most like as a life career.

More directly, individuals may derogate the self-evaluative standards by which they were judged wanting. Such an effect is apparent in experimental situation in which subjects were variously belittled or praised for their past performance. In response to the embarrassment presumed to be associated with belittlement by the group leader, subjects were observed to offer excuses for bad performance, to deny failure, *to devalue the task* (Modigliani, 1971), or to change behavioral preferences (Ludwig & Maehr, 1967). An interesting illustration of the derogation of a standard is provided in Gergen's (1981) discussion of the individual's ability to reject the views of others toward the self:

> One may avoid groups whose rules of meaning operate to one's disadvantage, or may attempt to change those rules. This latter choice has been made by those labelled sexually "queer" by mainstream society. In recent times such persons have banded together to redefine the character of their activities with an attempt to change the typical structure of meaning more common in society. They have developed a "homophobic" label to derogate those whose rules of meaning are repugnant to them, and remove homosexuality from the traditional nosology of character disorders. (p. 70)

Among the self-values of the individual are acceptance by specific individuals and groups. It is to be expected, then, that self-rejecting feelings would influence attitudes toward these others as well. Consistent with the view that individuals adopt evaluative standards by which they would be approved, Dittes (1959) observed that, to the extent that individuals were low in self-esteem, subjects showed more liking for group members who they were led to believe had positive attitudes toward them and a greater disliking for those who they were led to believe had rejected them. Similar results were obtained by others (Walster, 1965). These findings are compatible with the reasoning that people who are lowest in self-esteem will most need approval from others and will feel more threatened by disapproval from others. If differential attitudes toward the subject on the part of others are not clear, then the tendency of high self-esteem subjects to presume acceptance and the tendency of low self-esteem subjects to presume rejection by others would determine the person's responses to the others. However, where it was reasonably clear that others like or dislike the person, the person (particularly the low self-esteem person) would respond in kind (Berscheid & Walster, 1969).

Also relevant to the rejection of others' attitudes as standards for self-evaluation when the subject is found wanting by those standards, is Rosenberg's (1979) conclusion, from his data that

> the more the other person cirticizes or disapproves of him, the more will the individual try to shrug it off, discount their judgement, withdraw affect from them. Although he will not be entirely successful, the inclination is there. In the long run, then, he is likely to end up caring most about the opinions of those who, in his view, think well of him. (p. 90)

Further, Rosenberg notes that there is a tendency, through the mechanism of "selective credulity," to have "stronger faith in the judgments of those who appreciate our merits than in those more alert to our shortcomings."

Data from the longitudinal study (Kaplan, 1980) referred to earlier confirm these conclusions. Adolescents who, at an earlier point in time, had more negative self-feelings were more likely, later, to indicate devaluation of specific groups or, generally, other people who may be presumed to be implicated in the genesis of the person's negative self-feelings. Controlling on evaluation of others at an intermediate point in time (eighth grade), adolescents who in the seventh grade manifested more self-rejecting feelings were more likely in the ninth grade to indicate that they had disobeyed their parents, that they would respond to insults by thinking, "Who cares what he thinks," that they did not care much about other people's feelings, and that their experiences outside the home made them wonder whether their parents' ideas were right. Again, controlling on responses to the items at an intervening point in time, seventh-grade subjects who had more negative self-feelings were more likely in the ninth grade to deny that what their parents thought of them was important and that being kind to others was important (after stating in the eighth grade that what their parents thought of them was important and that being kind to others was important). Further, considering only those subjects who affirmed in the eighth grade that most of their close friends were also friends with each other, persons with increasingly greater levels of self-rejecting feelings in the seventh grade were increasingly likely to deny in the ninth grade that most of their close friends were also friends with each other. This indicates a change in interpersonal peer networks.

Changes in value systems and interpersonal networks frequently reflect deviation from conventional norms. The results of a study by Graf (1971) were compatible with the hypothesis that self-rejecting feelings lead to self-protective–self-enhancing responses reflected in revision of the personal value system. Through the use of false feedback of personality test scores to subjects, experimental induction of various self-esteem levels was accomplished. Dishonest behavior, defined in terms of whether the subject kept a dollar bill left on the floor near the door of the testing room following completion of the feedback of the positive, negative, or neutral personality descriptions, were significantly more likely to follow the low self-esteem induction. Although various interpretations are possible, the results are compatible with the interpretation that the dishonest behavior reflected a distancing from the conventional value system in terms of which the person must find himself wanting (insofar as the person believed he had undesirable test scores).

The relationship between self-rejecting feelings and the adoption of self-protective–self-enhancing patterns reflecting changes in the personal value system are apparent in data from the longitudinal study of junior high school students cited above (Kaplan, 1980). Individuals who displayed more self-rejecting feelings in the seventh grade were more likely to show high scores in the eighth grade on a measure of tendency to devalue the normative structure and to value contranormative patterns as potential sources of gratification, controlling for scores on these measures in the seventh grade. Other findings suggest that observed changes in interpersonal peer networks may involve gravitation toward more deviant value systems. Thus, seventh-graders with more negative self-feelings were increasingly likely to report in the ninth grade that many of their good friends smoked marijuana, that many of their good friends took narcotic drugs, and that most of their close friends were the kind of kids who got into trouble a lot. Since only students who denied these responses in the eighth grade were considered, the relationship between earlier self-rejection and later affiliation with deviant others could not be accounted for by their common relationship with earlier deviant affiliations.

The deviant manifestations of revised value systems toward self-enhancing goals are reflected also in changing self-values relating to economic, political, and religious institutions. The shifting of self-evaluative frames of reference as a self-protective response to negative self-feelings is nicely illustrated with reference to political affiliations. Della Fave (1980) argues that radical parties perform the vital function of raising self-evaluations of the disadvantaged:

> Marxist parties, for example, do this by promulgating the idea that the working class has a pivotal role in history, no less than that of ending oppression itself. The party can also make itself a powerful source of positive self-evaluation by actually being successful in wringing concession from the system. (p. 966)

The tendency of individuals with negative self-feelings to attack the value systems by which they would necessarily be judged to be wanting is reflected also in the observation that adolescents with low self-esteem were more likely to be disposed toward political protest activities than to adopt more conforming or conservative stances (Carmines, 1978).

Consistent with the expectation that negative self-feelings lead individuals to revise personal value systems are conjectures regarding the role of a search for identity (Klapp, 1969) or a need for a sense of personal worth and dignity (Turner, 1969, 1976). Zurcher and Snow (1981) comment that

> symptomatic of this theme is alienation from self and a corresponding search for a more satisfactory locus or base for reconstituting the self. Accordingly, participants in such movements as Hare Krishna, the Children of God, and the National Organization of Women are, hypothetically, individuals whose

experiences in the various institutional domains of life have not provided a sense of personal worth or dignity. They are thus seeking a new locus for identity, one that provides a sense of personal worth in a more satisfactory basis for organizing life. (pp. 450–451)

Such conclusions are compatible with earlier research findings. For example, a study of motivation to join charismatic religious groups is clearly relevant to the hypothesis that self-rejecting feelings lead to self-protective–self-enhancing responses reflected in the affiliation with new value systems (Freemesser & Kaplan, 1976). Individuals who join charismatic religious groups were expected to be motivated by an experience of negative self-attitudes and to have enjoyed salutary effects on level of self-esteem as a result of joining the groups. It was expected that joining charismatic religious groups would give such individuals the opportunity to avoid and attack the worthiness of the conventional value systems by the standards of which they were found wanting. At the same time, the religious groups would offer new evaluative standards, the approximation of which would permit favorable self-cognitions, self-evaluations, and self-feelings. The hypotheses were supported. Members of the charismatic religious communities, relative to comparison subjects, reported higher levels of self-derogation at the time they accepted membership in the charismatic group. Individuals who adopted membership in the charismatic cult displayed a significantly greater tendency to decrease the level of recalled self-rejection between the earlier point in time and the point in time at which they were interviewed. Thus, at the time of the interview, in this cross-sectional study, the charismatic and comparison groups had comparable levels of self-derogation.

Approximating Self-Values. In addition to forestalling self-devaluation and enhancing self-esteem through revision of self-referent cognitive responses and the personal need-value system, the person fulfills self-protective–self-enhancing objectives by attaining the attributes, performing the behaviors, and attracting the experiences that indicate approximation to self-values. Generally positive self-feelings *reinforce* the subject's earlier behaviors toward the goal of approximating self-values. Negative self-feelings stemming from self-recognition and self-evaluation lead to *increased* efforts to approximate the self-values, avoidance of circumstances that increase the likelihood of failure to do so, adopting response patterns that compensate for other failures to attain conventional self-values, attempts to adapt to conventional values through deviant means, or attempts to achieve newly adapted deviant values.

Positive self-feelings call forth responses that maintain self-accepting feelings. These are the responses that have proved rewarding in the past through the stimulus of positive self-evaluations and subsequent positive self-feelings. The same attributes, behaviors, and experiences that provoke positive self-feelings, because of their association with these feelings, come to be valued in their own right. They come to be standards against which the person evaluates himself on perceiving himself to possess these attributes, perform these behaviors, or to be the object of these experiences.

Self-rejecting feelings, however, provoke the need to take action in ways that will change either one's self-cognitions or the personal attributes, behaviors, and experiences that incite those self-cognitive responses. In short, positive self-feelings lead to the maintenance of behavioral response tendencies, whereas self-rejecting feelings lead to changes in efforts.

Since change, by definition, is more dramatic, negative self-feelings appear to have more significant motivational consequences than have positive self-feelings (Wicklund, 1979). However, positive self-feelings do reinforce tendencies to repeat behaviors (including self-cognitions) that evoke positive self-feelings. People become increasingly attracted to the standards and become increasingly motivated to approximate them. In effect, then, positive self-feelings would be expected to lead to responses that would endorse the normative system within which the individual was able to achieve gratification. Noting that there has been little investigation of the consequence of positive evaluations or of the circumstances under which these evaluations have consequences for others, Singer (1981) speculates that

> satisfaction with the outcome of a comparison involving the self would be accompanied by generally positive feelings toward those perceived as responsible for the favorable allocation of tangible or intangible goods. Under conditions of *relative gratification,* in other words, one would expect greater satisfaction with the "system," just as one would expect greater dissatisfaction under conditions of relative deprivation. (p. 85)

Consistent with the idea that *positive* self-feelings lead to *conventional* responses associated with securing valued attributes, performing valued behaviors, and eliciting positively valued environmental responses are findings that positive affect (indicated by feeling good and happy, feeling satisfied, having a sense of mastery) tended to be associated with the use of coping patterns (behavior aimed at producing changes in the objective self or in the objective environment) (Caplan *et al.*, 1984). Coping-like responses were indicated by paying attention to studies, getting help from others, asking questions in class, practicing skills, trying to locate one's faults, and resolving to do better in the future.

Also compatible with these findings are observations that (1) individuals with positive self-feelings are more likely to select occupations that reflect their self-concept, but such a relationship is not consistently observed for individuals with negative self-feelings (Dipboye, 1977); (2) self-concept of school ability, self-esteem, and satisfaction with school work independently contributed to a multiple regression equation predicting future educational attainment even after controlling on background characteristics, socioeconomic level, number of siblings, and ability (Bachman *et al.*, 1978); and (3) women who were labeled charitable, on donating money to a worthy cause, were more likely later to support another charity (Kraut, 1973). Under conditions suggesting positive self-feelings, responses associated with positive self-feelings tend to be reinforced. Also consistent with this conclusion is the observation that, with a *minimal* degree of self-awareness under nonevaluative conditions, self-awareness appears to have motivating properties insofar as performance was improved (Wicklund & Duval, 1971; Liebling & Shaver, 1973).

When *negative* self-feelings (prompted by recognition of failure to approximate self-values) are induced, individuals will be motivated to *adjust* their behavior so as to approximate the self-values. Support for the proposition that self-feelings motivated such self-protective–self-enhancing responses is provided by a study (Howe & Zanna, 1975) in which male and female subjects were observed to adjust their behavior, apparently in an effort to perceive themselves as having role-appropriate characteristics toward the goal of positive self-evaluation and the subsequent experience of positive self-feelings. The adjustive behavior constituted the self-enhancing response. In this study, male and female subjects were expected to perform an anagram task. The male and female subjects were variously led to believe that success at this task correlated highly with masculine interests and abilities or with feminine interests and abilities. Feedback regarding task performance led the subjects to believe that they had either done well or poorly on the task. They were then asked to complete the task. Males who were succeeding at a task they thought was appropriately feminine adjusted their behavior to do more poorly next time, whereas males who thought success was appropriate for their sex improved their performance. Female subjects who believed that success at the task was female-appropriate improved their performance in the second part of the study but decreased performance if they thought that the task was male-appropriate.

Grube, Greenstein, Kearney, and Rankin (1977) also report data that strongly suggest that self-dissatisfaction leads to self-protective responses in the form of behaviors the self-perception of which would lead to favorable self-evaluations. These authors suggest that a self-confrontation procedure

> served to reveal inconsistencies between behaviors and self-conceptions for those individuals who considered themselves to be egalitarian but who had not previously engaged in behaviors that were consistent with these self-conceptions. In accord with Rokeach's (1973) theory, we hypothesize that awareness of such inconsistencies aroused a state of self-dissatisfaction in these individuals because such information was threatening to their self-esteem or self-conceptions. As one means of reducing this dissatisfaction, some of these individuals changed their behaviors to become more consistent with their self-conceptions by responding favorably to the NAACP solicitation. (pp. 215–216)

Generally, then, under conditions in which individuals may be presumed to have enhanced needs for positive self-feelings, individuals tend to behave in ways, particularly by increasing conformity to normative standards, that would permit them to perceive themselves realistically in positive terms and to evaluate themselves in such terms. One such condition that enhances self-evaluation, and, consequently, self-feeling, is objective self-awareness, whereby an individual becomes increasingly cognizant of discrepancies between evaluative standards and personal attributes or behavior. Under conditions of high objective self-awareness, individuals are observed to *increasingly* comply with normaiive standards (Wegner & Vallacher, 1980; Wicklund, 1975). Reis (1981) reviews one study in which the facilitation of objective self-awareness (OSA), achieved by putting a mirror placed directly in the subjects' field of vision, apparently influenced behavior that reduced the discrepancy between internal standards of equity and personal involvement in an inequitable situation (being overpaid):

> If overpayment is truly discomforting, then the presence of self-focusing stimuli should lead to greater attempts at restitution. Results supported this prediction. Overpaid-Non OSA subjects did less but better quality work than their equitably paid controls. Overpaid-OSA subjects proofread significantly more material but made many more errors than their controls. Performing a greater quantity of work less well indicates more zealous attempts at greater output (Latta, 1976) commensurate with higher pay. Thus, calling attention to internal standards of a fair work exchange without altering the salience of others as a source of social approval prompted heightened restitutive actions. (p. 282)

Another study (Greenberg, 1980) examined the influence of heightened self-awareness and perceived personal responsibility (conditions that may be taken as reflecting a heightened need for positive self-feelings) on behaving justly. In addition, the subjects were either induced to be objectively self-aware or not. They were required to allocate a reward of 20 poker chips between themselves and a partner. It was expected and observed that self-focused attention would produce a discrepancy between real and ideal behavior, as expressed in conforming to equity norms in allocation only when the subjects would feel personally responsible for how they performed. The results supported the hypothesis, since allocations were more just in the objectively self-aware-responsible condition then in the not objectively self-aware-responsible condition, which, in turn, resulted in more equitable distribution than either of the groups of subjects who did not feel responsible for their behavior. These results were independent of whether the subjects (who allocated the chips) had earned higher or lower shares than their partners. Also interesting was the observation that the objectively self-aware subjects were more concerned than the non-self-aware subjects about the appropriateness of the allocations. This suggests that objectively self-aware individuals are more highly motivated to behave in ways that will evoke positive self-cognitions and self-evaluations.

Other studies also indicate that self-perceived failure to conform to a presumed self-value of equity leads to increase attempts to approximate the self-value. In response to being overpaid for a task, subjects who were told by the experimenter that they were unqualified tended to increase their productivity (Friedman & Goodman, 1967), and they responded with increased performance to a greater extent to overpayment on an ego-involving task than to overpayment on an ego-irrelevant task (Wiener, 1970).

As Reis (1981) notes, the need to live up to one's own standards leads to appropriate behavior. He proposes that justice-related behaviors

> are influenced by the desire to create a favorable impression in one's own eyes; in clumsier terms, self-presentation to the self. In this light, living up to one's own standards may be examined using the same processes that motivate self-presentation to others. As with equitable behavior generally, the sense of justice may be fashioned out of behavioral change or cognitive manipulation. Cognitive change is probably less extensive, as distortion must fall within the bounds of credibility and surveillance by others. Perhaps this accounts for Lerner's (1977) comment that most people usually behave fairly and the observation . . . that even in complete privacy, people do not increase their own rewards more than a little bit. (p. 282)

Generally, individuals are motivated to secure positive responses from others, since this represents one criterion, along with so many others, for self-evaluation. Under conditions in which negative self-feelings result from a threat to others' good opinions of the individual, individuals will behave in ways calculated to restore others' positive attiiudes toward them. One area of the research literature relating to this proposition concerns the frequently observed tendency to attribute the causes of benign outcomes to oneself and to attribute the causes of unwelcome outcomes to external circumstances. This literature is interpretable either in terms of the person's private attributions (that is, the person believes the attributions) or in terms of self-presentation (the person does not necessarily believe the attributions, but in any case is attempting to elicit approving responses from others by attributing positive outcomes to his own agency or to avoid disapproving responses of others by denying responsibility for negative outcomes). To the extent that the latter interpretation is warranted, this literature is compatible with the proposition that negative self-feelings stemming from threats to the need for approval of others motivates behaviors calculated to secure others' approval or to forestall others' disapproval. Bradley (1978) states that

> according to the self-presentation interpretation of defensive and counter-defensive attributions a public-esteem motive, or a desire to maintain or gain a positive public image, is assumed to mediate the self-serving bias effect; nonetheless, private self-esteem needs certainly may be implicated. For example, positive evaluations from others may serve to enhance the esteem an individual feels for himself and, conversely, negative evaluations from others may threaten the individual's positive, private self-image. (pp. 66–67)

The effect of self-rejecting feelings on self-protective responses reflected in self-presentational strategies is supported by observations from Kaplan's (1980) panel study of junior high school students. Consistent with the expectation that self-rejecting subjects would tend to present themselves to others in ways that would disguise their self-perceived shortcomings were observations that among subjects who denied these statements in the eighth grade, seventh-grade subjects who were more self-derogating were more likely to affirm in the ninth grade that they frequently told lies and that, to be liked, one has to tell others what they want to hear even if it is not the truth. Also consistent with the hypothesis that negative self-feelings increase self-protective responses in the form of positive self-presentational strategies are the observations that seventh-grade subjects with greater levels of self-derogation were more likely to deny in the ninth grade that they do what is right even when they are criticized for it and that they usually admit it, and take their punishment, when they do something wrong. These observations were made on subjects who, at an intervening point in time (eighth grade), affirmed these statements.

Self-rejecting feelings, then, lead to behaviors that appear calculated to approximate self-values when the feelings were perceived as occasioned by the failure to do so. The attempt to approximate the values is presumed to occur only if the person perceived these goals as attainable. In the absence of personal expectations of achieving these values, however, the person might adopt *avoidance strategies,* whereby he did not have to confront the demand to approximate the value. The predisposition to structure interpersonal transactions so as to avoid adverse outcomes, the perception of which leads to negative self-feelings, is suggested by the greater tendency on the part of more self-derogating seventh-graders to indicate the disposition, in the ninth grade (after having denied such a disposition in the eighth grade), to quit school, to avoid competitive situations, to spend a lot of time alone, to avoid talking to those who insult them, and to leave home (Kaplan, 1980). The tendency of more self-derogating subjects in the seventh grade to structure their lives so as to forestall events requiring novel responses (which might increase the risk of failure to make the required response) is suggested by the observation that, initially, greater levels of self-rejection are associated with increasingly greater rates of subsequent affirmation of the item "I get nervous when things aren't just right."

The avoidance mechanism appears to be present also in studies in which individuals who caused harm to others offered more help to victims if they did not have to make face-to-face contact with them then if they did have to make such contact with them (Freedman, Wallington, & Bless, 1967). The need to deny awareness of the negative behavior is also suggested by results reported by Carlsmith and Gross (1969), which suggested that, in guilt-inducing circumstances, a person was more likely to comply to a request from someone *other* than the victim.

Presenting oneself as less able has the effect of decreasing the likelihood that others will expect more of them and, therefore, apply negative sanctions to them when they fail. Thus, Marecek and Mettee (1972) reported that low self-esteem subjects rejected personal responsibility for increased performance, and, in fact, intentionally performed less well on subsequent trials, presumably to avoid high expectations of them by others as a result of their increased performance. However, the avoidance of responsibility for increased performance appears to be a function of the public nature of their improved performance (Sacco & Hokanson, 1978) and of the expectation of future evaluation by others (Mettee, 1971). Individuals with low self-esteem also are more likely to indicate avoidance of occupations in which leadership behavior, being subject to supervision, and competitive situations were involved (Rosenberg, 1965).

Other avoidance techniques in response to negative self-feelings have been described in studies such as those summarized by Arkin (1981):

> For instance, Dykman and Reis (1979) found that students who scored high on measures indicative of feelings of vulnerability and inadequacy showed a strong tendency to occupy seats near the rear and far sides of the classroom, presumably so that they could personally regulate the threat of interaction better. Similarly, Wine (1975) found that test-anxious students were less likely to become involved with another child when they were confronted with a highly evaluative experimental context, even though norms of helping supported such involvement. Likewise, McGovern (1976) found that socially anxious persons prefer to work alone rather than together with others. (p. 326)

When the goal is to attract approving responses of others, the avoidance of self-devaluing circumstances may take the form of conformity to the standards of others, not because the standards reflect self-values but, rather, because conformity represents a way of avoiding others' disapproval. It is others' disapproval that constitutes a threat to the person's self-value.

This is most likely to occur under conditions whereby an individual is motivated to reduce negative self-feelings. Consistent with this formulation are results reported by Carlsmith, Lepper, and Landauer (1974). Children were either exposed to an anxiety-provoking film (interpreted here as exciting a need to reduce negative self-feelings) or to a slightly amusing film. Under each condition, the children were either shown a videotape of an apparently punitive and threatening adult or of a rewarding and warm adult. When the children were shown an anxiety-provoking film, unlike when they were shown an amusing film, the children were observed to comply more frequently with the requests when the adult was presented as negative and threatening than when the adult was presented as warm and positive.

Conformity to the expectations of others, to be sure, may reflect a tendency to avoid the disapproval of others. However, it may also be interpreted as an alternate route to the fulfillment of a self-value. If the person experiences self-rejecting feelings as a result of the failure to approximate a self-value, he may attempt to restore his positive self-feelings by approximating an equivalent or more highly placed self-value in his system of values. If the frustrated value is reflected in the disapproval of others, the person may attempt to secure the approval in another way. Consistent with this interpretation, individuals who appear to be deviant relative to the group norms were more likely to conform to the expectations of others. Wicklund (1982) cites findings, by

Wegner and Schaefer (1978), to the effect that people who perceive themselves in the minority were more likely to display helping responses, and by Duval (1976), to the effect that the holding of minority opinions is related to susceptibility to influence. These findings are interpretable in terms of minority status leading to negative self-evaluations and accompanying negative self-feelings. The negative self-feelings, in turn, motivate the individual to behave in ways that will ultimately restore positive self-feelings or lead to their attainment. Conforming to the expectations of others represents to the person one such route to self-acceptance and positive self-feelings.

In general, self-enhancing functions may be served by behavior that is not at all relevant to the offensive attribute, behavior, or experience that eventuated in self-devaluation and self-rejecting feelings. Rather, the person may choose to behave in a way that is personally or socially valued and that (although unrelated to the offending object of self-perception) permits the person to perceive himself and evaluate himself as possessing positive social attributes or performing positive social behaviors. As Tedeschi and Riordan (1981) have noted: "Research has reliably established a positive relationship between transgression and subsequent prosocial behavior by the actor" (p. 223). This literature admits of a number of different interpretations, including that which suggests that the behavior serves to counterbalance the experience of disvalued self-perceptions and consequent self-rejecting feelings. Tedeschi & Riorden (1981) suggest that

> one set of theories dealing with posttransgression behaviors postulates mediating factors within the individual. Thus, a transgressor may engage in prosocial behavior to reduce his guilt, to promote a positive self-image, to restore belief in a just world, or to relieve himself of negative affect. The prosocial behavior serves the function in each of these theories of reducing some negative state that has been produced in the individual by the transgression. (p. 224)

A number of studies support the generalization that persons will respond to self-rejecting feelings, in the absence of mitigating self-enhancing experiences, with behaviors that compensate for the failure to approximate particular self-values with behaviors that approximate alternate self-evaluative standards. The tendency to comply with other people's requests, following self-devaluing experiences, is observed in a study (Koneske, Staple, & Graff, 1979) in which subjects were or were not induced to upset a graduate student's ordered IBM cards. The subjects were then asked to comply with a request involving either deceptive or nondeceptive activities. Subjects who had spilled the cards and were asked to cooperate in a nondeceptive activity were more willing to do so than subjects who were not induced to upset the IBM cards or who were asked to cooperate in a deceptive activity. This is what would be expected if individuals were trying to perform a worthy activity and were unwilling to perform another self-disvalued activity to counterbalance the negative self-feelings that accompanied the earlier self-disvalued activities.

The assertion that individuals who perform disvalued behaviors will attempt to compensate for their transgression by performing helping behaviors in order to bolster their negative self-feelings is supported also by results reported by McMillen (1970). Individuals who had been induced to lie were compared with those who had not been induced to lie with regard to subsequent compliance with the requests of others. No differences in compliance were observed between groups when subjects received feedback calculated to enhance self-esteem before being asked to comply with requests. However, in the absence of the feedback designed to enhance self-esteem, subjects who had lied previously were more likely to comply than those who had not lied. Similar effects for such manipulations were observed in a study in which subjects were variously induced to spill a deck of computer cards or witness the experimenter spill a deck of computer cards (Cialdini, Darby, & Vincent, 1973). In another variation, the subjects experienced a positive event in the form of social approval or a monetary reward, as opposed to not experiencing a positive event. The data indicated that subjects who had not experienced a positive event were more willing to help a fellow student then were subjects who had experienced a positive event. The willingness to comply with the request to help a fellow graduate student was unrelated to whether the mishap had been caused by the subject or by the experimenter. Although it was argued that this result suggested that self-esteem needs did not motivate the compliance behavior, it might be argued that this is not the case. Whether the individual performed the harmful act himself or stood by and watched other people perform a harmful act might constitute a self-disvalued behavior. In the latter case, either identifying with the experimenter (and, thereby, feeling guilt) or identifying with the victim (and, thereby, vicariously experiencing a disvalued circumstance) might exacerbate the need for esteem-giving consequences. Hence, in the *absence of an esteem-inducing circumstance* (receiving rewards), it might be expected that the individual would try to compensate for performing a disvalued behavior by performing a more positively valued act.

To the extent that the person is unable to approximate self-values through *legitimate* means, in an attempt to enhance self-attitudes, the individual may be forced to engage in *deviant* behavior to approximate the conventionally endorsed self-values. Insofar as the person had already adopted a deviant value system as a self-enhancing mechanism, the deviant behavior reflects appropriate self-enhancing responses toward the achievement of the new (deviant) self-evaluative criteria.

Among the strongest data in support of the hypothesis that negative self-feelings (stemming from perceived failure to approximate salient self-evaluative criteria) stimulate deviant orientations are those provided by longitudinal studies in which earlier levels of self-feelings are related to subsequent deviant responses while controlling on earlier levels of deviant response. In a longitudinal study of junior high school students, Kaplan (1976) observed that levels of self-rejecting feelings in the seventh grade were positively associated with self-reports of adopting each of a range of deviant responses between the seventh and eighth grade. For this analysis, only subjects who denied performing the deviant act during a specified period before the seventh-grade testing were considered. For example, 8 percent of the seventh-graders who had low scores on a measures of self-rejecting feelings, 11 percent of those who had medium scores, and 14 percent of those who had high scores reported in the eighth grade that during the preceding year they had stolen something worth between 2 and 50 dollars. Similarly, among seventh-graders who denied earlier suspension or expulsion from school, 5 percent of the seventh-graders who had low scores on an index of self-rejection, 7 percent of those who had medium scores, and 9 percent of those who had high scores reported in the eighth grade that during the preceding year they were suspended or expelled from school. Among individuals who, in the seventh grade, denied that they had cheated on exams during the preceding grading period, 32 percent of the low self-derogating individuals, 38 percent of the moderate self-rejecting individuals, and 43 percent of the highly self-rejecting individuals reported in the eighth grade that during the preceding year they had cheated on exams. Comparable relationships were observed for such patterns as using force to get money or valuables from another person, vandalism, stealing from other students' desks or lockers, using someone's car without permission, and beating up someone who had done nothing to the subject. In all, such results were observed for 28 different deviant patterns (Kaplan, 1976).

Not only do levels of self-rejecting feelings anticipate the adoption of deviant responses, but *changes* in self-rejecting feelings also anticipate the adoption of deviant responses. Using the same data, Kaplan (1975b) reported that among students who denied performing a deviant act before they entered the eighth grade, the students who reported performing the deviant acts during the period between the eighth and the ninth grades relative to those who denied performing the behavior during the same period had manifested higher residualized gain scores in self-rejecting feelings during the antecedent period between the seventh and eighth grade. Statistically significant differences were observed in 22 of the 28 comparisons.

Experimental evidence is available that suggests linkages between the need for positive self-feelings and deviant behavior as self-enhancing responses under conditions in which the behavior results in self-perceptions of positively valued attributes. Thus, under conditions of heightened self-awareness, individuals cheated when the result was to make them feel more competent but did not increase cheating behavior when the behavior was associated with being lucky (Vallacher & Solodky, 1979). The results of a study by Aronson and Mettee (1968) also may be taken as compatible with the proposition that negative self-feelings lead to deviant self-enhancing responses. The subjects were led to believe that the study in which they were participating concerned the relationship between personality test scores and extrasensory perception. The latter ability was said to be determined through the use of a modified game of blackjack. After taking a personality test, the subjects were provided with false feedback, which was intended to induce a temporary increase or decrease or no change in self-esteem. The subjects were randomly assigned to one of the three self-esteem conditions. During the blackjack game that followed, they were placed in situations in which they could cheat and win or not cheat and lose the game. People who received uncomplimentary feedback about themselves (the low self-esteem condition) were significantly more likely to cheat than were the subjects who received more positive information about themselves. Although the investigator did not interpret the results in these terms, since success at the blackjack game was thought to reflect a presumably desirable trait (extrasensory perception), the cheating behavior by the low self-esteem subjects may have been an attempt on the part of these subjects to provide evidence to themselves (or, perhaps, to others) that they possessed a desirable quality, thereby compensating for the self-devaluing experience they had undergone.

Also illustrative of deviant self-protective responses that lead to attributes interpretable as approximating conventional standards are the outcomes of delinquency. Thus, although delinquency is a negatively regarded role, it consists of such positively valued features as potency and daring (Gold & Mann, 1972).

The influence of self-rejecting feelings on the adoption of deviant self-protective responses is, perhaps, most clearly demonstrated in studies reporting association between antecedent self-rejecting feelings and subsequent adoption of deviant patterns (Kaplan, 1980; Kaplan, Martin, & Johnson, 1986; Kaplan, Johnson, & Bailey, 1986). However, another group of studies that also suggest the functional relationship of deviant self-protective responses to self-rejecting feelings included demonstrations of the effects of social success on the *prevention* of deviant adaptations. A large number of studies suggest that social skills training reduces illicit substance use, aggression, withdrawal, truancy, and stealing among adolescents. Whether the mastery of social skills are interpreted as intrinsically valued by individuals or as instrumental to the achievement of valued ends, these findings are compatible with the interpretation that enhancement of self-feelings, presumed to be associated with mastery of social skills, decreases the need to respond with deviant self-protective mechanisms and increases the need to behave in socially approved ways associated with positive self-feelings (i.e., proficiency in such skills as assertiveness, initiating conversations, expression of feelings, decision making) (Pentz, 1983).

The absence of such skills, however, appears to be associated with the need to adopt contranormative patterns, presumably to enhance self-feelings. The adoption of such deviant patterns as self-enhancing mechanisms is required in view of the inability to gain such self-feelings through the utilization of more conventional social skills. As Pentz (1983) observes:

> Some of the more notable social skills required in adolescence appear to be assertiveness, expression of opinion, ability to disagree and refuse, and ability to make requests and initiate conversation. Adolescents who experience delay in learning social skills or who remain skill deficient are prone to the development of such drug-use-related problems as delinquency, truancy, aggression, and academic and social withdrawal (Goldstein, Sherman, Gershaw, Sprafkin, & Glick, 1978; Quay & Quay 1965). (p. 196)

To summarize, more or less negative self-feelings, under different conditions, stimulate the person to adopt self-protective–self-enhancing responses in the form of conventional or deviant self-referent cognitive responses, revision of the need-value system, or purposive behaviors oriented to the approximation of self-evaluative criteria.

Self-Referent Cognitions

The nature of the person's self-protective–self-enhancing responses that are stimulated by self-feelings depend on the person's awareness and conceptualization of himself, both in terms of the situationally circumscribed self-values that guide his efforts relative to the individual's beliefs about his abilities to approximate those values and in terms of his more generalized expectancies regarding his capabilities to approximate his self-values.

Situationally Circumscribed Self-Cognition. The person's self-awareness stimulates awareness of the expectations that he holds of how he should behave in any given situation. Consistent with this proposition, increased self-awareness, facilitated by the use of mirror images and playback of subjects' voices, creates increased effort and conformity (Wicklund & Duval, 1971). With generalized self-awareness comes more specific self-perceptions. When individuals are more aware of themselves, they are more likely to describe themselves in ways that correspond to their true behavior patterns than under conditions when self-awareness is not stimulated. Pryor, Gibbons, Wickland, Fazio, and Hood (1977) report that self-descriptions of sociability were much more predictive of subsequent behavior when the individual's self-awareness was stimulated by confrontation with a mirror image.

How an individual behaves in response to his need to obtain positive self-feelings and to avoid negative self-feelings is, in part, a function of the individual's specific self-perceptions regarding his self-values and the means available to approximate the self-values. Combs (1981) suggests that

> these generalized perceptions about ends or means exert selective influences upon perceptions. Like self-concept, they are differentiated as a consequence of experience and serve thereafter as guidelines for both the selection of goals and appropriate behaviors for achieving them. Understanding the self in action requires understanding the organism's purposes or goals and the means which seem to him or her appropriate to achieve them. (pp. 12–13)

The specific beliefs that one has about one's self, then, determine how one will respond to the goal of protecting or enhancing one's self. And, depending on the response that an individual makes to his beliefs about himself, he will engender more or less self-enhancing experiences. According to Gergen (1981),

> as the meaning of one's actions or feelings are negotiated within the social milieu, one's personal state may be enhanced or diminished. Praise or criticism, pride or depression, stereotypy or enriched opportunities may all be generated by the particular concepts one employs in understanding oneself. If one believes oneself a failure, little may be attempted; if one fancies oneself a struggling romantic, mounting frustrations may be transformed into existential ecstasy; if people believe they need another's love, then they may organize their lives around the search. (p. 71)

The self-values toward which these more or less effective instrumental responses are oriented, as well as the appropriateness of the instrumental responses, depend on situational prescriptions, not the least important of which are those related to the particular identities the individual has in the situation. By recognizing an identity, the individual also recognizes a set of evaluative standards by which he appropriately judges himself. As McCall and Simmons (1966) note,

> the contents of a person's role-identities provide him with criteria for appraising his own actual performances. Those actions that are not consonant with one's imaginations of self as a person in a particular social position are regarded as embarrassing, threatening, and disconcerting; if possible they will be discontinued and superseded by actions more in keeping with one's view of self. (p. 69)

If the socialization experience is a successful one, the individual learns to accept and value his social identities and, therefore, to need to conform to the demands made on the individual that are associated with the various identities. As situations change, different identities among the person's repertoire of identities will become salient. As a particular identity becomes salient, so will the normative demands made on the person who has that identity become salient. To the extent that the individual successfully approximates the standards that apply to that identity in the particular situation, to that extent will the individual evaluate himself positively.

To the extent that the person evaluates himself in terms of situationally appropriate self-values, and to the extent that the person believes that he is able to behave in ways that will approximate those values, the person will be motivated to do so. This is suggested by the research literature dealing with student and occupational roles. Self-enhancing mechanisms take the form of using the capacities that one believes one has to approximate the role demands the fulfillment of which permits positive self-evaluation.

In relationship to the student role, the literature permits the conclusion that, to the extent the individual feels he is effective in certain areas, he is more likely to attempt to achieve in those areas. For example, in a longitudinal study of high school students, Bachman and his associates (1978) observed that self-concept of school ability was related to subsequent educational attainment. Junior high school students who had more favorable academic self-concepts achieved more in school than students with negative self-concepts. This relationship was observed independent of IQ (Brookover, Shailer, & Paterson, 1964). This suggests again that individuals who perceive themselves as having certain capabilities are more likely to behave in ways for which these capabilities are prerequisite. Presumably, individuals who do not believe that they have academic ability will not be as likely to attempt to achieve in school as will students who believe that they have the ability to succeed. Although alternative explanations are possible, this interpretation is compatible with the observation of Rosenthal and Jacobson (1968) that children who were reputed to have greater capabilities than other students showed a significantly greater improvement in IQ scores than did those for whom the expectations of greater performance were not present. This literature suggests that self-cognitions of possessing particular aptitudes will lead to the expenditure of efforts to realize those aptitudes, presumably toward the goal of achieving what will be recognized as personally valued states. In particular, Ballif (1981) drew the following conclusion on the basis of such studies:

> In combination, these studies suggest that the self-concept is a significant component in motivation for learning in students from four to seventy-five years of age, in students from low to upper middle socioeconomic backgrounds, for students in ghetto and private schools, for students in urban and rural areas, and for students from a variety of ethnic backgrounds. Clearly they argue that an individual's efforts to obtain knowledge and skill is dependent on how effective that person thinks he or she will be in doing so. (p. 255)

Similar conclusions appear to be appropriate with regard to occupational roles. Also consistent with the view that self-perception of abilities influence the individual's self-enhancing responses are the observations that self-perceptions of positive qualities influence expectations of occupational success (Rosenberg, 1965) as well as high occupational aspirations (Bedeian, 1977). Mortimer and Lorence (1979a) observed a direct effect of self-perceptions of competency and efficacy as college seniors on income in 1976, suggesting that

> those students who had a stronger sense of personal efficacy before college graduation have been successful in their early work careers in obtaining occupational positions involving high income. Adolescent orientations toward the self may thus have some importance for the attainment of future extrinsic occupational rewards. The individual's sense of competence in the senior year may reflect his actual competence, or have led to a more competent "presentation of self" to those supervisors, clients, and employers whose decisions can influence income. (p. 317)

Also consistent with the hypothesized influence of self-cognition on mode of self-enhancing response is the observation by Morrison (1977) of a relationship between willingness to take risks and successful adaptation to changing role demands among managers.

Although these findings suggest that people will conform to perceived demands when they perceive themselves as having the requisite abilities, and opportunities to do so, to achieve the goal of evaluating themselves positively, the same end may be achieved by tailoring their

self-values to their self-perceived abilities and opportunities. In this connection, Rosenberg (1981) concludes:

> People's self-concepts tend to match the stereotypical characteristics associ-
> ated with their chosen occupations. For example, students planning to enter
> the field of sales tend to describe themselves as sociable, talkative, ag-
> gressive, and having initiative, whereas those selecting accounting are likely
> to describe themselves as precise, self-controlled, organized, and thorough
> (Korman, 1969). Furthermore, the self-concept is not only consonant with
> prime occupational choice, but with second occupational choice (Leonard,
> Walsh, & Osipow, 1973). In selecting an occupation, people seek to achieve
> "self-role" congruence. (Sarbin & Allen, 1968) (p. 615)

Data from a study cited above (Mortimer & Lorence, 1979a) indicate
an effect of a sense of self-efficacy on the person's occupational values
that, in turn, influence the experiences he had of autonomy in the work
place. A higher sense of efficacy was associated with a high evaluation
of occupational choices that fit the person's abilities and skills, express
the person's interests, and permit the exercise of creativity and origi-
nality. Presumably, the person's expenditure of effort to meet the demands made on him depends on the person's expectation of success in
this regard. In the absence of expectations of success, the person may
revise his system of self-values, adopt deviant instrumental patterns,
distort his perceptions of success, avoid situations in which the self-
value is applicable, or, failing these, become depressed. As others have
noted (Wortman & Brehm, 1975), either effort or depression may follow
the inability to meet valued ends, depending on conditions relating to
evaluation and expectancy.

The person's expectations of success with regard to approximating
self-values depends on past experiences in this regard. Past experiences,
in turn, depend on the extent to which the circumstances are under that
person's control. Usually the person will expend effort in those situations when it is profitable to do so and will make appropriate adjustments otherwise. As Bandura (1977) summarizes these processes:

> In this conceptual system, expectations of personal mastery affect both initia-
> tion and persistence of coping behavior. The strength of people's convictions
> in their own effectiveness is likely to affect whether they will even try to cope
> with given situations. At this initial level, perceived self-efficacy influences
> choice of behavioral settings. People fear and tend to avoid threatening situa-
> tions they believe exceed their coping skills, whereas they get involved in
> activities and behave assuredly when they judge themselves capable of han-
> dling situations that would otherwise be intimidating.
>
> Not only can perceived self-efficacy have direct influence on choice of
> activities and settings, but through expectations of eventual success, it can
> affect coping efforts once they are initiated. Efficacy expectations determine

how much effort people will extend and how long they will persist in the face of obstacles and aversive experiences. The stronger the perceived self-efficacy, the more active the efforts. Those who persist in subjectively threatening activities that are in fact relatively safe will gain corrective experiences that reinforce their sense of efficacy thereby eventually eliminating their defensive behavior. Those who cease their coping efforts prematurely will retain their self-debilitating expectations and fears for a long time. (pp. 193–194)

On the basis of the person's earlier experiences, the person will form certain general self-perceptions of his or her ability to approximate self-values.

Generalized Self-Perceptions. One's broad experience of failing to approximate self-values because of self-perceived inability to do so will lead to generalized expectations of failure. As stated in current formulations of learned helplessness theory described by Lazarus and Folkman (1984):

Learned helplessness theorists are now saying . . . that when a negative outcome is thought to be a product of the person's effort (internality), there will be a loss of self-esteem and a greater likelihood of depression than if the outcome is seen as the result of external factors. If such attribution is viewed as the result of stable person factors, the cost of uncontrollability will be chronic as well. There is, moreover, an added attributional factor of "globality," that is, a generalization of helplessness from a specific context to the overall life context. . . .

The more a person expects not to have control, the greater will be the cognitive, emotional, and motivational deficits leading to nonadaptive behavior and depression. The *cognitive deficit* is that the person fails to notice that his or her coping response might be connected to a favorable outcome. The *motivational deficit* refers to passivity in the face of a condition of helplessness. (p. 202)

Short of depression, the person may adopt a behavioral orientation toward self-protection characterized by avoidance responses rather than toward self-enhancing problem-solving responses. Arkin (1981, p. 324) reviews a number of studies that suggest such avoidant tendencies.

A child punished (labeled inadequate) when her behavior does not live up to high parental standards and unrewarded when it does may easily acquire "fear of failure" (Canavan-Gumpert, 1977; Teevan & McGhee, 1972).Consistent rejection, or anticipated rejection (Jones and Berglas, 1978), coupled with reinforcement of the child for dependency (Weinstein, 1968, p. 772), may focus the child's attention on disapproval rather than approval. Attention to potential losses as opposed to potential gains have been shown to engender an increasingly conservative (e.g., hesitant) response style (Canavan-Gumpert, 1977; Thies & Chance, 1975). Such a style could easily generalize to other contexts in which evaluation is substantial. (Arkin, 1981, p. 324)

When the threats to self are severe, the avoidance tendencies may be manifested in regressive responses. Lazarus and Folkman (1984) note:

> The greater the threat, the more primitive, desperate, or regressive emotion-focused forms of coping tend to be and the more limited the range of problem-focused forms of coping. . . . Wheaton (1959) in a study of the effects of isolation, notes that as threats (such as hunger, thirst, injury, illness or physical discomforts) were added to the experiences of isolation, extreme pathological symptoms and "regression to a child-like type of emotional lability and behavior pattern" (p. 41) became more likely. He points out that the absence of any workable alternatives for coping encourages primitive defense activity. (p. 168)

Congruent with these observations, the perceived inability to resolve problems leads to mechanisms that facilitate the acceptance of the inevitable. Pearlin and Radabaugh (1976) observe that, for people who perceive themselves as being in control of the important circumstances in their lives, there is a relatively weak relationship between level of anxiety and the tendency to use alcohol in order to control feelings of distress. However, where a person perceives himself as necessarily submitting fatalistically to external forces, there is a relatively stronger relationship between the experience of intense anxiety and the disposition to use alcohol for distress control.

In contrast, if individuals characteristically perceive that the approximation of self-values is within their control and that attempts to approximate the value are likely to be acceptable, then negative self-feelings (that result from perceived distance from the self-values) will motivate conventional efforts to achieve the value rather than behavior that distorts self-referent cognition, deviates from conventional norms, reorders the value system, or avoids situations in which approximation to the self-value is appropriate. Thus, in a panel study, Andrisani & Nestel (1976) observed a relationship between earlier perceived internal control and later achievement. The relationship was interpreted in terms of the confidence, exploratory behavior, and tendency toward risk-taking behavior on the part of those individuals who could be characterized in terms of an internal locus of control. Further, Gore and Rotter (1963) found that participation in civil rights activity was more likely on the part of individuals who perceived themselves as having control over their environment, as independent of environmental forces. Those individuals who saw themselves as highly dependent on environmental forces were less likely to participate in civil rights activities.

Evaluation of Self-Protective–Self-Enhancing Patterns

The need to protect or enhance oneself that is stimulated by self-feelings may be expressed in a very broad range of behaviors. Among the determinants of the self-protective–self-enhancing patterns with which the person responds is the personal system of values. The system of self-values influences the manifestations of self-protective–self-enhancing mechanisms in the following ways. First, self-values orient the person to the range of behaviors that experience dictates are relevant to the achievement of characteristically or momentarily salient values. Second, among the various patterns that may serve self-protective–self-enhancing functions, some are more highly valued than others. Thus, those that are more situationally appropriate are more likely to be enacted. Third, among the responses that might otherwise serve self-protective–self-enhancing functions, some are disvalued by the person and thus are less likely to be enacted. Fourth, partly as a result of earlier experiences with the patterns, certain of the responses—because of their proven effectiveness or because of their new-found relevance for revised self-values—come to be increasingly valued. Each of these points will be considered in turn.

Relevance of Self-Enhancing Patterns. The particular self-protective–self-enhancing patterns that an individual adopts in response to more or less negative self-feelings depends, in large measure, on the individual's personal value system. To the extent that it is important to the individual to perceive himself as more closely approximating certain values than others, he will behave in ways that he perceives as reflecting those evaluative standards. Thus, Mortimer and Lorence (1979b) observed that work-related values or aspirations influence work-related experiences ten years later that reflect those values.

Insofar as the person evaluates himself according to his ability to fulfill the obligations of particular social identities, he will be sensitive and strive to conform to what are perceived as legitimate role demands for that identity. In short, self-enhancing mechanisms are defined in terms of the responses that are manifestly related to the approximation of the self-value.

Prescribed Self-Enhancing Patterns. Among the self-values according to which a person evaluates himself are those relating to the propriety of particular self-protective–self-enhancing mechanisms. This is illustrated by Jones and Pittman's (1982) discussion of self-presentational strategies toward the goal of ingratiating one's self with others:

> Each of us internalizes a set of moral standards defining the reprehensibility
> of dissimulation and deceit in human relations. The moral situation is com-

plicated, however, by the inculcation of other values favoring the promotion of self-interest and the legitimacy of self-salesmanship. Thus, out of a complex mixture of moral forces pushing here for "authenticity" and there for "impression management," the individual must decide on the best strategic combination in his dealings with others. (p. 237)

Also consistent with the hypothesis that personal evaluation of behavior patterns influences the adoption of particular modes of response to self-rejecting feelings are the several studies (Kaplan, 1972b) suggesting that aggressive behaviors in response to self-devaluing circumstances are adopted under conditions in which the patterns are provided within the social context and socially transmitted to the individual, when the responses are congruent with the individual's social identity, when the aggressive responses are viewed as appropriate within the context of the social relationship, and when the responses are already part of the individual's characteristic repertoire. Illustrative of the influence of the personal identity-appropriate values on self-protective mechanisms adopted in response to self-rejecting feelings are findings reported by Kaplan (1977) from analyses of the conditional relationships between sex and depressive affect. The findings are compatible with the conclusions that females, in the course of their socialization experiences, are more likely to be inhibited from adopting response patterns that would permit them to deflect blame from themselves in blameworthy circumstances and are more encouraged than males to employ intrapunitive responses in devaluing circumstances. Further, males may be more likely than females to defensively distort self-reports (Maccoby & Jacklin, 1974), and girls may be more likely than boys to present themselves in a favorable light (Bush, Simmons, Hutchinson, & Blyth, 1977–1978).

Occupation-related values also influence the disposition to use, and the effectiveness of, self-protective mechanisms. Thus, Speisman, Lazarus, Mordkoff, and Davison (1964) report that executives who were high in disposition to employ denial as a coping device manifested the greatest reduction of stress response on listening to a denial message emphasizing that the stimulus film was staged and the actors suffered no injury. In contrast, a student group that was relatively low in disposition to employ denial showed very little stress reduction in response to the denial message but did show a marked reduction to an "intellectualization" message encouraging a detached, analytic attitude toward the events and persons in the stress-inducing film.

Proscribed Self-Enhancing Patterns. The readiness to behave in certain ways that offer promise of serving self-protective or self-enhancing functions often does not find expression in overt responses because of the person's devaluation of the pattern itself. Although the expected effects of the pattern are acceptable, the means to the ends are not. The devaluation of the pattern by the individual acts as a personal constraint. Lazarus and Folkman (1984) observe that

> personal constraints refer to internalized cultural values and beliefs that proscribe certain types of action or feeling, and psychological deficits that are a product of the person's unique development. . . . Culturally derived values and beliefs serve as norms that determine when certain behaviors and feelings are appropriate and when they are not. . . . In an investigation by Klass (1981), women students who felt a high sense of guilt over assertive behavior reported being less assertive in social contexts than women with low guilt. The measure of guilt suggests a personal constraint, presumably derived from their process of socialization. Undoubtedly, there are some situations where an individual will be more influenced by cultural norms, depending in part on what is at stake and the consequences for violating them. Also, individuals differ in the extent to which they comply with norms. Nevertheless, even allowing for a wide range of situational and individual differences culturally derived values, beliefs, and norms operate as important constraints. (p. 165)

Similar constraints are postulated by Hirschi (1969): commitment to conventional goals, attachment to conventional persons, involvement in conventional activities, and belief in conventional norms. Partly as a result of such constraints, the most prevalent response to negative self-feelings is, when it is possible, to conform to expectations of self and others and thereby to reflect on one's self as having the characteristics that would lead to positive self-evaluation. This mode of response may be inferred, for example, from studies in which circumstances facilitating negative self-evaluations and (presumably) consequent negative self-feelings lead to conforming responses. Thus, Wicklund (1982) describes studies in which the placement of a mirror (presumably facilitating self-awareness and self-evaluation) markedly inhibited cheating behavior (Beaman, Klentz, Diener, & Svanum, 1979; Diener & Wallbom, 1976). These results are interpretable as suggesting that self-awareness leads the individual to reflect on himself from the perspectives of others, as these perspectives are reflected in internalized values. The self-awareness that was facilitated by the presence of a mirror influenced self-evaluations of anticipated cheating behavior. The consequent vicarious negative self-feelings led to self-protective responses in the form of self-control and conformity to expectations of honesty. The person will not use an illegitimate mechanism to achieve a valued end, if the use of that illegitimate mechanism will result in self-cognitions of performing disvalued behavior.

The normal tendency to conform to conventional expectations is exacerbated by the experience of self-devaluing circumstances. When the person perceives himself as doing something wrong, he is more motivated than usual to approximate self-values, including positive responses from others. Thus, self-rejecting individuals are expected to be somewhat inhibited from acting out dispositions to deviance by virtue of the increased sensitivity to the attitudes of others that follow on self-rejecting attitudes. This relationship is demonstrated by data from a three wave panel analysis of junior high school students (Kaplan, 1980). The students were tested at annual intervals during the junior high school years. Individuals who, in the seventh grade, were more highly self-derogating were increasingly likely to report in the ninth grade that they became deeply disturbed when someone laughed at them or blamed them for something they had done wrong. Only those subjects who, in the eighth grade, had denied that they became deeply disturbed when someone laughed at them for something they had done wrong were considered in the analysis. By virtue of excluding those who affirmed the dependent variable in the eighth grade, the observed relationship between earlier self-rejection and subsequent sensitivity to the negative responses of others could not be easily interpreted in terms of response bias or some other common factor that might be hypothesized to influence both self-derogation and sensitivity to the attitudes of others.

The observation (Kaplan & Robbins, 1983) of an inverse relationship between earlier self-rejecting feelings and later deviant outcomes was anticipated in earlier analyses in which hypothesized and observed positive bivariate relationships between self-derogation and later deviant behavior were transformed in the context of multivariate models:

> In effect, controlling for disposition to adopt deviant patterns resulting from the genesis of self-derogation in the context of normative membership groups, the inhibitory effects of self-derogation upon the adoption of deviant patterns are revealed. In the context of the full model, perhaps operating through such correlates of self-derogation as low sense of self-efficacy and sensitivity to adverse outcomes, self-derogation becomes inversely related to the adoption of a number of deviant patterns particularly those that appear to have a high risk of adverse outcomes for the subject. (p. 143)

Changing Valuation of Deviant Patterns. Frequently it happens that the person is unable to forestall or to reduce the intensity of distressful self-feelings through the use of heretofore positively valued, self-protective patterns. The proven ineffectiveness of self-protective–self-enhancing responses the individual characteristically subscribed to tends to reduce the individual's personal valuation of these self-protective–self-enhancing strategies. The individual loses motivation to conform to response patterns in which he continues to (1) perceive himself as possessing personally and socially disvalued attributes, performing disvalued behaviors, and being the object of negative attitudes by valued others; (2) endorse values that he cannot approximate and to value people who express negative attitudes toward him; (3) behave in ways that, in the past, were ineffective in facilitating the achievement of valued attributes and the performance of valued behaviors and that were ineffective, in the past, in forestalling, or reducing the effects of, expressions of negative self-attitudes. Given the disvaluation of these self-protective–self–enhancing patterns and the ongoing experience of self-rejecting feelings that motivate the individual to enhance self-feelings, the individual is motivated to seek out and adopt alternatives to these patterns that may fall outside the bounds of former limits of acceptability, whether socially or personally defined.

At the same time, however, although the individual may be motivated to dissociate himself from the perceived source of his distressful self-rejecting feelings and may seek deviant alternatives that will fulfill his need for self-acceptance, he cannot easily completely dissociate himself from the normative world. Having been socialized in a society, the individual has internalized a sense of identification and commitment to the society. A range of quotidian needs depends on the responses of the adults in his environment. To act out dispositions to deviate from normative expectations would threaten the person's sense of identity and commitment to the normative order, as well as the satisfaction of the needs that depend on the positive attitudes of the adults in the person's environment. The greater the projected deviation from normative expectations, the greater the inhibitory threat to the sense of identity and commitment. Both forces (the disposition to deviate, and the threat to one's sense of commitment and identity) are simultaneously operative. Lazarus and Folkman (1984) observe that

> society places many shifting and complex expectations on its members through the roles they are required to play. People may dissociate themselves psychologically from these demands through processes such as distancing or intellectualizing . . ., but when the sense of identification or commitment is lost through these self-protective processes, the person must often pay a price in low morale, impaired social functioning, and even damage to health. Furthermore, when social expectations are violated or demands not met, we are punished with expressions of disapproval that not only threaten our need to belong but also endanger the prospect of gaining the material and social advantages we require to meet central and sustaining life goals. (p. 238)

The conflict between using a disvalued behavior pattern to obtain a valued end versus resisting use of a disvalued (otherwise) self-enhancing pattern is nicely illustrated by the results of studies in which values regarding cheating and achievement were in conflict (Vallacher & Solodky, 1979). Wicklund (1982) observed that under conditions of high self-awareness, which stimulate self-evaluative responses, the increased salience of one or another standard evoked differential responses:

> The situation in which their subjects were working allowed and enticed a certain amount of cheating, and two elements were varied: The attractiveness of successful performance was varied, and subjects' self-awareness was also experimentally manipulated. If desire to perform well was relatively low, self-awareness had the same effect as in the experiments reported previously. The amount of cheating declined given self-awareness. But if achievement needs had been brought to the fore experimentally, self-aware subjects began to disregard the norm against cheating *in the interest of* making better progress in their achievements. This is to say that the achievement ethic won out over the non-cheating ethic as self-awareness rose. (p. 218).

The devaluation of conventional self-protective patterns and the adoption of deviant patterns are most likely to overcome personal constraints, in the form of devaluation of the deviant patterns, under the related conditions whereby the person (1) avoids self-perceptions of violating self-values by performing deviant behaviors either by redefining the behavior as valued or under circumstances that permit ignoring personal responsibility (as when deindividuation loosens inhibitions against aggressive responses), (2) perceives that the self-devaluing costs of remaining committed to the normative order are far greater than any potential threats to the self that may result from contravening the normative expectations defining the conventional order, and (3) perceives that deviant responses may be expected to have self-protective or self-enhancing consequences, whether measured against preexisting conventional or newly acquired deviant self-values.

SUMMARY

Self-protective–self-enhancing responses are behaviors by the person that are more or less consciously oriented toward the goal of (1) forestalling the experience of self-devaluing judgments and consequent distressful self-feelings (self-protective patterns) and (2) increasing the occasions for positive self-evaluations and self-accepting feelings (self-enhancing patterns). Self-protective–self-enhancing responses may take any or all of three forms variously relating to the person's self-referent cognitive responses, the person's revision of the need-value system, and the person's responses that are oriented to the approximation of salient self-values. Self-referent cognitive responses serve self-protective functions by permitting the person (1) to perceive himself as having positively valued qualities; (2) to deny negative attributes; and (3) to be sensitive to those personal attributes, behaviors, and experiences that have self-evaluative relevance. This last function orients the person to responses that are likely to forestall self-devaluing and to facilitate self-enhancing experiences. Revisions in the need-value system permit an individual to selectively order self-values so that they are compatible with the person's present and anticipated traits, behaviors, and experiences. The third major form of self-protective–self-enhancing responses encompass the person's purposive behaviors that are oriented to the approximation of self-evaluative standards. That is, the person behaves in ways that are instrumental in the attainment of, or intrinsically reflect, salient self-values. In all these ways (by perceiving oneself favorably, if not veridically, and by sensitizing the person to aspects of the self that have self-evaluative relevance; by reordering the personal system of self-values; and by behaving in ways that lead to or reflect the realistic approximation of self-values), the person is enabled (1) to forestall the self-perception of personal traits, behaviors, and experiences that are personally disvalued and evoked needs to attain positive self-feelings and (2) to facilitate the self-perception of traits, behaviors, and experiences that approximate salient self-values and, thereby, contribute to positive self-evaluation and self-accepting feelings.

The responses in all three formal categories may be expressed in ways that, in varying degrees, approximate conventional or deviant standards.

The occurrence and form of self-protective or self-enhancing responses are determined by the nature of the person's self-feelings, the person's beliefs about himself in relationship to his environment, and the person's evaluation of the projected self-protective–self-enhancing responses as more or less closely approximating self-evaluative criteria. To the extent that the individual variously experiences chronic self-rejecting feelings or situational exacerbation of self-rejecting feelings, the person will be motivated to adopt self-protective or self-enhancing responses that reflect changes in the person's cognitive orientations, need-value system, and behaviors oriented toward the approximation of the stable or newly revised system of self-values. The experience of positive self-feelings tends to reinforce those specific or general responses that the person associates with the experience of positive self-feelings. Within these contraints, the specific forms of the self-protective and self-enhancing patterns are influenced by the person's beliefs about his own capabilities in relationship to the mutability of reality. The person will tend to adopt those response patterns that, based on earlier experiences, are believed to be within the person's capabilities and that are expected to serve self-protective or self-enhancing functions. The form of the self-protective or self-enhancing responses is influenced, further, by the personal evaluation of responses that are expected to serve these functions. Although a person may anticipate that certain responses will serve self-enhancing functions, he may not perform those behaviors if they are judged to reflect or to be instrumental in the approximation of disvalued states. Those behaviors will be acted out to the extent that such judgments are not made, whether because they were already compatible with the person's self-values or because the person reorders his self-values in such a way that the projected self-enhancing patterns are no longer incompatible with the person's self-evaluative criteria.

CHAPTER 6

Toward a General Theory of Self-Referent Behavior

In this final chapter, I present the outline of a theoretical framework within which the preceding more detailed chapters may be interpreted and which serves as a device for ordering the relevant results of current and future research. The outline places self-referent behaviors in social psychological context as playing mediating roles between social influences on the person and personal influences on social systems. In considering their mediating roles, each mode of self-referent response is viewed as the product of social psychological influences, including other modes of self-referent behaviors, and as having social psychological consequences, including effects on other modes of self-referent responses. Among these consequences, particularly as these are manifested in certain self-protective–self-enhancing responses, are influences on the functioning of the social systems in which the person participates.

SELF-REFERENT BEHAVIOR IN SOCIAL PSYCHOLOGICAL CONTEXT

In social psychological context, the person, as a psychological structure, is viewed in terms of the profound influence exerted on him by his past and continuing participation in social systems. The person, as a product of past and contemporary social influences, in turn, behaves in ways that have consequences for the social system. Mediating the processes by which the person is influenced by his past and current participation in interpersonal networks, and his behavior that has consequences for the social systems in which he participates, are the person's self-referent behaviors, that is, his behaviors that are oriented toward his own person.

The Person as Social Product

The person is born into functioning social systems and continues to participate in such systems throughout his life. As a result of his participation in these systems, the individual has experiences that determine, in large measure, the form of that psychological entity that we call "the person." In the course of socialization experiences, the person is the object of behaviors by others. These behaviors, partly in response to the person's attributes, influence the person's outcomes. In addition, the person's outcomes are influenced by ongoing macrosocial forces that are responsive to laws of their own and are little influenced by the behavior of individuals.

In the course of the person's social experience, in the contexts of dynamically evolving interlocking interpersonal systems, his biogenetically given capabilities are actualized. He learns to view the world through a system of concepts, internalizes needs, symbolizes the needs as values, accepts social identities, and develops response dispositions. These relatively stable psychological structures are stimulated by contemporary social situations that have symbolic significance for the individual and, as such, evoke predictable personal responses. Over time, these same social situations stimulate personal change.

The Person as Social Force

The person, however, is more than a passive product of social experiences. The person is also a social force. As a participant in ongoing interpersonal systems, the person, in his behaviors, stimulates responses from other participants in the system. As the person conforms to situation-specific demands on his social identities, he evokes complementary responses from others in their capacities as possessing complementary social identities. Further, to the extent that the interpersonal system consists of persons playing interlocking roles, the person's role behavior may have indirect effects on others' role functioning, depending on the extent to which and how the person conforms to the situationally relevant, identity-specific expectations.

The person, of course, has most direct impact on interpersonal systems, that is, on systems of individuals who engage in long-term or short-term interactions that are governed by shared situation-specific, identity-specific, or person-specific expectations. To the extent that shared social experiences lead to patterned responses by large numbers of individuals, to that extent will the predictable behaviors influence the structure and functioning of the more abstract social systems the interpersonal systems exemplify.

Intervening Influences of Self-Referent Behaviors

The processes by which the person, as a product of past socialization experiences and as stimulated by contemporary social situations, comes to behave in ways that influence the functioning of interpersonal systems (or, in the case of *patterns*, of personal responses, social systems) are mediated by self-referent responses. The person, as the outcome of past and current social experiences, comes to influence current and future functioning of interpersonal systems by first becoming self-aware and conceiving of himself in particular ways, by evaluating himself as more or less closely approximating personal standards, and by experiencing self-feelings that stimulate self-protective and self-enhancing responses, some of which directly and indirectly affect the functioning of the interpersonal or social systems in which he participates. Our understanding of how the self-referent responses mediate the relationships between the person as the object of socioenvironmental influences and as an influence on the social environment constitutes the social psychology of self-referent behaviors.

SOCIAL PSYCHOLOGICAL ANTECEDENTS AND CONSEQUENCES OF SELF-REFERENT BEHAVIORS

Self-referent behaviors, the responses of individuals to themselves, are outcomes of the person's history of experiences in social contexts. How an individual thinks about, evaluates, feels toward, and otherwise responds to his own person are the consequences of the facts of being born into, raised in, and living with social groups. And how these groups function is directly influenced by the individual and collective responses of the participants to themselves, particularly with regard to their attempts to protect themselves from self-devaluing experiences and to increase the likelihood of self-enhancing experiences. Less directly, the functioning of interpersonal or social systems are the consequence of the social psychological influences on the self-protective–self-enhancing responses (including other self-referent responses and their determinants). These determinants of each mode of self-referent behavior were considered in detail in earlier chapters. Here, I review the social psychological influences on each mode of self-referent behavior and consider the implications of individual and collective self-referent responses for the functioning of interpersonal and social systems.

The Person in Social Context as Influencing Self-Referent Behaviors

Self-referent responses are the direct effects of psychological structures and processes and the indirect effects of the social structures and processes that give rise to these psychological structures and processes. Thus, self-referent cognitive responses are directly affected by the person's own traits, the system of concepts the person uses to structure his perceptions of these traits, the person's perceptions of the situational context that defines the social significance of these traits, and the self-protective responses that influence favorable self-perceptions. These influences, in turn, are socially determined. From a diachronic point of view, the personal behavior pattern, its evaluative significance, and the system of concepts that gives structure to personal awareness of the pattern are all learned in the course of the socialization process. From a synchronic point of view, the perceptual and evaluative significance of a person's behaviors and attributes varies according to the social context.

I review, in turn, the social psychological antecedents (including other self-referent behaviors) of each of four categories of self-referent responses: self-referent cognitive responses, self-evaluation, self-feeling, and self-enhancing–self-protective responses.

Self-Referent Cognition. Self-awareness, self-conceiving, and other self-referent cognitive responses are influenced by (1) the person's socially derived traits, behaviors, and experiences; (2) the social context in which they are perceived; (3) the system of concepts that structures the self-perceptions; and (4) the person's self-protective–self-enhancing responses.

The person's objectively given, socially derived traits, behaviors, and experiences directly or indirectly (through their stimulation of other traits, behaviors, or experiences) stimulate self-awareness and self-conceiving responses, either in terms of their objectively given forms or in terms of other unobserved or unobservable traits, behaviors, or experiences that are implied by the objectively given phenomena. The meanings of the phenomena are enhanced by the situational context in which they appear. The situational context provides symbolic cues that specify the relevance of particular, from among a myriad of, personal traits, behaviors, and experiences for the person's immediate life situation. Further, the situational context provides a range and distribution of values along specific dimensions that permit and stimulate the person to identify the particular values along those dimensions that characterize the individual.

The individual uses a relatively stable, shared system of concepts to select from and structure his perceptions of personal traits, behaviors, and experiences. The system of concepts is influenced by the stability of personal characteristics and by social reinforcement. The use of certain concepts in conceiving the self elicits social rewards directly and is of instrumental value in permitting the person to anticipate others' responses to the person.

The person's need for positive self-evaluation motivates the person (1) to be aware of those personal traits, behaviors, and experiences that are most relevant to self-evaluation; (2) to perceive himself in ways that will elicit positive self-evaluative responses; and (3) to behave in ways that, in fact, lead to the approximation of self-values and that, thereby, stimulate self-referent cognitions in these terms.

Self-Evaluative Responses. Self-judgments of the extent to which the person approximates desirable states is a learned disposition that is stimulated by self-awareness, in general, or by self-conceptualization, in particular. The nature of the self-evaluative responses is a function of the person's specific self-referent cognitions and of the system of self-evaluative standards (self-values) that are the criteria for more or less positive self-evaluative judgments. The specific self-perceiving–self-conceiving responses, in conjunction with social situational cues, stimulate self-judgments of approximating or being distant from those self-evaluative standards that are personally defined as applicable in the particular situation. The most inclusive and superordinate self-value in the person's system of self-values is positive self-evaluation. The individual's overall self-evaluation is a function of the frequency and duration of self-perceptions of approximating self-evaluative standards that are more or less salient in the personal hierarchy of values.

Indirectly, past and current social circumstances influence self-evaluative judgments by (1) socializing the person to evaluate himself as well as to accept and to assign specific priorities to particular self-values; (2) defining the situational relevance of particular self-values; and (3) influencing the personal traits, behaviors, and experiences, the self-awareness and self-conceptualization of which stimulate self-evaluation.

Self-Feelings. Self-feeling reflects the stimulation of need dispositions occasioned by self-evaluations of being more or less distant from self-values. Need dispositions are internalized self-values and, as such, imply a readiness to behave in ways that permit the person to approximate valued states and to distance himself from disvalued states. The self-feelings, as affective or emotional experiences of the stimulation of need dispositions by self-evaluative judgments, are personally and socially conceptualized in qualitatively distinct terms, depending on such circumstances as the nature of the evaluative criterion and whether the judgment is being made regarding past, present, or future circumstances. The intensity and the more or less distressful nature of the self-feelings are influenced by the salience of the self-evaluative criterion and the judgment of being proximate to or distant from the valued or disvalued state. The experience of self-feelings stimulated by self-judgments of being more or less proximate to salient self-evaluative criteria contributes to the person's overall self-evaluation and, thereby, influences the stimulation of the need for positive self-evaluation.

Social circumstances, in addition to influencing the cognitive experience of self-feelings, indirectly affect the stimulation of need dispositions by facilitating the internalization of self-values, defining the situational appropriateness of self-evaluative judgments and influencing the likelihood of approximating the more or less salient evaluative criteria.

Self-Protective–Self-Enhancing Responses. The intensification of self-feelings that is stimulated by self-evaluative judgments motivates the person to engage in self-protective–self-enhancing responses. Such responses are behaviors by the person that are more or less consciously oriented toward the goal of forestalling the experience of self-devaluing judgments, and consequent distressful self-feelings (self-protective patterns), or increasing the occasions for positive self-evaluations and self-accepting feelings (self-enhancing responses).

The chronic experience or situational exacerbation of self-rejecting feelings motivates the person to adopt self-protective or self-enhancing responses that reflects a change in level of effort or kind of activity that promises to assuage the self-rejecting feelings. The experience of positive self-feelings tends to reinforce those response tendencies that are subjectively associated with positive self-feelings.

The specific behaviors that are undertaken are a function of the person's beliefs about his capabilities in relationship to the mutability of reality and of the intrinsic value placed on the self-protective or self-enhancing response. The individual will tend to behave in ways that, based on earlier experiences, are thought to be within his capabilities and are expected to serve self-enhancing functions. Further, the person will tend to respond in ways that are not incompatible with and, in fact, are positively valued, according to salient self-evaluative standards.

Self-protective–self-enhancing responses may take any or all of three forms variously relating to the person's (1) self-referent cognitive responses, (2) revision of the need-value system, and (3) responses oriented to the approximation of salient self-values.

Self-referent cognitive responses serve self-protective–self-enhancing responses by facilitating the perception of valued personal qualities and the denial of personal disvalued attributes and by sensitizing the individual to personal attributes, behaviors, or experiences that have self-evaluative relevance. Sensitization to aspects of one's own experience permits the person to behave effectively in ways that will lead to the achievement of, and consequent self-recognition of having achieved, desirable states.

By revising the need-value system, the person is able to assign higher evaluative priority to those standards that are compatible with his current perceptions and anticipation of personal traits, behaviors, and experiences.

The third category encompasses the person's purposive behaviors that lead to or reflect the realistic approximation of self-evaluative standards.

The responses in each of the three categories may be expressed in ways that, in varying degrees, reflect approximation to or deviation from conventional standards of behaviors. Severe distortion of reality, rejection of conventional and adoption of contranormative value systems, behavior that deviates from conventional standards toward the goals of achieving conventional goals, or behavior that reflects approximation to newly adopted contranormative standards are likely to occur to the extent that the person's experiences lead him to believe that conventional responses will eventuate in self-rejecting feelings, whereas deviant responses offer the promise of facilitating positive self-evaluation and self-accepting feelings.

Social circumstances influence self-protective–self-enhancing responses by socializing the person with regard to attitudes toward, and beliefs about, the efficacy of such responses and by influencing the occurrences of the circumstances that ultimately stimulate the need for positive self-evaluation.

Self-Protective–Self-Enhancing Responses as Influencing the Social System

Self-referent behavior influences the functioning of interpersonal systems either because the self-referent behaviors are visible to others and stimulate responses on their part or because even if the self-referent behaviors are not recognized by others, the behaviors influence functioning of others either by facilitating or constraining their responses. In the former instance, a person may behave hostilely and stimulate a similar response on the part of the others with whom the person interacts. Alternatively, the person may take an action that affects others' comes, although these others are unaware of the person's action. A person in a position of authority in a corporation may give an order that, when ultimately carried out, will influence the occupational role of a participant in the organization, although the participant might not recognize the sequence of events that led to the change in his behavior. Self-referent cognitions, self-evaluative responses, and self-feelings *in themselves* have no direct impact on the functioning of the social systems. These responses, by their very nature, are covert and, hence, do not (by their visible nature) stimulate responses, nor do they have direct impact on the outcomes of others. It is only when these responses have visible consequences or lead to behaviors by the person that have consequences for others that they exercise *indirect* effects on the functioning of interpersonal or social systems. To be sure, the communication of self-referent cognitions, self-evaluations, or self-feelings may stimulate others' responses or influence others' outcomes. However, these behaviors no longer may be described as self-referent cognitions, self-evaluations, or self-feelings. Rather, they are intentional or unintentional *communications* about the person.

All self-referent responses that influence the interpersonal systems in which the individual participates fall within the category of self-protective–self-enhancing responses. Of course, not all these behaviors stimulate responses or influence outcomes of others directly. Many self-protective responses can only have indirect influences, insofar as they are covert responses. Changes in self-referent cognitions and in self-evaluative responses are cases in point. However, self-protective–self-enhancing responses that are reflected in visible behaviors or otherwise influence what befalls other people, by definition, influence the functioning of interpersonal systems and the social systems that are individuated by these interpersonal systems. Whereas such self-referent responses may be stimulated by other self-referent responses, it is these overt and consequential responses that are relevant as direct influences on the functioning of interpersonal and social systems.

As noted above, although it may be proper to speak of the consequences of an individual's self-protective–self-enhancing responses for interpersonal systems in which the person participates, to speak of the consequences for the functioning of the more abstract social system that the interpersonal systems express requires that we consider *patterns* of self-referent responses. To the extent that common social influences lead to prevalent experiences of self-rejecting feelings and to the adoption of similar self-protective–self-enhancing responses, it might be expected that the self-referent response pattern might have some influence on the form, functioning, and stability of the social systems in which the population under consideration functions.

Perhaps the most important general consequence of self-referent behaviors, from the point of view of the functioning and stability of interpersonal and social systems, is the extent to which self-protective–self-enhancing responses are reflected in the conformity to or deviation from the expectations of the others who participate in the system. Insofar as the person's self-protective–self-enhancing responses take the form of avoidance of interpersonal systems in which the individual participates, the functioning of other individuals will be disrupted to the extent that the performance of others is contingent on the person's conformity to their expectations. Conversely, the functioning of the interpersonal system will be facilitated to the extent that the individual is motivated (to protect or enhance self-feelings) to conform to the system of expectations that the person views as applicable to him in a given situational context. The degree to which the person conforms to the expectations and the way in which he interprets the expectations will be a function of his self-referent responses. The more prevalent the experience of self-rejecting feelings, and, therefore, the more prevalent the alienation from normative standards and the greater the readiness to adopt deviant patterns in an attempt to serve self-protective–self-enhancing functions, the greater is the likelihood that (1) the functioning of those social positions that the alienated individuals occupy, or that depend on the functioning of these individuals in complementary statuses, will be disrupted, and (2) the system will be less resistant to changes in functional patterns.

The motivation to conform to the expectations that others have of them depends on the extent to which conformity to the expectations serves the self-enhancing–self-protective functions of individuals. If individuals are expected to internalize, as desirable values, the same attributes and behaviors that are shared by others and that are relevant to the fulfillment of existing social functions, then these values cannot pose strong threats to individuals' need for self-acceptance. An individual will tend to assign high priority to those social values that he is likely to approximate and to reject those values for which he has no opportunity or talent for approximating. If the inability to approximate a talent is widespread in a segment of the population, then it is to be anticipated that this value will be rejected by that segment of the population. If the value is a central one for the more inclusive social system, then this could be quite dysfunctional for the achievement of social goals. It is inevitable, given the strength of the self-esteem motive (even stronger among individuals whose desire for self-acceptance is most frustrated), that people will behave in ways that will maximize their self-acceptance. This includes rejection of criteria for self-evaluation by which they must be found wanting and acceptance of those values (including deviant ones) that will permit positive self-feelings. A person will strive to excel at that which he values. To the extent that a person rejects basic social values, the kinds of individual activity that are required by society to fulfill its basic goals will be wanting.

To the extent that the basis for self-rejection is generalized to that group, self-feelings will have important implications for group identity. Whether dealing with race, religion, or society at large, if we identify the collectivity as the source of our self-devaluation and consequent subjectively distressful self-feelings, then, lacking alternatives, one possible response mechanism is to reject the basis of one's self-devaluation. The group becomes a negative reference group. The standards, behaviors, and attributes that are accepted as the defining characteristics of the group, whether they have any basis in reality as characterizing the group, are rejected. Identification with the aggressor occurs. By sharing the attitudes of the aggressor, we applaud ourselves as we believe we would be lauded were our attitudes apparent to the aggressor.

Alternatively, the person may "overidentify" with the "offending" group membership. The greater the *need* to justify one's behavior, that is, the more self-devaluing implications the (unavoidable) behavior has, the more the individual will attempt to justify the behavior by committing himself to its rightness. Since the person cannot tolerate self-devaluation, he will act to deny that the behavior, in fact, has self-devaluing implications. Thus, since responses generally are selected to serve self-enhancing goals, in an era in which one is applauded for identifying with one's roots, identification with the "disvalued" group may be a more profitable means of self-enhancement than identification with the attitudes of the aggressor. The conditions under which each of these responses will occur are still matters for speculation.

In like manner, intergroup relations are influenced by self-feelings. Recourse to projection as a self-enhancing mechanism has important implications for the expression of aggressive impulses toward segments of the population. Since projection involves attribution to others of traits or behaviors that, in fact, characterize the self but that would result in self-devaluation if recognized, the projection of these traits or behaviors on others would justify the expression of aggressive impulses. Since the populations most likely to be selected for this treatment are least able to defend themselves, it is to be anticipated that the ordinary powerlessness of these segments of the populace would be exacerbated, an experience that might be expected to increase self-rejecting feelings and self-protective adaptations among them.

More specifically, the performance of roles in a variety of social institutional contexts (economic, political, religious, etc.) is influenced by self-feelings and consequent self-protective–self-enhancing responses. In the economic realm, for example, Rosenberg (1965) reports that adolescents with lower self-esteem were more likely to report lower expectations of success in work, getting ahead in life, being as successful as most people seem to be, or going into the business or profession they would most like as a life career (pp. 232–239). Rasmussen and Zander (1954) reported that teachers who had high failure scores (discrepancy between real and ideal levels of classroom performance) were significantly less likely than those with low failure scores to indicate that they would choose teaching if they could begin their professional careers over again.

Within the political realm, early commentators have viewed power seeking as a compensatory reaction against low estimates of the self (Lasswell, 1948) or as the reflection of a deeper need for reassurance about the self (Lane, 1959). Rosenberg (1965) later reported that the adolescent with low self-esteem tends to lack interest in matters of national or international significance, is less likely to follow such issues in newspapers and broadcasts, and tends to be more ignorant of such subjects. He participates less frequently in discussions of such questions and is unlikely to take on a forceful or dominant role in these discussions. Nor is he likely to be called on by others for his advice and opinions on these matters. Presumably it is the personal concern with his own inadequacies that precludes his taking an interest in affairs beyond his own personal concerns, such as social and political issues.

In addition to influencing political understanding, level of self-esteem and consequent self-protective–self-enhancing strategies might also be expected to influence such matters as feelings of political cynicism and political efficacy, with higher self-esteem individuals being less distrustful toward political authorities and showing a greater sense of political effectiveness. In their feelings of vulnerability, self-rejecting people are unlikely to trust others, including political authorities, and, having no confidence in their own abilities or worth, they are not likely to see these qualities in others, including government officials. In contrast, with regard to political efficacy, the high self-esteem adolescent, considering himself worthy and capable of efficient action within his environment, will likely have a similar conception of his potential political role (Carmines, 1978).

Low self-esteem subjects might also be expected to be less involved in political activities, since, feeling vulnerable, they will avoid further exposure to interpersonal relationships, which, of course, is frequently required in political activities. Finally, adolescents with low self-esteem, feeling neither politically effective nor trusting, would be disposed to protest actions if they participated at all in political activities.

All the above relationships would be expected to hold insofar as political activities were salient, that is, were felt to be important, evoked interest, and were invested with psychic energy. As expected, Carmines (1978) found that level of self-esteem influences the political orientations, attitudes, and beliefs of those adolescents for whom politics is salient but not of those adolescents for whom politics is not salient. More specifically, low self-esteem adolescents were more likely to hold a vague, unclear, and inaccurate view of the political world; low self-esteem adolescents were more politically cynical or distrustful; and high self-esteem adolescents were less likely to engage in protest activities than were low self-esteem adolescents.

In the religious sphere, I reported earlier that self-rejecting attitudes were associated with the adoption of membership in any of a variety of charismatic religious movements existing in the contemporary world, such as the Catholic and Protestant charismatic communities, "Jesus Freaks," and evangelistic communities (Freemesser & Kaplan, 1976).

The preceding discussion, of course, is intended to illustrate rather than exhaust the implications of self-feelings and consequent self-protective–self-enhancing responses for personal behavior in various social institutional contexts, for the functioning of the social institutions, and for the functioning and stability of the more inclusive social system.

CONCLUSION: THEORY AND RESEARCH IN THE STUDY OF SELF-REFERENT BEHAVIOR

I present the foregoing chapters as a beginning stage in the formulation of a theory of self-referent behaviors that defines these behaviors as mediating the influence of the person (conceived of as a social product) on the interpersonal and social systems in which the person participates. The emerging theoretical framework derives from a consideration of the literature detailing the social psychological antecedents and consequences of the interacting patterns of self-referent behavior and is intended to serve as a structure for (1) incorporating new theoretical assertions and research findings relating to the social psychology of self-referent constructs; (2) sensitizing the investigator to the relevance of theoretical formulations and research findings for the understanding of self-referent constructs, when the relationship of these phenomena to self-referent responses is not immediately apparent; and (3) identifying lacunae in our understanding of the social psychological antecedents and consequences of self-referent behavior.

The need for such a tentative framework and for the structuring of disparate observations, which would presumably be facilitated by such a framework, is implied in the comments of other reviewers in the area of self-referent constructs. Wylie (1974) has commented on the "persisting primitive state of theory" (p. 315) in this area and the maleficent effects of this situation on research activities. She argues that

> planning adequate research procedures for studies relevant to self-concept theories is hampered because the theories as presented often imply no precise hypotheses concerning the mode of functional relationship of allegedly important variables. Especially noteworthy is the lack of theoretical guidance for stating testable multivariate hypotheses which predict interactions between construct variables and between these variables and situation variables. (p. 329)

Wells and Marwell (1976), while commenting on self-esteem research, in particular, offer an opinion that appears to have broader applicability to all self-referent constructs:

> The future development of self-esteem research will depend on two key factors—*consensus* and *accumulation*. The task is to combat the disparateness of the literature, where much of the research is carried on in analytical and empirical isolation from the remainder, and cross-comparisons are difficult. Hopefully, review efforts such as this one will be instrumental in this task. (p. 251)

The tentative theoretical framework frequently rested on untested causal assertions out of necessity, since relatively few definitive findings have been reported and most of the studies reviewed are directed toward hypothesized antecedents of self-referent responses rather than the influence of these responses on behavioral consequences or the mutual influences among self-referent phenomena and other variables (Wylie, 1979).

The discussion was based on a consideration of the social antecedents and consequences of four categories of often-studied, mutually influential self-referent responses: self-conceiving, self-evaluating, self-feeling, and self-protective–self-enhancing mechanisms. Each mode of self-referent response, in addition to being viewed as more or less directly influencing and being influenced by other modes of self-referent response, was viewed as more or less directly influencing and being influenced by numerous interacting social patterns.

This review reflects the complexity of the subject matter. Indeed, so complex is the field that the mutual interaction among self-referent responses and their various social antecedents and consequences could not be properly examined except by examining each mode of self-referent response separately with regard to its more or less direct social psychological and self-referent antecedents and responses. The effect is of having a set of "simultaneous equations" centering about various modes of self-referent responses. What has been presented, in non-statistical terms, is a set of "equations" in which certain self-referent responses appear as dependent variables in one equation and as independent or moderating variables, or both, in another equation. However, the set is not yet complete. Nor have all the explanatory factors been entered in the equations. At this point, we have a limited view of how the social psychological implications of self-referent responses might be structured, taking into account what is currently suspected or accepted as known about these phenomena. Whether the preceding treatment will continue to be a useful representation of reality will be determined by the future stimulus value it might have for new research activities and its capability of easily incorporating the fruits of these activities. What is certain however, is that our understanding of these phenomena will not proceed at any rapid rate without employing some such working representation of reality as a starting point.

References

Allport, G. (1943). The ego in contemporary psychology. *Psychological Review, 50,* 451–479.
Allport, G. W. (1961). *Pattern and growth in personality.* New York: Holt, Rinehart & Winston.
Andrisani, P. J., & Abeles, R. P. (1976, September). *Locus of control and work experience: Cohort and race differences.* Paper presented at the meeting of the American Psychological Association, Washington, D.C.
Andrisani, P. J. and Nestel, G. (1976). Internal-external control as contributor to the outcome of work experience. *Journal of Applied Psychology, 61,* 156–165.
Archer, D. (1974). Power in groups: Self-concept changes of powerful and powerless group members. *Journal of Applied Behavioral Science, 10,* 208–220.
Arieti, S. (1967). Some elements of cognitive psychiatry. *American Journal of Psychotherapy, 124,* 723–736.
Arkin, R. M. (1981). Self-presentation styles. In J. T. Tedeschi (ed.). *Impression management theory and social psychological research* (pp. 311–333). New York: Academic Press.
Arkin, R. M., Appelman, A. J., & Burger, J. M. (1980). Social anxiety, self-preservation, and the self-serving bias in causal attribution. *Journal of Personality and Social Psychology, 38,* 23–35.
Aronson, E., & Mettee, D. R. (1968). Dishonest behavior as a function of differential levels of induced self-esteem. *Journal of Personality and Social Psychology, 9,* 121–127.
Austin, W. & Walster, E. (1974). Reactions to confirmations and disconfirmations of expectancies of equity and inequity. *Journal of Personality and Social Psychology, 30,* 208–216.
Bachman, J. G. (1982). Family relationships and self-esteem. In M. Rosenberg & H. B. Kaplan (eds.). *Social Psychology of the Self Concept* (pp. 356–364). Arlington Heights, IL: Harlan Davidson, Inc.
Bachman, J. G., & O'Malley, P. M. (1977). Self-esteem in young men: A longitudinal analysis of the impact of educational and occupational attainment. *Journal of Personality and Social Psychology, 35,* 365–380.
Bachman, J. G., O'Malley, P. M., & Johnston, J. (1978). *Adolescence to adulthood—change and stability in the lives of young men.* Ann Arbor, MI: Survey Research Center.
Back, K. W., & Bogdonoff, M. (1964). Plasma lipid responses to leadership, conformity, and deviation. In P. H. Leiderman and D. Shapiro (eds.). *Psychobiological Approaches to Social Behavior* (pp. 24–42). Stanford, CA.: Stanford University Press.
Backman, C. W., Secord, P. F., & Pierce, J. R. (1963). Resistance to change in the self-concept as a function of consensus among significant others. *Sociometry, 26,* 102–111.

Ballif, B. L. (1981). The significance of the self-concept in the knowledge society. In M. D. Lynch, A. A. Norem-Hebeisen, and K. J. Gergen (eds.). *Self-Concept, Advances in Theory and Research* (pp. 251–260). Cambridge, MA: Ballinger Publishing Company.

Bandura, A. (1977). Self-efficacy: Toward a unifying theory of behavioral change. *Psychological Review, 84*, 191–215.

Bassis, M. S. (1977). The campus as a frog pond: A theoretical and empirical reassessment. *American Journal of Sociology, 82:* 1318–1326.

Beaman, A. L., Klentz, B., Diener, E., & Svanum, S. (1979). Self-awareness and transgression in children: Two field studies. *Journal of Personality and Social Psychology, 37*, 1835–1846.

Becker, H. S. (1963). *Outsiders: Studies in the sociology of deviance.* New York: The Free Press.

Bedeian, A. G. (1977). The roles of self-esteem and N achievement in aspiring to prestigious vocations. *Journal of Vocational Behavior, 11*, 109–119.

Bell, P. A. (1978). Affective state, attraction, and affiliation. *Personality and Social Psychology Bulletin, 4*, 616–619.

Bem, D. J. (1972). Self-perception theory. In Leonard Berkowitz, (ed.). *Advances in Experimental Social Psychology* (Vol. 6, pp. 2–62). New York: Academic Press.

Berg, N. L. (1971). Effects of alcohol intoxication of self-concept. *Quarterly Journal of Studies on Alcohol, 32*, 442–453.

Berscheid, E., & Walster, E. H. (1969). *Interpersonal attraction.* Reading, MA: Addison-Wesley.

Billings, A. G., & Moos, R. H. (1981). The role of coping responses and social resources in attenuating the stress of life events. *Journal of Behavioral Medicine, 4*, 139–157.

Blumberg, H. H. (1972). Communication of interpersonal evaluations. *Journal of Personality and Social Psychology, 23*, 157–162.

Bohrnstedt, G. W., & Felson, R. B. (1983). Explaining the relationships among childrens' actual and perceived performances and self-esteem: A comparison of causal models. *Journal of Personality and Social Psychology, 45*, 43–56.

Bourne, P. G., Coli, W. M., & Datel, W. E. (1968). Affect levels of Special Forces soldiers under threat of attack. *Psychological Reports, 22*, 363–366.

Bradley, G. W. (1978). Self-serving biases in the attribution process: A reexamination of the fact or fiction question. *Journal of Personality and Social Psychology, 36*, 56–71.

Bramel, D. A. (1962). A dissonance theory approach to defensive projection. *Journal of Abnormal and Social Psychology, 64*, 121–129.

Brewer, M. B., & Campbell, D. T. (1976). *Ethnocentrism and intergroup attitudes: East African evidence.* New York: Halstead Press.

Brookover, W. B., & Passalacqua, J. (1981). Comparison of aggregate self-concepts for populations with different reference groups. In M. D. Lynch, A. A. Norem-Hebeisen, and K. J. Gergen (eds.). *Self-concept, advances in theory and research* (pp. 283–294). Cambridge, MA: Ballinger Publishing Company.

Brookover, W. B., Shailer, T., & Paterson, A. (1964). Self-concept and school achievement. *Sociology of Education, 37*, 271–278.

Burish, T. G., & Houston, B. K. (1979). Causal projection, similarity projection, coping with threat to self-esteem. *Journal of Personality, 47*, 57–70.

Burnstein, E., & Zajonc, R. B. (1965). Individual task performance in a changing social structure. *Sociometry, 28*, 16–29.

Bush, D. E., Simmons, R. G., Hutchinson, B., & Blyth, D. (1977–1978). Adolescent perception of sex-roles in 1968 and 1975. *Public Opinion Quarterly, 41*, 459–474.

Canavan-Gumpert, D. (1977). Generating reward and cost orientations through praise and criticism. *Journal of Personality and Social Psychology, 35*, 501–513.

Caplan, R. D., Naidu, R. K., & Tripathi, R. C. (1984). Coping and defense: Constellations vs. components. *Journal of Health and Social Behavior, 25,* 303–320.

Carlsmith, J. M., & Gross, A. E. (1969). Some effects of guilt on compliance. *Journal of Personality and Social Psychology, 11,* 240–244.

Carlsmith, J. M., Lepper, M. R., & Landauer, T. K. (1974). Children's obedience to adult requests: Interactive effects of anxiety, arousal, and apparent punitiveness of the adult. *Journal of Personality and Social Psychology, 30,* 822–828.

Carmines, E. G. (1978). Psychological origins of adolescent political attitudes. *American Politics Quarterly, 6,* 167–186.

Carver, C. S. (1975). Physical aggression as a function of objective self-awareness and attitudes toward punishment. *Journal of Experimental Psychology, 11,* 510–519.

Carver, C. S., & Ganellen, R. J. (1983). Depression and components of self-punitiveness: High standards, self-criticism, and over-generalization. *Journal of Abnormal Psychology, 92,* 330–337.

Cialdini, R. B., Borden, R. J., Thorne, A., Walker, M. R., Freeman, S., & Sloane, L. R. (1976). Basking in reflected glory: Three (football) field studies. *Journal of Personality and Social Psychology, 34,* 366–374.

Cialdini, R. B., Darby, B. L., & Vincent, J. E. (1973). Transgression and altruism: A case for hedonism. *Journal of Experimental Social Psychology, 9,* 502–516.

Cialdini, R. B., & Richardson, K. D. (1980). Two indirect tactics of image management: Basking and blasting. *Journal of Personality and Social Psychology, 39,* 406–415.

Cohn, R. M. (1978). The effect of employment change on self-attitudes. *Social Psychology, 41,* 81–93.

Combs, A. W. (1981). Some observations of self-concept research and theory. In M. D. Lynch, A. A. Norem-Hebeisen, and K. J. Gergen (eds.). *Self-concept, advances in theory and research* (pp. 5–16). Cambridge, MA: Ballinger Publishing Company.

Cooley, C. H. (1902). *Human nature and the social order.* New York: Charles Scribner's Sons.

Coopersmith, S. (1967). *The antecedents of self-esteem.* San Francisco: W. H. Freeman.

Cottrell, N. B., & Epley, S. W. (1977). Affiliation, social comparison, and socially mediated stress reduction. In J. M. Suls and R. L. Miller (eds.). *Social comparison processes: Theoretical and empirical perspectives* (pp. 43–68). Washington, DC: Hemisphere.

Covington, M. V., & Beery, R. G. (1976). *Self worth and school learning.* New York: Holt, Rinehart & Winston.

Cozby, P. C. (1973). Self-disclosure: A literature review. *Psychological Bulletin, 79,* 73–91.

Craig, H. B. (1965). A sociometric investigation of the self-concept of the deaf child. *American Annals of the Deaf, 110,* 456–478.

Della Fave, L. R. (1980). The meek shall not inherit the earth: Self-evaluation and the legitimacy of stratification. *American Sociological Review, 45,* 955–971.

Demo, D. H., & Savin-Williams, R. C. (1983). Early adolescent self-esteem as a function of social class: Rosenberg and Pearlin revisited. *American Journal of Sociology, 88,* 763–774.

Denzin, N. K. (1972). The genesis of self in early childhood. *Sociological Quarterly, 13,* 291–314.

Denzin, N. K. (1983). A note on emotionality, self, and interaction. *American Journal of Sociology, 89,* 402–409.

Diener, E., & Wallbom, M. (1976). Effects of self-awareness on antinormative behavior. *Journal of Research in Personality, 10,* 107–111.

Diller, L. (1954). Conscious and unconscious self-attitudes after success and failure. *Journal of Personality, 23,* 1–12.

Dipboye, R. L. (1977). A critical review of Korman's self-consistency theory of work motivation and occupational choice. *Organizational Behavior and Human Performance, 18*, 108–126.

Dittes, J. E. (1959). Attractiveness of group as a function of self-esteem and acceptance by group. *Journal of Abnormal and Social Psychology, 59*, 77–82.

Duval, S. (1976). Conformity on a visual task as a function of personal novelty on attitudinal dimensions and being reminded of the object status of self. *Journal of Experimental Social Psychology, 12*, 87–98.

Duval, S. & Wicklund, R. A. (1972). *A theory of objective self-awareness*. New York: Academic Press.

Duval, S., & Wicklund, R. A. (1973). Effects of objective self-awareness on attribution of causality. *Journal of Experimental Social Psychology, 9*, 17–31.

Dykman, B., & Reis, H. T. (1979). Personality correlates of classroom seating position. *Journal of Educational Psychology, 71*, 346–354.

Ehrlich, H. J. (1973). *The social psychology of prejudice*. New York: Wiley.

Elder, G. H., Jr. (1969). Occupational mobility, life patterns, and personality. *Journal of Health and Social Behavior, 10*, 308–323.

Feather, N. T., & Simon, J. G. (1975). Reactions to male and female success and failure in sex-linked occupations: Impressions of personality causal attributions, and perceived likelihood of different consequences. *Journal of Personality and Social Psychology, 31*, 20–31.

Federoff, N. A., & Harvey, J. H. (1976). Focus of attention, self-esteem, and attribution of causality. *Journal of Research in Personality, 10*, 336–345.

Fellner, C. H., & Marshall, J. R. (1970). Kidney donors. In J. Macaulay and L. Berkowitz (eds.). *Altruism and helping behavior* (pp. 269–281). New York: Academic Press.

Felson, R. B. (1981). Ambiguity and bias in the self-concept. *Social Psychology Quarterly, 44*, 64–69.

Felson, R. B. (1985). Reflected appraisal and the development of self. *Social Psychology Quarterly, 48*, 71–78.

Felton, B. J., Revenson, T. A., & Hinrichsen, G. A. (1984). Stress and coping in the explanation of psychological adjustment among chronically ill adults. *Social Science and Medicine, 18*, 889–898.

Festinger, L. (1957). *A theory of cognitive dissonance*. Stanford, CA: Stanford University Press.

Fitts, W. H. (1981). Issues regarding self-concept change. In M. D. Lynch, A. A. Norem-Hebeisen, and K. J. Gergen (eds.), *Self-concept, advances in theory and research* (pp. 261–272). Cambridge, MA: Ballinger Publishing Company.

Franks, D. D., & Marolla, J. (1976). Efficacious action and social approval as interacting dimensions of self-esteem: A tentative formulation through construct validation. *Sociometry, 39*, 324–341.

Freedman, J. L., Wallington, S. A., & Bless, E. (1967). Compliance without pressure: The effects of guilt. *Journal of Personality and Social Psychology, 7*, 117–124.

Freemesser, G. F., & Kaplan, H. B. (1976). Self-attitudes and deviant behavior: The case of the charismatic religious movement. *Journal of Youth and Adolescence, 5*, 1–9.

Friedman, A., & Goodman, P. S. (1967). Wage inequity, self-qualifications, and productivity. *Organizational Behavior and Human Performance, 2*, 406–417.

Friend, R. M., & Gilbert, J. (1973). Threat and fear of negative evaluation as determinants of locus of social comparison. *Journal of Personality, 41*, 328–340.

Gecas, V. (1981). Contexts of socialization. In M. Rosenberg and R. H. Turner (eds.). *Social psychology, sociological perspectives* (pp. 165–199). New York: Basic Books, Inc.

Gecas, V. (1982). The self-concept. *Annual Review of Sociology, 8*, 1–33.

Gergen, K. (1971). *The concept of self.* New York: Holt, Rinehart & Winston.

Gergen, K. J. (1981). The functions and foibles of negotiating self-conception. In M. D. Lynch, A. A. Norem-Bebeisen, and K. J. Gergen (eds.). *Self-concept, advances in theory and research* (pp. 59–74). Cambridge, MA: Ballinger Publishing Company.

Gibbons, F. X. (1978). Sexual standards and reactions to pornography: Enhancing behavioral consistency through self-focused attention. *Journal of Personality and Social Psychology, 36*, 976–987.

Gibbons, F. X., & Wicklund, R. A. (1976). Selective exposure to self. *Journal of Research in Personality, 10*, 98–106.

Gibby, R. G., Sr., & Gibby, R. G. Jr., (1967). The effects of stress resulting from academic failure. *Journal of Clinical Psychology, 23*, 35–37.

Goffman, E. (1955). On face-work: An analysis of ritual elements in social interaction. *Psychiatry: Journal for the Study of Interpersonal Processes, 18*, 213–231.

Goffman, E. (1959). *The presentation of self in everyday life.* Garden City, NY: Doubleday.

Gold, M. (1978). Scholastic experiences, self-esteem, and delinquent behavior: A theory for alternative schools. *Crime and Delinquency, 254*, 290–308.

Gold, M., & Mann, D. (1972). Delinquency as defense. *American Journal of Orthopsychiatry, 42*, 463–479.

Goldstein, A. P., Sherman, M., Gershaw, N. J., Sprafkin, R. P., & Glick, B. (1978). Training aggressive adolescents in prosocial behavior. *Journal of Youth and Adolescence, 1*, 73–92.

Gordon, C. (1968). Self-conceptions: Configurations of content. In C. Gordon and K. Gergen (eds.). *The self in social interaction* (Vol. I, pp. 115–136). New York: Wiley.

Gordon, S. L. (1981). The sociology of sentiments and emotion. In M. Rosenberg and R. H. Turner (eds.). *Social psychology, sociological perspectives* (pp. 562–592). New York: Basic Books, Inc.

Gore, P. M., & Rotter, J. B. (1963). A personality correlate of social action. *Journal of Personality, 31*, 58–64.

Graf, R. G. (1971). Induced self-esteem as a determinant of behavior. *Journal of Social Psychology, 85*, 213–217.

Greenberg, J. (1980). Attentional focus and locus of performance causality as determinants of equity behavior. *Journal of Personality and Social Psychology, 38*, 579–585.

Greenberg, J., & Musham, C. (1981). Avoiding and seeking self-focused attention. *Journal of Research in Personality, 15*, 191–200.

Greenwald, A. G., & Ronis, D. L. (1978). Twenty years of cognitive dissonance: Case study of the evolution of a theory. *Psychological Review, 85*, 53–57.

Grube, J. W., Greenstein, T. N., Kearney, K. A., & Rankin, W. L. (1977). Behavior change following self-confrontation: A test of the value-mediation hypothesis. *Journal of Personality and Social Psychology, 35*, 212–216.

Haemmerlie, F. M., & Montgomery, R. L. (1982). Self-perception theory and unobtrusively biased interactions: A treatment for heterosexual anxiety. *Journal of Counseling Psychology, 29*, 362–370.

Hakmiller, K. L. (1966). Threat as a determinant of downward comparison. *Journal of Experimental Social Psychology, 2*(Suppl.), 32–39.

Hammersmith, S. K., & Weinberg, M. S. (1973). Homosexual identity: Commitment, adjustment, and significant others. *Sociometry, 36*, 56–79.

Heider, F. (1958). *The psychology of interpersonal relations.* New York: Wiley.

Helmreich, R. (1972). Stress, self-esteem, and attitudes. In B. T. King and E. McGinnies (eds.). *Attitudes, conflict and social change* (pp. 33–48). New York: Academic Press.

Hess, R. D. (1970). Social class and ethnic influences on socialization. In P. H. Mussen (ed.). *Carmichael's manual of child psychology* (pp. 457–557). New York: Wiley.

Hewitt, J. P., & Stokes, R. (1975). Disclaimers. *American Sociological Review, 40,* 1–6.

Hilgard, E. R. (1949). Human motives and the concept of the self. *American Psychologist, 4,* 374–382.

Hirschi, T. (1969). *Causes of delinquency.* Berkeley: University of California Press.

Holmes, D. S. (1978). Projection as a defense mechanism. *Psychological Bulletin, 85,* 677–688.

Howe, K. G., & Zanna, M. P. (1975). Sex-appropriateness of the task and achievement behavior. Paper read at the Meeting of the Eastern Psychological Association, New York.

James, W. (1890). *Principles of psychology* (Vol. I). New York: Henry Holt.

Jellison, J. M. (1977). *I'm sorry I didn't mean to and other lies we love to tell.* New York: Chatham.

Jensen, G. F., White, C. S., & Galliher, J. M. (1982). Ethnic status and adolescent self-evaluations: An extension of research on minority self-esteem. *Social Problems, 30,* 221–239.

Jones, E. E., & Berglas, S. (1978). Control of attributions about the self through self-handicapping strategies: The appeal of alcohol and the role of underachievement. *Personality and Social Psychology Bulletin, 4,* 200–206.

Jones, E. E., & Gerard, H. B. (1967). *Foundations of social psychology.* New York: Wiley.

Jones, E. E., & Pittman, T. S. (1982). Toward a general theory of strategic self-presentation. In J. Suls (ed.). *Psychological perspectives on the self* (Vol. 1, pp. 231–262). Hillsdale, NJ: Erlbaum Associates.

Jones, S. C. (1973). Self and interpersonal evaluations: Esteem theories versus consistency theories. *Psychological Bulletin, 79,* 185–199.

Jourard, S. (1957). Identification, parent-cathexis, and self-esteem. *Journal of Consulting Psychology, 21,* 375–380.

Jourard, S. M. (1964). *The transparent self.* Princeton, NJ: Van Nostrand.

Kagan, J. (1964). Acquisition and significance of sex typing and sex role identity. In M. Hoffman and L. Hoffman (eds.). *Review of child development research* (Vol. 1, pp. 137–165). New York: Russell Sage Foundation.

Kaplan, H. B. (1970). Self-derogation and adjustment to recent life experiences. *Archives of General Psychiatry, 22,* 324–331.

Kaplan, H. B. (1971a). Age-related correlates of self-derogation: Contemporary life space characteristics. *Aging and Human Development, 2,* 305–313.

Kaplan, H. B. (1971b). Social class and self-derogation: A conditional relationship. *Sociometry, 34,* 41–64.

Kaplan, H. B. (1972a). Studies in sociophysiology. In E. G. Jaco (ed.). *Patients, physicians and illness* (pp. 86–92). New York: The Free Press.

Kaplan, H. B. (1972b). Toward a general theory of psychosocial deviance: The case of aggressive behavior. *Social Science and Medicine, 6,* 593–617.

Kaplan, H. B. (1973). Self-derogation and social position: Interaction effects of sex, race, education and age. *Social Psychiatry, 8,* 92–99.

Kaplan, H. B. (1975a). Increase in self-rejection as an antecedent of deviant responses. *Journal of Youth and Adolescence, 4,* 281–292.

Kaplan, H. B. (1975b). *Self-attitudes and deviant behavior.* Pacific Palisades, CA.: Goodyear.

Kaplan, H. B. (1976). Self-attitudes and deviant responses. *Social Forces, 54,* 788–801.

Kaplan, H. B. (1977). Gender and depression: A sociological analysis of a conditional relationship. In W. E. Fann, A. D. Pokorny, I. Karacan, and R. L. Williams (eds.). *Phenomenology and treatment of depression* (pp. 81–113). New York: Spectrum Publishing Co.

Kaplan, H. B. (1980). *Deviant behavior in defense of self.* New York: Academic Press.

Kaplan, H. B. (1982). Self-Attitudes and deviant behavior: New directions for theory and research. *Youth and Society, 14,* 185–211.

Kaplan, H. B. (1983). Psychological stress in sociological context: Toward a theory of psychosocial stress. In H. B. Kaplan (ed.). *Psychosocial stress: Trends in theory and research* (pp. 195–264). New York: Academic Press.

Kaplan, H. B. (1984). *Patterns of juvenile delinquency.* Beverly Hills, CA.: Sage.

Kaplan, H. B., Boyd, I., & Bloom, S. W. (1964). Patient culture and the evaluation of self. *Psychiatry, 27,* 116–126.

Kaplan, H. B., Burch, N. R., Bedner, T. D., & Trenda, J. D. (1965). Physiological (GSR) activity and perceptions of social behavior in positive, negative and neutral pairs. *Journal of Nervous and Mental Disease, 140,* 457–463.

Kaplan, H. B., Burch, N. R., Bloom, S. W., & Edelberg, R. (1963). Affective orientation and physiological activity in small peer groups. *Psychosomatic Medicine, 25,* 245–252.

Kaplan, H. B., Johnson, R. J., & Bailey, C. A. (1986). Self-rejection and the explanation of deviance: Refinement and elaboration of a latent structure. *Social Psychology Quarterly, 49,* 110–128.

Kaplan, H. B., Martin, S. S., & Johnson, R. J. (1986). Self-rejection and the explanation of deviance: Specification of the structure among latent constructs. *American Journal of Sociology, 92,* 384–411.

Kaplan, H. B., & Pokorny, A. D. (1970a). Age-related correlates of self-derogation: Reports of childhood experiences. *British Journal of Psychiatry, 117,* 533.

Kaplan, H. B., & Pokorny, A. D. (1970b). Aging and self-attitudes: A conditional relationship. *Aging and Human Development, 1,* 241–250.

Kaplan, H. B., & Pokorny, A. D. (1972). Sex-related correlates of adult self-derogation: Reports of childhood experiences. *Developmental Psychology, 6,* 536.

Kaplan, H. B. & Robbins, C. (1983). Testing a general theory of deviant behavior in longitudinal perspective. In K. Van Dusen and S. A. Mednick (eds.). *Prospective studies in delinquent and criminal behavior* (pp. 117–146). Boston, MA: Kluwer-Nijhoff.

Kaplan, H. B., Robbins, C., & Martin, S. S. (1983). Antecedents of psychological distress in young adults: Self-rejection, deprivation of social support, and life-events. *Journal of Health and Social Behavior, 24,* 230–244.

Kasl, S. V., Gore, S., & Cobb, S. (1975). The experience of losing a job: Reported changes in health, symptoms, and illness behavior. *Psychosomatic Medicine, 37,* 106–121.

Kemper, T. D. (1978). *A social interactional theory of emotions.* New York: Wiley.

Kiesler, S. B., & Baral, R. L. (1970). The search for a romantic partner: The effects of self-esteem and physical attractiveness on romantic behavior. In K. J. Gergen and D. Marlow (eds.). *Personality and social behavior* (pp. 155–165). Reading, MA: Addison-Wesley.

Kinch, J. W. (1963). A formalized theory of the self-concept. *American Journal of Sociology, 68,* 481–486.

Kirchner, E. P., & Vondracek, S. I. (1975). Perceived sources of esteem in early childhood. *Journal of Genetic Psychology, 126,* 169–179.

Kiritz, S., & Moos, R. (1974). Physiological effects of social environments. *Psychosomatic Medicine, 36,* 96–114.

Kitsuse, J. I. (1962). Societal reaction to deviant behavior: Problems of theory and method. *Social Problems, 9,* 247–257.

Klapp, O. (1969). *Collective search for identity*. New York: Holt, Rinehart & Winston.

Klass, E. T. (1981). A cognitive analysis of guilt over assertion. *Cognitive Therapy and Research, 5*, 293–297.

Kleinke, C. L. (1975). Effects of false feedback about response length on subjects' perception of an interview. *Journal of Social Psychology, 95*, 99–104.

Kohlberg, L. (1966). A cognitive-developmental analysis of children's sex-role concepts and attitudes. In E. Maccoby (ed.). *The development of sex differences* (pp. 82–173). Stanford, CA: Stanford University Press.

Koneske, P., Staple, S., & Graff, R. G. (1979). Compliant reactions to guilt: Self-esteem or punishment. *The Journal of Social Psychology, 108*, 207–211.

Korman, A. H. (1969). Self-esteem as a moderator in vocational choice: Replications and extensions. *Journal of Applied Psychology, 53*, 188–192.

Kraut, R. E. (1973). Effects of social labeling on giving to charity. *Journal of Experimental Social Psychology, 9*, 551–562.

Lane, R. E. (1959). *Political life*. New York: The Free Press.

Lasswell, H. D. (1948). *Power and personality*. New York: Norton.

Latta, R. M. (1976). Differential tests of two cognitive theories of performance: Weiner vs. Kukla. *Journal of Personality and Social Psychology, 34*, 295–304.

Lazarus, R. S., & Folkman, S. (1984). *Stress, appraisal, and coping*. New York: Springer.

Lemert, E. M. (1951). *Social pathology*. New York: McGraw-Hill.

Leon, C. A. (1969). Unusual patterns of crime during *La Violencia* in Colombia. *American Journal of Psychiatry, 125*, 1564–1575.

Leonard, R. L., Walsh, W. B., & Osipow, S. H. (1973). Self-esteem, self-consistency, and second vocational choice. *Journal of Counseling Psychology, 20*, 91–93.

Lerner, M. J. (1977). The justice motive: Some hypotheses as to its origins and forms. *Journal of Personality, 45*, 1–52.

Lewinsohn, P. M., & Mischel, W. (1980). Social competence and depression: The role of illusory self-perceptions. *Journal of Abnormal Psychology, 89*, 203–212.

Liebling, B. A., & Shaver, P. (1973). Evaluation, self-awareness, and task performance. *Journal of Experimental Social Psychology, 9*, 297–306.

Ludwig, D. J., & Maehr, M. L. (1967). Changes in self-concept and stated behavioral preferences. *Child Development, 38*, 453–467.

Lynd, H. (1958). On shame and the search for identity. New York: Harcourt Brace and World.

McCall, G. J., & Simmons, J. L. (1966). *Identities and interactions*. New York: The Free Press.

Maccoby, E. E., & Jacklin, C. N. (1974). *The psychology of sex differences*. Stanford, CA: Stanford University Press.

Mackie, M. (1983). The domestication of self: Gender comparisons of self-imagery and self-esteem. *Social Psychology Quarterly, 46*, 343–350.

McGovern, L. B. (1976). Dispositional social anxiety and helping behavior under three conditions of threat. *Journal of Personality and Social Psychology, 44*, 84–97.

McGuire, W. J., & McGuire, C. V. (1982). Significant others in self-space: Sex differences and developmental trends in the social self. In J. Suls (ed.). *Psychological perspectives on the self* (Vol. I, pp. 71–96). Hillsdale, NJ: Lawrence Erlbaum Associates.

McGuire, W. J., McGuire, C. V., Child, P., & Fujioka, T. (1978). Salience of ethnicity in the spontaneous self-concept as a function of one's ethnic distinctiveness in the social environment. *Journal of Personality and Social Psychology, 36*, 511–520.

McGuire, W. J., & Padawer-Singer, A. (1976). Trait salience in the spontaneous self-concept. *Journal of Personality and Social Psychology, 33*, 743–754.

McMillen D. L. (1970). Transgression, fate control, and compliant behavior. *Psychonomic Science, 21,* 103–104.

Maehr, M. L., Mensing, J., & Nafzger, S. (1962). Concept of self and the reaction of others. *Sociometry, 25,* 353–357.

Marecek, J., & Mettee, D. R. (1972). Avoidance of continued success as a function of self-esteem, level of esteem uncertainty, and responsibility for success. *Journal of Personality and Social Psychology, 29,* 98–107.

Marks, P. A., & Seeman, W. (1963). *The actuarial description of abnormal personality.* Baltimore: Williams & Wilkins.

Markus, H. (1977). Self-schemata and processing information about the self. *Journal of Personality and Social Psychology, 35,* 63–78.

Maslach, C. (1974). Social and personal bases of individuation. *Journal of Personality and Social Psychology, 29,* 411–425.

May, R. (1980). Value conflicts and anxiety. In Irwin L. Kutash and L. B. Schlesinger (eds.). *Handbook on stress and anxiety.* (pp. 241–248). San Francisco: Jossey-Bass.

Mead, G. H. (1934). *Mind, self, and society.* Chicago: University of Chicago Press.

Meadow, K. P. (1969). Self-image, family climate, and deafness. *Social Forces, 47,* 428–438.

Merton, R. K., & Rossi, A. S. (1950). Contributions to the theory of reference group behavior. In R. K. Merton and P. F. Lazarsfeld (eds.) *Continuities in social research: Studies in the scope and method of "The American Soldier"* (pp. 40–105). Glencoe, IL: The Free Press.

Mettee, D. R. (1971). Rejection of unexpected success as a function of the negative consequences of accepting success. *Journal of Personality and Social Psychology, 17,* 332–341.

Miller, D. T. (1976). Ego involvement and attributions for success and failure. *Journal of Personality and Social Psychology, 34,* 901–906.

Miller, D. T., & Ross, M. (1975). Self-serving biases in the attribution of causality. Fact or fiction? *Psychological Bulletin, 27,* 154–164.

Mirels, H. L., & McPeek, R. W. (1977). Self-advocacy and self-esteem. *Journal of Consulting and Clinical Psychology, 45,* 1132–1138.

Modigliani, A. (1971). Embarrassment, face-work and eye-contact: Testing a theory of embarrassment. *Journal of Personality and Social Psychology, 17,* 15–24.

Montemayor, R., & Eisen, M. (1977). The development of self-conceptions from childhood to adolescence. *Developmental Psychology, 31,* 314–319.

Morrison, R. F. (1977). Career adaptivity: The effective adaptation of managers to changing role demands. *Journal of Applied Psychology, 62,* 549–558.

Morse, S., & Gergen, K. J. (1970). Social Comparison, self-consistency, and the concept of self. *Journal of Personality and Social Psychology, 16,* 148–156.

Mortimer, J. T., & Lorence, J. (1979a). Occupational experience and the self-concept: A longitudinal study. *Social Psychology Quarterly, 42,* 307–323.

Mortimer, J. T., & Lorence, J. (1979b). Work experience and occupational value socialization: A longitudinal study. *American Journal of Sociology, 84,* 1361–1385.

Murphy, G. (1974). Personality: A biosocial approach to origins and structure. New York: Harper.

Mussen, P. H., Conger, J. J., & Kagen, J. (1969). *Child Development and personality.* New York: Harper & Row.

Newcomb, T. M. (1961). *The acquaintance process.* New York: Holt, Rinehart & Winston.

Norem-Hebeisen, A. A. (1981). A maximization model of self-concept. In M. D. Lynch, A. A. Norem-Hebeisen, and K. J. Gergen (eds.). *Self-concept, advances in theory and research* (pp. 133–146). Cambridge, MA: Ballinger Publishing Company.

Notterman, J. M., Schoenfeld, W. N., and Bersh, P. J., 1952. A comparison of three extinction procedures following heart rate conditioning. *Journal of Abnormal and Social Psychology, 47,* 674–677.

O'Malley, P. M., & Bachman, J. G. (1979). "Self-esteem and education: Sex and cohort comparisons among high school seniors. *Journal of Personality and Social Psychology, 37,* 1153–1159.

Pearlin, L. I. (1980). Life strains and psychological distress among adults. In N. J. Smelser and E. H. Erikson (eds.). *Themes of work and love in adulthood* (pp. 174–192). Cambridge, MA: Harvard University Press.

Pearlin, L. I., & Lieberman, M. A. (1979). Social sources of emotional distress. In R. G. Simmons (ed.). *Research in community and mental health (Vol. I),* (pp. 217–248). Greenwich, CT: JAI Press.

Pearlin, L. I., & Radabaugh, C. W. (1976). Economic strains and the coping functions of alcohol. *American Journal of Sociology, 82,* 652–663.

Pearlin, L. I., & Schooler, C. (1978). The structure of coping. *Journal of Health and Social Behavior, 19,* 2–21.

Pentz, M. A. (1983). Prevention of adolescent substance abuse through social skill development. In T. J. Glynn, C. G. Leukefeld, and J. P. Ludford (eds.). *Preventing adolescent drug abuse: Intervention strategies. Research Monograph Series 47* (pp. 195–225). Rockville MD: National Institute on Drug Abuse.

Pepitone, A. (1968). An experimental analysis of self-dynamics. In C. Gordon and K. Gergen (eds.). *The self in social interaction* (Vol. 1, pp. 347–354). New York: Wiley.

Petersen, A. C., & Kellam, S. G. (1977). Measurement of the psychological well-being of adolescents. The psychometric properties and assessment procedures of the how I feel. *Journal of Youth and Adolescence, 6,* 229–247.

Pitts, R. A. (1978). The effects of exclusively French language schooling on self-esteem in Quebec. *Canadian Modern Language Review, 34,* 372–380.

Pryor, J. B., Gibbons, F. X., Wicklund, R. A., Fazio, R. H., and Hood, R. (1977). Self-focused attention and self-report validity. *Journal of Personality, 45,* 513–527.

Purkey, W. W. (1970). *Self-concept and school achievement.* Englewood Cliffs, NJ: Prentice-Hall.

Quay, H. C., & Quay, L. C. (1965). Behavior problems in early adolescence. *Child Development, 36,* 215–220.

Rand, C. S., & Hall, J. A. (1983). Sex differences in the accuracy of self-perceived attractiveness. *Social Psychology Quarterly, 46,* 359–363.

Rasmussen, G., & Zander, A. (1954). Group membership and self-evaluation. *Human Relations, 7,* 239–251.

Reis, H. T. (1981). Self-presentation and distributive justice. In J. T. Tedeschi (ed.). *Impression management theory and social psychological research* (pp. 269–291). New York: Academic Press.

Rogers, C. M., Smith, M. D., & Coleman, J. M. (1978). Social comparison in the classroom: The relationship between academic achievement and self-concept. *Journal of Educational Psychology, 70,* 50–57.

Rokeach, M. (1973). The nature of human values. New York: The Free Press.

Rokeach, M. (1983). A value approach to the prevention and reduction of drug abuse. In T. J. Glynn, C. G. Leukefeld, and J. P. Ludford (eds.). *Preventing adolescent drug abuse: Intervention strategies. Research Monograph Series 47* (pp. 172–192). Rockville, MD: National Institute on Drug Abuse.

Rosen, G. M., & Ross, O. A. (1968). Relationship of body image to self-concept. *Journal of Consulting and Clinical Psychology, 32,* 100.

Rosenberg, M. (1965). *Society and the adolescent self-image.* Princeton, NJ: Princeton University Press.

Rosenberg, M. (1973). Which significant others? *American Behavioral Scientist, 16,* 829–860.

Rosenberg, M. (1979). Conceiving the self. New York: Basic Books, Inc.

Rosenberg, M. (1981). The self-concept: Social product and social force. In M. Rosenberg and R. H. Turner (eds.). *Social psychology, Sociological Perspectives* (pp. 593–624). New York: Basic Books, Inc.

Rosenberg, M., & Kaplan, H. B. (1982). *Social psychology of the self concept.* Arlington Heights, IL: Harlan Davidson, Inc.

Rosenberg, M., & Pearlin, L. I. (1978). Social class and self-esteem among children and adults. *American Journal of Sociology, 84,* 53–77.

Rosenberg, M., & Simmons, R. G. (1972). Black and white self-esteem: The urban school child. American Sociological Association, Washington, DC: Arnold & Caroline.

Rosenthal, R., & Jacobson, L. (1968). *Pygmalion in the classroom: Teacher expectations and pupil's intellectual development.* New York: Holt, Rinehart & Winston.

Rubin, R. T. (1974). Biochemical and neuroendocrine responses to severe psychological stress: 1. U.S. Navy Aviator Study, 2. Some general observations. In E. K. Gunderson and R. H. Rahe (eds.). *Life stress and illness,* (pp. 227–274). Springfield, IL: Charles C Thomas.

Sacco, W. P., & Hokanson, J. E. (1978). Expectations of success and anagram performances of depressives in a public and private setting. *Journal of Abnormal Psychology, 87,* 122–130.

Salzman, L. (1965). Obsessions and phobias. *Contemporary Psychoanalysis, 2,* 1–15.

Sarbin, T. R., & Allen, V. L. (1968). Role theory. In G. Lindzey and E. Aronson (eds.). *Handbook of social psychology* (Vol. 1, Reading, MA: pp. 488–567). (2nd ed.). Addison-Wesley.

Scheff, T. (1966). *Being mentally ill: A sociological theory.* Chicago: Aldine.

Schwartz, M., & Stryker, S. (1970). *Deviance, selves and others.* Washington, DC: American Sociological Association.

Scott, M. R., & Lyman, S. M. (1968). Accounts. *American Sociological Review, 33,* 46–62.

Sears, R. R. (1970). Relation of early socialization experiences to self-concepts and gender role in middle childhood. *Child Development, 41,* 267–289.

Secord, P. F., & Backman, C. W. (1964). Interpersonal congruency, perceived similarity, and friendship. *Sociometry, 27,* 115–127.

Seligman, M. E. P. (1975). *Helplessness: On depression, development, and death.* San Francisco, CA: Freeman Press.

Sharoff, R. L. (1969). Character problems and their relationship to drug abuse. *American Journal of Psychoanalysis, 29,* 189–193.

Shrauger, J. S., & Schoeneman, T. J. (1979). Symbolic interactionist view of self-concept: Through the looking glass darkly. *Psychological Bulletin, 86,* 549–573.

Simmons, R. G., Brown, L., Bush, D., & Blyth, D. A. (1978). Self-esteem and achievement of black and white adolescents. *Social Problems, 26,* 86–96.

Simmons, R. G., Rosenberg, F., & Rosenberg, M. (1973). Disturbance in the self-image at adolescence. *American Sociological Review, 38,* 533–568.

Singer, E. (1981). Reference groups and social evaluations. In M. Rosenberg and R. H. Turner (eds.). *Social psychology, Sociological perspectives* (pp. 66–93). New York: Basic Books, Inc.

Slaughter, D. T. (1977). Relation of early parent–teacher socialization influences to achievement orientation and self-esteem in middle childhood among low-income black children. In J. C. Glidewell (ed.). *The social context of learning and development* (pp. 101–132). New York: Gardner Press.

Smedley, J. W., & Bayton, J. A. (1978). Evaluative race–class sterotypes by race and perceived class of subjects. *Journal of Personality and Social Psychology, 36,* 530–535.

Snyder, M. (1974). Self-monitoring of expressive behavior. *Journal of Personality and Social Psychology, 30,* 526–537.

Speisman, J. C., Lazarus, R. S., Mordkoff, A., & Davison, L. (1964). Experimental reduction of stress based on ego-defense theory. *Journal of Abnormal and Social Psychology, 68,* 367–380.

Staples, C. L., Schwalbe, M. L., & Gecas, V. (1984). Social class, occupational conditions, and efficacy-based self-esteem. *Sociological Perspectives, 27,* 85–109.

Stephan, W. G., & Rosenfield, D. (1978). Effects of desegregation on racial attitudes. *Journal of Personality and Social Psychology, 36,* 795–804.

Stryker, S. (1968). Identity salience and role performance: The relevance of symbolic interaction theory for family research. *Journal of Marriage and the Family, 30,* 558–564.

Stryker, S. (1977). Developments in "two social psychologies": Toward an appreciation of mutual releveance. *Sociometry, 40,* 145–160.

Sweet, J. R., & Thornburg, K. R. (1971). Preschooler's self and social identity within the family structure. *Journal of Negro Education, 40,* 22–27.

Sykes, G., & Matza, D. (1957). Techniques of neutralization: A theory of delinquency. *American Journal of Sociology, 22,* 664–670.

Taylor, D. G., Sheatsley, P. B., & Greeley, A. M. (1978). Attitudes toward racial integration. *Scientific American, 238,* 42–49.

Taylor, R. (1964). Personality traits and discrepant achievement: A review. *Journal of Counseling Psychology, 11,* 78–81.

Tedeschi, J. T. (ed.) (1981). *Impression management theory and social psychological research.* New York: Academic Press.

Tedeschi, J. T., & Riess, M. (1981). Identities, the phenomenal self, and laboratory research. In J. T. Tedeschi (ed.). *Impression management theory and social psychological research* (pp. 3–22). New York: Academic Press.

Tedeschi, J. T., & Riordan, C. A. (1981). Impression management and prosocial behavior following transgression. In J. T. Tedeschi (ed.). *Impression management theory and social psychological research* (pp. 223–244). New York: Academic Press.

Teevan, R. C., & McGhee, P. E. (1972). Childhood development of fear of failure motivation. *Journal of Personality and Social Psychology, 21,* 345–348.

Thies, A., & Chance, J. (1975). Potential losses versus potential gains as determinants of behavior. *Journal of Psychology, 89,* 81–88.

Thomas, D. L., Gecas, V., Weigert, A., & Rooney, E. (1974). *Family socialization and the adolescent.* Lexington, MA: D. C. Heath and Company.

Tippett, J. S., & Silber, E. (1966). Autonomy of self-esteem. *Archives of General Psychiatry, 14,* 372–385.

Turner, R. H. (1969). The theme of contemporary social movements. *British Journal of Sociology, 20,* 390–405.

Turner, R. H. (1976). The real self: From institution to impulse. *American Journal of Sociology, 82,* 989–1016.

Vallacher, R. R., & Solodky, M. (1979). Objective self-awareness, standards of evaluation, and moral behavior. *Journal of Experimental Social Psychology, 15,* 254–262.

Videbeck, R. (1960). Self-conception and the reactions of others. *Sociometry, 23,* 351–359.

Walster, E. (1965). The effect of self-esteem on romantic liking. *Journal of Experimental Social Psychology, 1,* 184–197.

Washburn, W. C. (1962). Patterns of protective attitudes in relation to difference in self-evaluation and anxiety level among high school students. *California Journal of Education Research, 13,* 84–94.

Wegner, D. M., & Schaefer, D. (1978). The concentration of responsibility: An objective self-awareness analysis of group sizes effects in helping situations. *Journal of Personality and Social Psychology, 36,* 147–155.

Wegner, D. M., & Vallacher, R. R. (1980). *The self in social psychology.* London and New York: Oxford University Press.

Weinstein, S. R. (1968). The development of interpersonal competence. In D. Goslin (Ed.). *Handbook of socialization theory and research* (pp. 753–775). Chicago: Rand McNally.

Wells, L. E., & Marwell, G. (1976). *Self-esteem, its conceptualization and measurement.* Beverly Hills, CA: Sage.

Wheaton, J. L. (1959). Fact and fancy in sensory deprivation studies. School of Aviation Medicine Reports, Brooks Air Force Base, Texas, no. 5–59, 60.

White, W. F., & Gaier, E. L. (1965). Assessment of body image and self-concept among alcoholics with different intervals of sobriety. *Journal of Clinical Psychology, 21,* 374–377.

White, W. F., & Porter, T. L. (1966). Self-concept reports among hospitalized alcoholics during early periods of sobriety. *Journal of Counseling Psychology, 31,* 352–355.

Wicklund, R. A. (1975). Objective self-awareness. In L. Berkowitz (ed.). *Advances in experimental social psychology* (Vol. 8, pp. 233–275). New York: Academic Press.

Wicklund, R. A. (1979). The influence of self-awareness of human behavior. *American Scientist, 67,* 187–193.

Wicklund, R. A. (1982). How society uses self-awareness. In J. Suls (ed.). *Psychological perspectives on the self* (Vol. 1, pp. 209–230). Hillsdale, NJ: Lawrence Erlbaum Associates.

Wicklund, R. A., & Duval, S. (1971). Opinion change and performance facilitation as a result of objective self-awareness. *Journal of Experimental Social Psychology, 7,* 319–342.

Wicklund, R. A., & Frey, D. (1980). Self-awareness theory: When the self makes a difference. In D. M. Wegner and R. R. Vallacher (eds.). *The self in social psychology* (pp. 31–45). New York: Oxford University Press.

Wiener, Y. (1970). The effects of "task and ego-oriented" performance on two kinds of overcompensation inequity. *Organizational Behavior and Human Performance, 5,* 191–208.

Williams, R., Kimball, C., & Williard, H. (1972). The influence of interpersonal interaction on diastolic blood pressure. *Psychosomatic Medicine, 34,* 194–198.

Wills, T. A. (1981). Downward comparison principles in social psychology. *Psychological Bulletin, 90,* 245–271.

Wilson, S. R., & Benner, L. A. (1971). The effects of self-esteem and situation upon comparison choices during ability evaluation. *Sociometry, 34,* 381–397.

Wine, J. D. (1975). Test-anxiety and helping behavior. *Canadian Journal of Behavioral Sciences, 7,* 216–222.

Wortman, C. B., & Brehm, J. W. (1975). Responses to uncontrollable outcomes. An integration of reactance theory and the learned helplessness model. In L. Berkowitz (ed.). *Advances in experimental Social psychology* (Vol. 8, pp. 227–336). New York: Academic Press.

Wylie, R. (1974). *The self-concept* (Vol. I). Lincoln: University of Nebraska Press.

Wylie, R. C. (1979). *The self-concept. (Vol. 2). Theory and research on selected topics.* Lincoln: University of Nebraska Press.

Zanna, M., Goethals, G. R., & Hill, J. (1975). Evaluating a sex-related ability: Social comparison with similar others and standards setters. *Journal of Experimental Social Psychology, 11,* 86–93.

Ziller, R. C., & Golding, L. H. (1969). Political personality. *Proceedings of the 77th Annual Convention of the American Psychological Association* 441–442.

Zimbardo, P. G. (1982). Shyness and the stress of the human connection. In L. Goldberger and S. Breznitz (eds.). *Handbook of stress, theoretical and clinical aspects* (pp. 466–481). New York: The Free Press.

Zurcher, L. A., & Snow, D. A. (1981). Collective behavior: Social movements. In M. Rosenberg and R. H. Turner (eds.). *Social psychology, Sociological perspectives* (pp. 447–482). New York: Basic Books, Inc.

Author Index

Subject Index